CHILD WELFARE
IN THE UNITED STATES

Sylvia I. Mignon, MSW, PhD, is professor of human services, and director of the MS in Human Services Program and the Forensic Services Graduate Certificate Program at the University of Massachusetts Boston. She has many years of experience in the human services field in settings such as hospitals, substance abuse treatment programs, and correctional facilities. Her research and publication specialty areas include family violence, child welfare, substance abuse, and criminal justice. She is the author of three other books: *Family Abuse: Consequences, Theories, and Responses*; *Substance Use and Abuse: Exploring Alcohol and Drug Issues*; and *Substance Abuse Treatment: Options, Challenges, and Effectiveness* (2015, Springer Publishing Company).

CHILD WELFARE IN THE UNITED STATES

CHALLENGES, POLICY, AND PRACTICE

Sylvia I. Mignon, MSW, PhD

SPRINGER PUBLISHING COMPANY

NEW YORK

Springer Publishing Company, LLC
11 West 42nd Street
New York, NY 10036
www.springerpub.com

Acquisitions Editor: Stephanie Drew
Compositor: S4Carlisle Publishing Services

ISBN: 9780826126429
e-book ISBN: 9780826126474
Instructor's Manual ISBN: 9780826134028
PowerPoints ISBN: 9780826134035

Instructors' Materials: Qualified instructors may request supplements by e-mailing textbook@springerpub.com

16 17 18 19 20/5 4 3 2 1

The author and the publisher of this Work have made every effort to use sources believed to be reliable to provide information that is accurate and compatible with the standards generally accepted at the time of publication. The author and publisher shall not be liable for any special, consequential, or exemplary damages resulting, in whole or in part, from the readers' use of, or reliance on, the information contained in this book. The publisher has no responsibility for the persistence or accuracy of URLs for external or third-party Internet websites referred to in this publication and does not guarantee that any content on such websites is, or will remain, accurate or appropriate.

Library of Congress Cataloging-in-Publication Data

Names: Mignon, Sylvia I., author.
Title: Child welfare in the United States : challenges, policy, and practice
  / Sylvia I. Mignon, MSW, PhD.
Description: New York : Springer Publishing Company, [2017] | Includes
  bibliographical references and index.
Identifiers: LCCN 2016034236 | ISBN 9780826126429
Subjects: LCSH: Child welfare—United States. | Children—Services
  for—United States.
Classification: LCC HV741 .M54 2017 | DDC 362.70973—dc23 LC record available at https://
lccn.loc.gov/2016034236

Printed in the United States of America by Gasch Printing.

For All the Children

Let us put our minds together and see
what life we can make for our children.

Sitting Bull

CONTENTS

PREFACE

On Wednesday, April 30, 2014, I picked up the morning newspaper to see the lead article on the front page of *The Boston Globe*, titled "Child Agency Gets a Change at the Top." The article chronicled the succession of tragic deaths within the Massachusetts Department of Children and Families (DCF), such that the commissioner "resigned under fire" and was replaced by an interim DCF commissioner. The *Globe* story reported that the interim commissioner "has no experience in child welfare issues, but developed a reputation as a hardworking manager who helped modernize the Registry's (Massachusetts Department of Motor Vehicles) computer system, allowing drivers to renew licenses and registrations online" (Levenson & Wen, 2014, p. A1). I could not remember a time when I was more enraged. Did the safety and health of children have no more importance than online renewal of drivers' licenses and car registrations? Were there no child welfare professionals for the job? Were no credentials needed for child protection and safety? And thus the idea for this book took hold.

This textbook represents a culmination of the author's many years of academic and clinical experience addressing the needs of abused and neglected children as well as collaborating with child protection systems to assist them in their important work. In my first job after receiving an MSW degree, I worked as a clinical social worker for a state department of corrections in a facility that performed a 30-day study and evaluation of children referred by family courts. Many years later, the stories of child abuse and neglect are still as shocking, including some children experiencing up to 15 different foster home placements. There were endless stories of parents with few emotional and physical resources who were childhood abuse and neglect victims themselves, struggling to provide for their children. The stories of poverty were overwhelming, and I quickly learned how few resources were available to help needy children and their families. Like many, I felt the full weight of the awesome responsibility to determine the plan for a child's future.

After a year, it was evident to me that even hard work and high hopes for the future could not overcome the lack of funding and the lack of interest by the child welfare and juvenile justice systems. They seemed more concerned with perpetuating the bureaucracies and giving professionals job security and the hope of a very comfortable pension. Here I saw firsthand the "revolving door" of families and children cycling through the system, often being pulled into more serious kinds of trouble. No matter how hardworking, I came to see that I was part of the endless machinery of misery from which very few clients seemed to escape into healthier lives. We are continually reminded of the limitations we have in addressing child maltreatment.

Although child protection agencies claim to focus on the "needs of the children," there are many factors that come into play in determining the type and quality of services provided. Some workers and programs are helpful in keeping families together; others assist children who have been determined to need removal from their families. Still other workers and programs can perpetuate and even exacerbate the problems of children and families. We often have unrealistic notions about what child welfare systems can accomplish, especially because poverty is a pervasive problem in the United States, engulfing almost one quarter of the total population.

The purpose of the book is to highlight the enormity of the problems of child maltreatment and their relationship to poverty and other social ills. The main themes of the book include the challenges in developing appropriate federal, state, and local policies that address child welfare issues, and the ways these policies impact the provision of services. It reveals that there is no national policy on children to ensure that their basic needs are met. Policies and practices can serve to meet the needs of the systems, as well as the professionals who work within them, rather than providing for children. Another theme is the importance of coordination among human service professionals and organizations. Yet another theme is to examine improvements to the system by considering innovative approaches and programs.

Chapter 1 provides a general overview of the topics covered in the book. It introduces the reader to the issues that impact children, such as poverty, lack of education, and myriad other problems of child maltreatment, including physical, emotional, and sexual abuse; physical and emotional neglect; as well as parental substance abuse and mental health problems. The chapter places the issues of child welfare within a general cultural and cross-cultural context. It examines children who are treated as the property of adults and exploited for sex and slave labor.

Chapter 2 examines the development of the contemporary child welfare system in the United States. It addresses the rich history of "child saving" of the 19th century and the orphan train experience. It looks at the private efforts to provide services to abused and neglected children that have transitioned through the years into significantly greater governmental roles. The chapter offers a chronological perspective on laws, policies, and practices that have developed in the United States.

Chapter 3 addresses the fact that the majority of families known to the child welfare system live in poverty. The chapter examines the relationship between poverty and child abuse and neglect, and the increased risk of coming into contact with child protection agencies. Not surprisingly, the prevalence of all types of childhood abuse and neglect is higher among families living in poverty. The chapter also teases out the relationship among poverty, race/ethnicity, and child maltreatment. Experts have suggested that reducing poverty in the United States could be the most important way to prevent child abuse and neglect.

Chapter 4 examines the relationship among schools, educational opportunities and attainment, and the child protection system. In our society, it is accepted that families with financial resources can buy the best education for their children, whereas those in poverty have far more limited educational opportunities. It is significantly harder for a child to get a good education when he or she has to endure multiple foster placements and is denied continuity of education in a supportive environment. Overall, these children are more likely to have poorer academic skills, lower standardized test scores, lower graduation rates, reduced opportunities for college, and fewer career options. Education can be especially tough for homeless children forced to live in shelters.

Chapter 5 examines the health issues that are likely to be present in families known to child protection agencies. Children who have been maltreated have higher rates of health services use, and Medicaid expenditures are significantly higher for this group. Parental substance abuse and mental health problems can be significant contributors to children becoming known to child welfare agencies. Children in the child welfare system are more likely to be on psychotropic medications to address a variety of issues of the child or family. Homelessness of children known to child protection agencies flies in the face of all we know about the need for consistency and appropriate structure and support for children. Housing instability can be a major factor in why families become known to child welfare agencies.

Chapter 6 examines the strong relationship between child and adolescent delinquent behaviors and becoming known to child welfare agencies. It addresses the impact of parental incarceration on children. Children intersect with both the child welfare system and the juvenile justice system in a variety of ways. The chapter examines the increased likelihood of delinquent and maltreated children moving into the adult criminal justice system. It concludes with recommendations for how the juvenile justice and child welfare systems can integrate their delivery of services.

Chapter 7 examines the many facets of foster care—the consequences for children who have numerous unsuccessful foster care placements, and the long-term impacts of negative foster care experiences. The chapter reviews lawsuits that have been filed to address the inadequacies of the foster care system. It examines kinship care and its successes, the plight of older children as they age out of foster care, and the difficulties of transitioning into independent adulthood.

Chapter 8 reviews the various kinds of adoption with an emphasis on situations where biological parents are unable to care for their children. It addresses the barriers to adoption as well as the positive and negative aspects of adoption. The chapter grapples with issues of race and ethnicity in adoption. One such issue is whether it is preferable to place a child with a family of a different race or ethnicity if a family of the same race or ethnicity is unavailable. An overview of international adoption is provided as an illustration that only those with the ability to pay very high fees, and jump through many hoops, are eligible for out-of-country adoptions.

Chapter 9 examines the experiences of parents and children receiving interventions and services from the child protection agencies. Surprisingly little information and research exist on parental and child experiences within the child protection system. Certainly, parents and children can have remarkably different perceptions of services received, and perceptions far different from those of their child protection workers. The chapter offers case illustrations and examines the challenges parents and children face when receiving services from child protection agencies, often under legal supervision. Effective engagement between child welfare workers and biological parents can be made more difficult when parental substance abuse, mental illness, and/or violence are present in the family.

Chapter 10 addresses the professional and personal realities of those who work within the child welfare system. Expected to adhere to agency policies, child protection workers can feel caught between the bureaucracy and doing what they feel is necessary to address the issues of their client families. Many factors determine the professionalism of child welfare workers. These factors include the personality of the worker, the level of job interest, the type and level of education, and the kind of training offered by child welfare agencies. Typically, child welfare workers who thrive in their work possess strong coping strategies including positive organizational characteristics and strong social and emotional support.

Chapter 11 examines the most recent literature regarding innovative and effective child welfare intervention practices that promote healthy families and children. The chapter highlights the importance of family engagement in appropriate planning for children. The values underlying these innovative practices feature cooperation and collaboration within a mutually trusting relationship between the worker and the family. The chapter examines the need for continued advocacy and the future of public and private partnerships in the development of community-based programs. The chapter also showcases examples of private and public programs that successfully meet the needs of children and families.

Chapter 12 addresses the prevention activities and strategies to reduce child maltreatment. *Primary prevention* is defined as keeping child maltreatment from developing at all. *Secondary prevention* is defined as early intervention into families at risk for child maltreatment that can provide helpful supports. *Tertiary prevention* is defined as services that treat child maltreatment to prevent abuse and neglect from becoming worse. The chapter also addresses future issues in child protection and identifies further steps to better protect children and ensure that they are living in safe and loving homes.

An Instructor's Manual also accompanies this text. The manual provides PowerPoint slides for each chapter, learning objectives, brief chapter summaries, key concepts, test questions, and a list of current resources. **Qualified instructors may request these ancillaries by e-mail: textbook@springerpub.com.**

REFERENCE

Levenson, M., & Wen, P. (2014, April 30). Child agency gets a change at the top. *The Boston Globe*, p. A1.

ACKNOWLEDGMENTS

I appreciate the support and patience of my husband John and my children Anna and Cameron. John Kohler reviewed the manuscript and contributed his wisdom about the importance of healthy families. Anna Mignon, who is preparing for her own career helping children, shared her insights about the needs of children and made significant contributions to the clarity of the manuscript. I also deeply appreciate Marcia Colagiovanni's comments on the entire manuscript and her outstanding editing skills.

OVERVIEW OF THE AMERICAN CHILD WELFARE SYSTEM

Children not having enough food to eat? Children whose parents are unable to provide the basics of food, clothing, and shelter? Children as victims of violence within their own homes? Children without homes sleeping in cars or on the streets? Children without access to health care? Child prostitutes on American city streets? Can this happen to children in the United States? Unfortunately, yes.

There are few things in the world, and perhaps none, as important as the life of a child. Yet it is surprising how little is done in the United States, and around the world, to ensure that the needs of children are met. There are no national or international policies to ensure the well-being of children or even that children have enough to eat, a place to live, access to health care, and access to quality education.

This chapter presents an overview of child welfare issues including the international context of child welfare, the reporting of child abuse and neglect cases within states, the national picture of childhood maltreatment, legal issues in child welfare, and opportunities to strengthen American families that can reduce child abuse and neglect.

In the United States, policies are often enacted in response to horrific cases of abuse and neglect, making child welfare a reactive rather than a proactive system. For example, it took the disappearance and death of Jeremiah Oliver, a 4-year-old boy who went missing in 2013 and whose remains were not found until April 2014, to prompt a review of the Massachusetts child welfare system. This boy's family had received intensive services from the Massachusetts

1

Department of Children and Families (DCF) for several years, and it required this deeply disturbing case to jolt Massachusetts into an evaluation of child welfare services (Child Welfare League of America, 2014). Major problems continued for Massachusetts child welfare services as the body of 2-year-old Bella Bond washed up on the shores of Boston Harbor in May 2015. Bella's older siblings were removed from the home owing to abuse and neglect, and twice the DCF had intervened with her mother on child abuse and neglect complaints. See Box 1.1 for the case of Bella Bond, known as "Baby Doe."

We do not have to dig deep to understand the importance in every culture of taking care of children. It is very easy to provide justification for making the needs of children paramount in every society. Children are the most likely victims of all kinds of maltreatment including physical, emotional, and sexual abuse as well as physical and emotional neglect. Not surprisingly, the youngest children are the most vulnerable to maltreatment and the least able to protect themselves (Stepleton, McIntosh, & Corrington, 2010).

The failure to provide a safe and loving home environment has lifelong consequences for children and their families. Brain development is adversely affected by abuse and neglect, and maltreated children are set up for a lifetime of difficulties (Center for the Study of Social Policy, 2013; Fang, Brown, Florence, & Mercy, 2012; Stepleton et al., 2010). More recent research correlates poverty with problems with brain development (Hair, Hanson, Wolfe, & Pollak, 2015). This does not mean that children cannot overcome an abusive childhood. We are all aware of situations of remarkable resilience where children successfully overcome their challenging and abusive childhoods. However, these successes of individuals tend to be memorable because they are outside of the norm.

A myriad of issues impact children that are associated with poverty and propel them toward involvement in the child welfare system. Parental substance abuse and parental mental illness can be contributors to abusive and neglectful family situations. Indeed, children in the child welfare system are significantly more likely to have emotional and behavioral problems, health care issues, and educational challenges (Kortenkamp & Ehrle, 2002).

The economic costs of child maltreatment in the United States are huge. It is estimated that the economic burden to the United States in 2008 was $124 billion (Fang et al., 2012). An economic analysis can encourage increased public attention to this very important social problem, and places child maltreatment in the broader context of public health problems—the short- and long-term medical costs and loss of productivity that already command attention owing to the costs of intervention and treatment. The "substantial economic burden" of child maltreatment should encourage prevention efforts (Fang et al., 2012, p. 163).

Family structure has changed enormously over the years, especially since the 1960s. Today, marriage and childbearing are no longer closely associated,

BOX 1.1 "Baby Doe" in Boston

Bela Bond was known only as "Baby Doe" when her body washed up on the shores of Deer Island in Boston Harbor in May 2015. The body of the 2½-year old was found in a plastic bag. For 3 months, her identity remained a mystery, despite extraordinary media attention. No one claimed to know the child whose likeness produced by a forensic artist bore an extraordinary resemblance to the photographs of Bella Bond. As this very disturbing story unfolded, it was learned that Bella's mother was a drug addict whose drug-addicted boyfriend murdered the child because he thought she was possessed by demons. The boyfriend and mother then stashed the small child's body in the refrigerator of their apartment until they dumped Bella into Boston Harbor. The boyfriend faces murder charges, and Bella's mother is charged with being an accessory after the fact.

Almost equally astonishing is that those who knew Bella, including other tenants in their apartment building, failed to make the connection between the disappearance of a child they knew and the likeness they saw perhaps daily on the news and area billboards. Although there had been many tips to the police, it took three months to identify Bella's body. Although there had been talk that perhaps this child was from some far-off place, Bella had spent her short life in the Dorchester neighborhood of Boston.

Bella had two older half-siblings who were taken away from their mother by the Massachusetts DCF. Two reports had been made for neglect or abuse of Bella, resulting in a short period of intervention by DCF before the cases were closed.

Is the blame for Bella's death to be shared by the mother's boyfriend, Bella's mother, and the DCF?

———

Source: Wen, Allen, and Ramos (2015).

especially among the poor (Furstenberg, 2014; Lopoo & Raissian, 2014). The nuclear family does not exist as it did until the 1960s, and the American family has had to adapt to numerous economic, technological, demographic, and cultural changes (Furstenberg, 2014). These changes can be attributed mostly to the feminist revolution and the reduction in the division of labor according to gender (Furstenberg, 2014; Putnam, 2015). Employment rates for all women increased after 1960 and were especially evident among women with college degrees (Putnam, 2015). While women continue to earn only three quarters of what men do for comparable work, women have made significant strides in the workplace. Yet the income inequality between men and women continues and is referred to by Mink (2010) as "sex-based occupational segregation" (p. 38).

Single parenthood is no longer severely stigmatized. We did get over the Murphy Brown television show flap in 1992 when Vice President Dan Quayle criticized the fictitious Murphy Brown character for choosing to have a child out of wedlock. Today, those who want to continue to stigmatize single-parenting often give religious reasons for doing so. Indeed, childbearing among single women has risen in all Western nations (Furstenberg, 2014). A variety of issues can help explain the changes. Contraceptives, especially oral contraceptives, which were developed in the late 1960s, have become widely available and have had a major impact on declining births. Within marriage, couples are having children at older ages as they take time to build their careers.

Overall, social class differences in families have become wider as inequality has grown in the wealthiest countries (Furstenberg, 2014). In fact, ". . . the United States has moved toward a two-tier family system in which practices in establishing and maintaining families among the affluent and the disadvantaged have become more dissimilar" (Furstenberg, 2014, p. 18). Those with low incomes do not have the opportunity to achieve economic security and have far fewer opportunities to move into the middle class. The affluent have the resources that support family stability, whereas those in poverty continue to struggle and have greater difficulty in achieving economic and family security. In comparison with other rich nations, the United States offers an "unusually small cash benefit package" (Garfinkel & Zilanawala, 2015, p. 211). More generous European and Nordic countries with stronger safety support networks include Austria, Germany, France, Norway, Sweden, and Denmark.

The single most important reason that families come to the attention of child welfare agencies is that they are poor—poverty and child welfare cases go hand in hand. Foster care in the 1960s as well as today is primarily for children of those living in poverty (Davidson, 2008). Indeed, the child welfare system "is the final social safety net that a family arrives at after falling through all other safety nets" (Pelton, 2010, p. 272). Typically, all facets of the child welfare system deal with poverty as an underlying issue with the exception of some types of adoption. Adoption of American-born infants and international adoption are typically available only to those with sufficient funds to pay the very high adoption fees, specifically the upper middle class and the wealthy.

Statistics regarding sex trafficking are probably underestimates of the true picture, and a significant number of child victims of sexual exploitation have been involved with child protective services (Walker & Quraishi, 2014). The National Center of Missing and Exploited Children estimated that in 2014, approximately 17% of runaway children were victims of sex trafficking (Child Welfare Information Gateway, 2015). Children in foster care are among the most vulnerable to abuse and are more likely to go missing than other children. In June 2014, 168 juveniles were found by the Federal Bureau of Investigation (FBI) to be involved in just one specific child sex trafficking case, a number of whom had never been reported as missing (Tucker, 2014). The National Center of Missing and Exploited Children has supported legislation to require child protection agencies to notify them at the same time police are notified. Clearly, better tracking of missing children is needed.

CHILD WELFARE IN AN INTERNATIONAL CONTEXT

Child welfare within an international context looks at the enormous problems of human trafficking, sexual exploitation, and child slave labor that exist in the world today. The United Nations Declaration of the Rights of the Child was adopted in 1959. After ratification by the required number of nations, the UN General Assembly adopted the Convention on the Rights of the Child that came into force in September 1990. This is the first treaty to set minimum protections for the rights of children around the world. Currently, 194 countries have signed it, including every member of the United Nations, except Somalia and the United States. The process is onerous, and the executive branch of the U.S. government must initiate the process to ratify a treaty. It must then be reviewed by the Senate Foreign Relations Committee and by the State Department. Then it must receive at least a two thirds vote by the full Senate, and finally be signed by the U.S. President (National Council of Juvenile and Family Court Judges, 2012). Again we see that children are not a priority, especially in the world of politics. The chairwoman of the National Association of Social Workers International Committee, Robin Mama, declared: "The U.S. is such a supporter of children's rights and is seen as a leader in international human rights" (Malai, 2014). This statement seems unduly optimistic and does not reflect reality.

According to the 2015 World Report on Child Labour, there are approximately 168 million child laborers, mostly working in agriculture, with 85 million children engaged in work that is considered hazardous (International Labour Organization, 2015). Child laborers face both health and safety risks and lower educational attainment, and are less likely to find better work in the future. Despite such adverse impacts, child labor issues around the world are unlikely to be resolved anytime soon.

Walmart has long been known to use child slave labor from other countries, even while boasting that their products are made in the United States. In an exposé of Walmart by *Dateline NBC* in 1992, Walmart denied that it used child slave labor in Bangladesh (*Dateline NBC*, 1992). When confronted with evidence of children working in factories making clothing for Walmart, then Chief Executive Officer David Glass terminated the television interview with NBC journalist Brian Ross. Mr. Glass asked to return 2 weeks later to continue the *Dateline NBC* interview, stating he could not verify that children were making clothes for Walmart in factories in Bangladesh. Even when looking at photographs of children of about the age of 12 seated at sewing machines, Mr. Glass continued his denial by stating: "Children. You and I might perhaps define children differently."

In some countries, the economy has come to rely on the labor of children. For example, in Honduras, 15% of children in the country, about 500,00 children, have jobs (Arce, 2014). According to the United Nations International Children's Fund (UNICEF), a spokesperson for Honduras stated: "Children need to support their families and themselves, and escape the gangs. You can prohibit child labor, but if the state does not take care of families, there are no options for the children but to work" (Arce, 2014, p. A7).

Examples abound of international abuses of children. In 2015, French soldiers were accused of sexually abusing children they were sent to protect in the Central African Republic (Charlton, 2015). In the aftermath of the 2015 earthquake in Nepal, orphaned children were sold by traffickers in to the work and sex industries (Rossington, 2015). UNICEF estimates that approximately 14 million children in Syria and Iraq have been traumatized by war (Cumming-Bruce, 2015). The UNICEF director stated: "Violence and suffering have not only scarred their past; they are shaping their futures" (Cumming-Bruce, 2015, p. A9). Currently, children are being groomed as perpetrators of violence and subjected to military training and indoctrination by the Islamic State.

The term Commercial Sexual Exploitation of Children (CSEC) refers to sexual abuse of children up to the age of 18 in exchange for money or another form of compensation. This includes exploitation of girls and boys who are engaged in prostitution on the streets or in brothels, or are the subject of pornographic materials. Initial sexual victimization and exploitation can be a setup for continued sexual abuse in adulthood (Mignon, Larson, & Holmes, 2002). See Box 1.2 for a description of a young girl in the United Kingdom who was a victim of sexual exploitation.

Children may not understand that their experiences constitute sexual exploitation. One 16-year-old who had been abused, neglected, and abandoned by her parents found herself taken in by a pimp and his girlfriend (Featherstone, 2015). She had sex with the pimp regularly, and then he was present while another man had sex with her in a hotel room. She did not see any money change hands and at the time, did not recognize this as prostitution. Later, the pimp and his girlfriend decided that because she was only 16 and had a warrant out for her arrest, she was not "ready to work yet."

BOX 1.2 Sexual Exploitation: A Setup for Future Troubles

Kim, one of the youngest of seven children, was 14 years old when she started staying out very late and "partying" with older boys and men. She lacked parental supervision because her father and oldest brother were in prison and her mother was often out of the home. Kim's school referred her to a counselor specializing in sexual exploitation who started working with Kim on "staying safe" and "appropriate sexual relationships." The counselor described Kim as "very difficult to engage" because she felt that her lifestyle was not a problem.

Kim fell into a relationship with a 35-year-old man who bought her alcohol, took her shopping, and told her he loved her. This was compelling for a young girl who felt this was the first time anyone had paid attention to her. Subsequently, Kim got into a fight with a neighbor and was arrested. The arrest served as her entrée into the juvenile justice system.

When Kim was age 15, her "boyfriend" took her to a house in a different city to meet another man. That man took her shopping and then wanted to have sex with her. When Kim refused to have sex, she was raped. She told no one about the rape, but decided to end the relationship with her boyfriend. She began partying again, hanging out with older boys, drinking, and exchanging sex for drugs.

By the time she was 18 years old, Kim was regularly exchanging sex for money and drugs, and had been raped several more times. She also had several charges for being drunk and disorderly, criminal damage of the car of one of her rapists, and continuously violating her juvenile justice orders.

Source: Phoenix (n.d.).

CHILD ABUSE REPORTING

The first federal laws requiring mandated child abuse reporting were enacted in 1990 (Davidson, 2008). Individual states have the primary responsibility for intervening in cases of child abuse and neglect with legislation and funding provided by the federal government (Child Welfare Information Gateway, 2013). The "system" is not simply one organization, but a variety of organizations to address the multiple needs of children and their families. Each state has its own state child protection agency or local agencies charged with investigating reports of suspected abuse and/or neglect of children by parents or other caregivers. When children are harmed by others outside of the family or by strangers, these cases are handled by law enforcement organizations including the police and court systems (Child Welfare Information Gateway, 2013).

State or county child protection agencies are responsible for receiving reports of child abuse and/or neglect from other family members, and from professionals or others, typically through an initial telephone call. These state agencies are often named the Department of Children and Families or the Department of Social Services. Reports of suspected abuse or neglect can be made anonymously. The child protection agency then determines whether the allegations of abuse and/or neglect warrant an investigation by a child protection worker. Unsubstantiated cases are those where the child protection agency has determined there is insufficient evidence of abuse or neglect. (Remember that insufficient evidence is not the same thing as no evidence.) Substantiated cases are those where the child welfare agency has determined there is the likelihood that abuse and/or neglect did occur, and intervention is needed (Child Welfare Information Gateway, 2013). Families that are "screened in" can be offered supportive services, or in the most serious cases, the child or children can be removed and placed with other relatives or in a state-approved foster home.

A variety of professionals are "mandated reporters," meaning that they are required by law to notify the state or local child protection agency if they suspect child abuse or neglect. Mandated reporters include physicians, nurses, teachers, police officers, social workers, and psychologists. Mandated reporters are often unclear about their role and responsibility, and can erroneously assume they need to produce proof of abuse or neglect before making a report. Again, it is the "suspicion" that requires the report, and it is the responsibility of the child protection agency to determine whether actual abuse and/or neglect occurred.

How the child protection agency responds to reports of suspected abuse or neglect can be problematic. For example, in Vermont in 2013, of 17,458 telephone reports regarding suspected abuse or neglect, 70% were "screened out" and found not to warrant any assessment or investigation (Rathke, 2014). It is exceedingly hard to imagine that among those 70% of reports, no abuse and/or neglect problems existed. In Arizona in 2015, the director of the child welfare agency planned to reduce the number of cases initially screened in by making the criteria more stringent to cope with a backlog of 14,635 cases, where no worker had examined the file or been in touch with the child for over 60 days (Fischer, 2015). The simple explanation is that an already overworked staff and overloaded agency screens out all but the most severe cases. These examples are strong indicators of foundering child welfare systems.

As early as the 1970s, it was noted that there was little public understanding of the child welfare system. Kadushin (1974) found "a low level of public knowledge about child welfare services" (p. 46). Protective services, followed by adoption services, were considered to be the most important by the child welfare system. The same lack of knowledge about and support for child welfare services appears to be true today. There is an acknowledgment that these services are important, yet little is known about them, and they are not a top social or political priority.

THE NATIONAL PICTURE

National data on the numbers of children in child protective systems provides a picture of the types and severity of child maltreatment. The Child Welfare Outcomes 2009 to 2012 Report to Congress found that nationally in 2012, there were approximately 679,000 cases where abuse or neglect was substantiated by a child protection agency (Child Welfare Information Gateway, 2013). This translates into 9.2 child victims of maltreatment for every 1,000 children in the United States.

The first national survey of well-being of children served by child welfare agencies found a troubling picture (Kortenkamp & Ehrle, 2002). Regarding education, 39% of children in the child welfare system had academic challenges, whereas 28% had a learning, physical, or mental health problem that "limits their activities" (p. 5). Twenty-seven percent had significant emotional and behavioral problems, yet one third of this group did not receive mental health services. One quarter of children did not receive adequate cognitive stimulation.

The National Survey of Child and Adolescent Well-Being II (NSCAW II) is a national longitudinal study of children and families who have been investigated by child protection agencies. Data is collected from children and parents as well as from teachers and child protection workers for two cohorts of children. The NSCAW II studied 5,873 children, ranging in age from 2 months to 17.5 years old, who had contact with the child welfare system between 2008 and 2009 (Stambaugh et al., 2013). More than half of the children in the NSCAW II sample reported four or more adverse childhood experiences by the time the abuse/neglect was reported to child protection agencies. The NSCAW II also found that children involved with child protective services subsequently acquired additional risk factors including poverty, frequent moves to foster placements, and lack of needed health and social services (Stambaugh et al., 2013).

We have long known the negative consequences for children living in homes with intimate partner or other kinds of violence. The 2011 data from the National Survey of Children's Exposure to Violence found that approximately 25% of children in the United States have been exposed to violence involving weapons, as victims or witnesses (Mitchell, Hamby, Turner, Shattuck, & Jones, 2015).

In 2013, 31% of children were living in a family household where no adult had a full-time year-round job (Annie E. Casey Foundation, 2015). Nationally, 22% of children were living in poverty, a rate that should be unacceptable in one of the richest countries in the world. This breaks down to 39% of African American children living in poverty, 37% of Native Americans, 33% of Hispanics, and 14% of Whites (Annie E. Casey Foundation, 2015). The Department of Health and Human Services defines the federal poverty level as $24,250 for a family with four members, "an inadequate measure of a minimally decent standard of living" (Annie E. Casey Foundation, 2015, p. 6). An in-depth examination of the relationship between poverty and child maltreatment is the subject of Chapter 3.

Although there are innovative approaches to child welfare issues that will be described in Chapter 11, there is consensus that state and local systems do not function as well as they should to keep children safe. Although child protection systems and agencies get media attention when things go awry, often when children die of neglect or are murdered, there are very few opportunities for the public and the media to see appropriate child welfare interventions that benefit children.

LEGAL ISSUES

It has been only since 1974, with the Child Abuse Prevention and Treatment Act (CAPTA), that the federal government created federal definitions of child abuse and neglect, with state laws following federal laws in order to receive federal funds (Davidson, 2008). Davidson (2008) described federal funding as "woefully deficient" (p. 490) to assist states in bolstering casework interventions.

Legal issues and dilemmas abound within the child welfare system. As Davidson (2008) noted: "A system that both rests on legal standards and affords an immense amount of discretion in its operation is one that is likely (especially if underfunded) to be troubled" (p. 481). Typically, public attention is stirred only when there is media attention to a horrific case. In general, juvenile courts have been "complacent" in addressing the issues of abused and neglected children (Davidson, 2008, p. 482). A child welfare–related lawsuit is likely to lead to an increase in legislation; however, that does not mean that states add more financial support to address child welfare issues (Gainsborough, 2009).

A number of court cases and media exposés have been designed to pressure individual states to do a better job in child protection efforts. For example, in Florida, an official report acknowledged 79 child deaths in the year 2008. Yet a review by the *Miami Herald* newspaper counted 103 child deaths on the basis of records from the child protection agency itself, the DCF (Miller & Burch, 2014). It is troubling when lawsuits and media attention must be relied upon to pressure child protection agencies to provide adequate child welfare services. See Box 1.3.

BOX. 1.3 *Lawsuit Against the Department of Children and Families in Massachusetts*

In April 2010, Children's Rights of New York filed a class action lawsuit to force Massachusetts to improve its foster care placements for children. One case that spurred this lawsuit was that of Connor, who was first placed in a foster home at age 6 and had 4 different foster placements within a year. Although still only 6 years old, Connor spent 4½ months in a locked psychiatric unit.

Testimony revealed that in 2011, Massachusetts had the seventh highest rate of child abuse in foster care of 49 reporting states. Massachusetts ranked 49th of 52 reporting jurisdictions on timeliness of adoptions. And between 2008 and 2011, no more than 50% of children in the custody of the DCF received monthly caseworker visits; DCF failed miserably to meet the federal government's benchmark of at least 90%.

The lawsuit was dismissed by the district court judge. In December 2014, on appeal, the Chief Judge of the U.S. First Circuit Court of Appeals upheld the dismissal and wrote:

> The plaintiffs have articulated moral arguments that Massachusetts should do better. But they have not established, based on facts, that there have been constitutional violations as to the class of foster children, so they are not entitled to an injunction or federal court oversight. Improvements in the system must come through the normal state political processes. The problems are now for the Governor and the legislature of Massachusetts to resolve. (McKim, 2014, p. 1)

Sources: Children's Rights Organization (2015); McKim (2014); Vennochi (2014).

Often, caseloads are very high, and the workload for child welfare workers can be overwhelming. The sheer number of cases is exacerbated by the seriousness of the abuse and neglect cases (Child Welfare Information Gateway, 2010; Smith & Donovan, 2003). As discussed in Chapter 10, child welfare workers can feel caught between the bureaucratic rules and doing what they think is right to help maltreated children.

Much more can and must be done to support children and families within the child welfare system. This includes shared philosophical principles as well as the provision of practical supports such as financial assistance, availability of childcare and counseling services, and the entire range of services to address problems within a coordinated framework. See Box 1.4 for principles to guide child welfare efforts to strengthen families.

Although it is a cliché, children are the future of every society. Thus, the goals of child welfare services are to provide the services for families that focus on the "safety, permanency, and well-being of their children with equal emphasis on all three" (Child Welfare League of America, 2013, p. 3). Inroads have been made by advocacy organizations such as the Child Welfare League of America, the Children's Defense Fund, the National Indian Child Welfare Association, and the Casey Family Program National Center for Resource Family Support. However, so much more needs to be done to improve child protection services.

BOX 1.4 Guiding Principles for Strengthening Families in Child Welfare

1. Families, as first teachers and primary protectors, are fundamental to children's optimal development.
2. Building protective factors as well as reducing risk factors strengthens a family's ability to promote optimal development for their children.
3. Relationships—within families and communities, between families and providers, and across systems—are essential as vehicles of change.
4. Systematic and intentional coordination promotes healthy cross-system relationships, and maximizes the ability of systems and services to support families and children.
5. Shared accountability for optimal development and strengthened family functioning across broad networks of services and opportunities is essential at all levels.

Source: Stepleton, McIntosh, and Corrington (2010).

By necessity, child welfare work focuses on risk factors for abuse and neglect. It is important to develop assessment protocols for suspected child physical abuse that can foster clarity and agreement in diagnosis as well as standardize and improve the quality of research (Campbell, Olson, & Keenan, 2015). Child protection is a very delicate balance between the conflicting goals of providing safety for children and the professional efforts to preserve the family system. It is important to acknowledge family strengths and work with them, as well as support their development. The challenges are to strengthen families by developing parental resilience including increased knowledge of parenting and child development, fostering social connections, providing concrete services when the family has specific needs, and developing emotional and social competence in children (Stepleton et al., 2010). Yet there are dire situations that require removal of children for their safety.

The child welfare system should promote strong family relationships and good physical and mental health within a nurturing and consistent environment. The quality of services these children receive has a tremendous impact on their ability to become fully functioning and independent adults (Gainsborough, 2009). See Box 1.5 for a description of the National Blueprint of the Child Welfare League to improve child welfare services nationally.

BOX 1.5 *The National Blueprint of the Child Welfare League of America*

The National Blueprint of the Child Welfare League is an effort by a coalition of federal, state, and local agencies to advance the field of child welfare through advocacy, providing standards of excellence, and the development of best practices.

There are eight core principles of the National Blueprint:

1. All citizens should participate in advancing the rights and needs of children.
2. The responsibility for ensuring the well-being of children lies within individuals, families, organizations, and communities.
3. Families and organizations need to participate and engage communities so that their voices are heard and the physical and psychological safety of children is ensured.
4. Supports and services are developed and implemented to meet the needs of children and their families and communities participate in policy and program development.

(continued)

> **BOX 1.5 The National Blueprint of the Child Welfare League of America (continued)**
>
> 5. Quality improvement efforts ensure that the needs of children and their families are actually met by evaluating programs and implementing only those that show concrete evidence of effectiveness.
> 6. Workforce development includes providing the appropriate level of education and training for child welfare workers to have strong and up-to-date skills in working with children and families.
> 7. Equality must be promoted through the understanding of racial, ethnic, and cultural differences.
> 8. Funding and resources are critical and must be secured at the federal, state, local, and tribal levels and through the development of public–private partnerships.
>
> _____
> Adapted from the Child Welfare League of America (2013).

SUMMARY AND CONCLUSION

The American child welfare system consists of a variety of organizations that have been challenged in keeping children safe and ensuring their rights to food, clothing, shelter, and emotional support within a healthy family. However, as described later, there is great variation in the types of services and levels of funding by individual states. There are no simple fixes for a challenged child welfare system to adequately meet the needs of the families they are to serve. Often, changes to systems are forced through legal cases, hardly the optimal way to improve a system.

As we will see in the following chapters, child maltreatment does not occur in a vacuum, but instead is correlated with critical social ills such as poverty, racism, substance abuse, and mental illness. A multipronged approach is necessary on the federal, state, and local levels, and must also include private foundations. The National Blueprint of the Child Welfare League of America offers important recommendations to strengthen child welfare systems and the specific services they offer.

DISCUSSION QUESTIONS

1. Why are children not a top priority in U.S. social policy?
2. Describe some of the challenges of child welfare work for social workers.

3. What are the duties of mandated reporters? Give examples of those designated as mandated reporters.

4. Why is child slave labor such a big problem in the world today?

5. Why has the United States not adopted the UN Convention on the Rights of the Child?

6. Discuss how child maltreatment impacts adulthood of abuse victims/survivors.

7. How has the American family structure changed since the 1960s?

8. How does social inequality impact child abuse and neglect?

9. Why does child welfare policy seem to be a reaction to serious cases of abuse rather than the product of strategic planning?

10. In what ways can child welfare organizations strengthen families?

REFERENCES

Annie E. Casey Foundation. (2015). *The 2015 KIDS COUNT data book: State trends in child well-being*. Baltimore, MD: Author.

Arce, A. (2014, December 25). Child labor is a necessity for many: A job can mean survival in places such as Honduras. *The Boston Globe*, p. A7.

Campbell, K. A., Olson, L. M., & Keenan, H. T. (2015). Critical elements in the medical evaluation of suspected child physical abuse. *Pediatrics, 136*(1), 35–43. doi:10.1542/peds.2014-4192

Center for the Study of Social Policy. (2013, July). *Raising the bar: Child welfare's shift toward well-being*. Washington, DC: State Policy and Advocacy Reform Center.

Charlton, A. (2015, April 30). French soldiers accused of abuses: African children allege sex assault. *The Boston Globe*, p. A6.

Children's Rights Organization. (2015). Class actions: MA—*Connor B. v. Patrick*. Retrieved from http://childrensrights.org/class_action/massachusetts

Child Welfare Information Gateway. (2010, April). *Issue Briefs: Caseload and workload management*. Washington, DC: U.S. Department of Health and Human Services, Children's Bureau. Retrieved from www.childwelfare.gov/pubs/case-work-management

Child Welfare Information Gateway. (2013). *Factsheets: How the child welfare system works*. Washington, DC: U.S. Department of Health and Human Services, Children's Bureau.

Child Welfare Information Gateway. (2015, July). *Issue Briefs: Child welfare and human trafficking*. Washington, DC: U.S. Department of Health and Human Services, Children's Bureau. Retrieved from https://www.childwelfare.gov/pubs/issue-briefs/trafficking

Child Welfare League of America. (2013). *National Blueprint for Excellence in Child Welfare. Executive Summary: Raising the bar for children, families and communities*. Washington, DC: Author.

Child Welfare League of America. (2014, May 22). *Quality improvement report*. Washington, DC: Author.

Cumming-Bruce, N. (2015, March 13). UN report warns of a lost generation: Trauma routine for 14m children in Syria and Iraq. *The Boston Globe*, p. A9.

Dateline NBC. (1992). Walmart "Buy American" campaign exposed.

Davidson, H. (2008, Fall). Federal law and state intervention when parents fail: Has national guidance of our child welfare system been successful? *Family Law Quarterly, 42*(3), 481–510.

Fang, X., Brown, D. S., Florence, C., & Mercy, J. A. (2012). The economic burden of child maltreatment in the United States and implications for prevention. *Child Abuse & Neglect, 36*(2), 156–165. doi:10.1016/j.chiabu.2011.10.006

Featherstone, A. (2015, August 8). I didn't realize I was being trafficked. *Salon.com*. Retrieved from www.salon.com/2015/08/09/i_didnt_realize_I_was_being_sex_trafficked_partner

Fischer, H. (2015). *Arizona to take on fewer child-abuse cases*. Retrieved from http://tucson.com/news/state-and-regional/arizona-to-take-on-fewer-child-abuse-cases/article

Furstenberg, F. F. (2014). Fifty years of family change: From consensus to complexity. *Annals of the American Academy of Political and Social Science, 654*, 12–30. doi:10.1177/0002716214524521

Gainsborough, J. F. (2009, Fall). Scandals, lawsuits, and politics: Child welfare policy in the U.S. states. *State Politics and Policy Quarterly, 9*(3), 325–355.

Garfinkel, I., & Zilanawala, A. (2015). Fragile families in the American welfare state. *Children and Youth Service Review, 55*, 210–221.

Hair, N. L., Hanson, J. L., Wolfe, B. L., & Pollak, S. D. (2015). Association of child poverty, brain development, and academic achievement. *JAMA Pediatrics, 169*(9), 822–829. doi:10.1001/jamapediatrics.2015.1475

International Labour Organization. (2015, June 10). *World report on child labour 2015*. Geneva, Switzerland: Author.

Kadushin, A. (1974, Winter). Public perception of child welfare services: Results of a student survey. *Journal of Education for Social Work, 10*(1), 42–47.

Kortenkamp, K., & Ehrle, J. (2002). The well-being of children involved with the child welfare system: A national overview. In *New Federalism: National Survey of America's Families* (The Urban Institute, Series B, B-43. Assessing the New Federalism: An

Urban Institute Program to Assess Changing Social Policies). Washington, DC: The Urban Institute.

Lopoo, L. M., & Raissian, K. M. (2014). U.S. social policy and family complexity. *Annals of the American Academy of Political and Social Science, 654*, 213–230. doi:10.1177/0002716214530372

Malai, R. (2014, November). International committee supports child rights treaty adoption. *NASW News, 59*(10), 1.

McKim, J. (2014, December 16). *Mass. appeals court upholds ruling dismissing DCF lawsuit.* Retrieved from http://eye.necir.org/2014/12/16/ma-appeals-court-upholds-rulingdismissing-dcf-lawsuit

Meltzer, J., & Paletta, R. (2014, September). *From crisis to opportunity: Child welfare reform in Massachusetts.* Boston, MA: The Center for the Study of Social Policy for the Boston Foundation and Strategic Grant Partners.

Mignon, S. I., Larson, C. J., & Holmes, W. M. (2002). *Family abuse: Consequences, theories, and responses.* Boston, MA: Allyn & Bacon.

Miller, C. M., & Burch, A. D. S. (2014, March 22). Florida's undercount of child abuse deaths. *The Miami Herald.* Retrieved from http://media.miamiherald.com/static/media/projects/2014/innocents-lost/stories/undercount

Mink, G. (2010). Women's work, mother's poverty: Are men's wages the best cure for women's economic insecurity? In B. R. Mandell (Ed.), *The crisis of caregiving: Social welfare policy in the United States* (pp. 33–46). New York, NY: Palgrave Macmillan.

Mitchell, K. J., Hamby, S. L., Turner, H. A., Shattuck, A., & Jones, L. M. (2015). Weapon involvement in the victimization of children. *Pediatrics, 136*(1), 10–17. doi:10.1542/peds.2014-3966

National Council of Juvenile and Family Court Judges. (2012, February 28). *U.S. still has not ratified United Nations Convention on the Rights of the Child.* Retrieved from www.ncjfcj.org/us-still-has-not-ratified-united-nations-convention-rights-child

Office of Planning, Research and Evaluation. (2013, August 8). *National Survey of Child and Adolescent Well-Being (NSCAW), No. 20: Adverse child experiences in NSCAW.* Washington, DC: U.S. Department of Health and Human Services.

Pelton, L. H. (2010, Winter). Introduction: Race, class and the child welfare system. *Journal of Health and Human Services Administration, 33*(3), 270–276.

Phoenix, J. (n.d.). *Out of place: The policing and criminalization of sexually exploited girls and young women.* London, UK: The Howard League for Penal Reform.

Putnam, R. D. (2015). *Our kids: The American dream in crisis.* New York, NY: Simon & Schuster.

Rathke, L. (2014, September 22). Vermont legislators question rate of child abuse intervention. *The Boston Globe,* p. B12.

Rossington, B. (2015, August 12). *Child traffickers preying on earthquake orphans left to fend for themselves in Nepal*. Retrieved from www.mirror.co.uk/news/world-news/child-traffickers-preying-earthquake-orphans-6242777

Smith, B. D., & Donovan, S. E. F. (2003). Child welfare practice in organizational and institutional context. *Social Service Review, 77*(4), 541–563.

Stambaugh, L. F., Ringeisen, H., Casanueva, C. C., Tueller, S., Smith, K. E., & Dolan, M. (2013). *Adverse childhood experiences in NSCAW* (OPRE Report No. 2013-26). Washington, DC: Office of Planning, Research and Evaluation, Administration for Children and Families, U.S. Department of Health and Human Services.

Stepleton, K., McIntosh, J., & Corrington, B. (2010, August). *Allied for better outcomes: Child welfare and early childhood* (pp. 9–10). Washington, DC: Center for the Study of Social Policy. Retrieved from www.strengtheningfamilies.net/images/uploads/pdf_uploads/allied_for_better_outcomes.pdf

Tucker, E. (2014, July 14). Some missing children are never reported. *The Boston Globe*, p. A11.

Vennochi, J. (2014, May 1). Will DCF case taint Coakley? *The Boston Globe*. Retrieved from http://www.bostonglobe.com/opinion/2014/05/01/dcf/coakley/rBvAOAP5kbgAbm3tQKpQsM/story.html

Walker, K., & Quraishi, F. (2014, August). *From abused and neglected to abused and exploited: The intersection of the child welfare system with the commercial sexual exploitation of children*. Oakland, CA: National Center for Youth Law. Retrieved from http://youthlaw.org/wp-content/uploads/2015/03/FROM-ABUSED-AND-NEGLECTED-TO-ABUSED-AND-EXPLOITED.pdf

Wen, P., Allen, E., & Ramos, N. (2015, October 3). A look at Bella before she was Baby Doe. *The Boston Globe*. Retrieved from https://www.bostonglobe.com/metro/2015/10/03/before-she-was-baby-doe/dLTwKDG6aRL3QO4qHdb5nJ/story.html

A BRIEF HISTORY OF THE CHILD WELFARE SYSTEM

*T*he concerns and problems of child welfare systems today have their seeds in the unresolved issues of the past (McGowan, 2005). These issues include the needs of children versus the rights of parents, in-home services and family preservation versus foster care and adoption, and issues of federal, state, and local child welfare responsibility and funding.

Chapter 2 examines the development of the contemporary child welfare system in the United States, including the rich history of "child saving" of the 19th century. It reviews the private efforts to provide services to abused and neglected children that have transitioned into significantly greater governmental roles through the years. Overall, this chapter offers a brief chronological perspective on laws, policies, and practices that have developed in the United States.

The history of child protection has been divided into three eras, a useful way to examine the history of social and child welfare (Myers, 2008/2009). The first era, up to 1875, focused on the period before child protection efforts and programs became organized. The second era, between 1875 and 1962, brought the development of private charitable child protection efforts. The third era, from 1962 up to the present, has focused on the roles of state and federal governments in child protection services (Myers, 2008/2009).

CHILD PROTECTION BEFORE 1875

The initial era of child protection focused on private efforts to aid the children of the poor, if children received any protection at all (Myers, 2008/2009). The English Poor Law of 1562 required a weekly charitable contribution to the poor. Failure to give voluntarily could result in increased taxes and even imprisonment in England. These laws allowed poor children to be placed in homes to perform indentured service until they reached adulthood. This arrangement extended to the United States. Some children came alone to the United States. It is not known how many came voluntarily and how many were compelled to come, although, clearly, poor children did not come voluntarily (Mason, 1994). These forms of "apprenticeship" were based on the English custom of placing children in the home of a master. The master and his family were obligated to provide food, clothing, and shelter as well as some form of training in return for services.

Organized services for children did not exist in the United States in the 1600s and 1700s (McGowan, 2010). The first orphanage was founded in 1727 in New Orleans by the Ursuline Convent; the children typically remained only until the age of 8 or 9 and were then indentured to families (McGowan, 2010).

Concerns about child labor emerged in the 1800s in the United Kingdom. The Report of the Select Committee on Factory Children's Labour, better known as the Sadler Report, was written in 1832 by Michael Sadler, the chairman of a United Kingdom parliamentary committee. Mr. Sadler introduced a legislative bill seeking to limit the hours children could work in textile mills and factories (Grundfossen, 1965). Mr. Sadler obtained testimony of child laborers describing long working hours under bleak and abusive conditions. For example, Mathew Crabtree, a child laborer, testified that he began work in a factory at the age of 8 and worked 14 hours each day, with 1 hour for a break. If deemed necessary, Mathew was required to work 16 hours a day. Mathew testified that if he was late to work, he was beaten with a strap (Sadler Report, 1832). The English Parliament did not directly act as a result of the Sadler Report, citing imbalances in the testimony; however, this did lead to the passage of the Factory Act of 1833, which began the era of modern factory legislation (Grundfossen, 1965). In the 1800s in the United States, decreased numbers of White children became indentured as a result of the rise of the large slave industry (McGowan, 2010).

Nineteenth century life in America emphasized the "good family life and childhood" (Holt, 1992, p. 11). This was a time when child-rearing practices and the education of children received close attention, and literature burgeoned on the topic. Industrialization and the movement West encouraged paying more attention to children, especially the societal expectations for them to have a positive childhood, which in turn would make for healthy and positive adults.

Clearly, not all children had the benefit of families that could provide for them in loving homes. Cases of child abuse could mean criminal prosecution of the abuser. For example, in Massachusetts in 1866, a law was passed that authorized judges to intervene when parents failed to provide appropriate parenting or education, when parents had alcohol problems, or when parents engaged in criminal activity (Myers, 2008/2009). In Illinois in 1869, a father was criminally prosecuted for keeping his blind son in a cold basement in the wintertime. Although the defense attorney argued that parents had the right to parent their children as they wish, the Illinois Supreme Court decided that parents must use reason and not commit cruelty toward their children (Myers, 2008/2009). These cases in the 1860s brought greater awareness of the responsibility of society to intervene when parents were not providing proper care of their children.

According to the Children's Aid Society, in New York City in the mid-1800s, approximately 30,000 children were homeless. The Society founder, Protestant minister Charles Loring Brace, thought that instead of remaining in the poverty-stricken and chaotic streets of the city, children could escape by being sent to the West by train to live and work on farms. The orphan trains ran from 1853 into the early 1900s, stopping in more than 45 states, transporting some 100,000 to 120,000 children (Children's Aid Society, n.d.; Mandell, 2010). However, not all shared the same view of Charles Loring Brace, and not all agree that children were sent on the orphan trains because they were homeless. Indeed, Reverend Brace preached that immigrants to New York were "genetically inferior," and that children needed to be removed from their poor parents to give them hope for a better future. Over time, Reverend Brace came to think that it would be useless to try to help poor adults (Holt, 1992). Reverend Brace "hated" Catholics, and most of the children on the trains were children of Catholic parents who were sent to Protestant homes (Mandell, 2010, p. 113). Many of the children had to do difficult labor in their families, and some were physically and sexually abused. Rather than being "child savers," the members of the Children's Aid Society on New York City streets looking for children were considered by some to be "child stealers" (Mandell, 2010).

Issues of race and ethnicity were concerns during this period. One disturbing episode was the case of Catholic nuns taking 40 Catholic children, most of whom were Irish, to settle with previously chosen Mexican families in Arizona in 1904 (Gordon, 1999). Upon arrival, there was a strong outcry from White families that Mexican families were adopting the children. The Mexican families were forced to return the children, or in some cases, children were kidnapped, and the children were then reassigned to White families. The case was taken up by the Arizona Supreme Court, and it was decided that Mexicans were "unfit" to raise White children, and that it was right to take the children away from the Mexican families. Many would like to think that this kind of discrimination in the child protection system is a thing of the past. We will see that discrimination is alive and well today.

The orphan trains ended when the entire system received criticism, the Catholic Church objected to placements in Protestant homes, and expansion westward was coming to a close (Cook, 1995; Holt, 1992). Other reasons included increased industrialization and development of child labor laws, as well as the rise of social work as a profession that offered services to families to help keep them together (Cook, 1995). Cook (1995), in an interview with 25 individuals who were subjected to the orphan train experience, learned that they had been torn from their parents and siblings, experienced prejudice in their new homes and communities, and were neglected by agencies: "Some interviewees described circumstances in which they were treated by their adoptive or foster families as unpaid workers, more like slaves than family members" (p. 4). See Box. 2.1 for a description of the experiences of two children on the orphan trains.

BOX 2.1 The Orphan Trains

A boy on a train that stopped in Benton County, Arkansas, had this to say:

> We were taken from the train to the Methodist church. Speeches were made and folks were asked to take an orphan home for dinner. Later that afternoon we were brought back for the selection process. . .. I felt sorry for the others because some of them were not chosen. I know now how it must have hurt them to feel that no one wanted them.

Another boy actually refused to be taken in until he felt comfortable with the adults:

> I refused to go home with two different farmers . . . but I was fortunate I did not. The two boys the farmers adopted were hardly more than slaves to them. . . . Everyone seemed to think I was a very bad character and I was left alone on stage that day alone, with no place to go. . . . A 60 year-old couple heard about me and . . . persuaded me to go home with them . . . as it turned out, I had the best home of all the orphans. . . .

Source: Holt (1992).

In general, because there were few complaints, it was assumed that the orphan train experience worked well for all. The children found homes, and the families benefited from their contributions, despite evidence to the contrary (Holt, 1992). The orphan train experience is considered the precursor to the foster care system of today (Children's Aid Society, n.d.; McGowan, 2005).

Thus, it was the children of the poor in cities that bore the brunt of the child-saving efforts through "control, constraint, and punishment" (Platt, 1977, p. 177), and who were denied the opportunity for "initiative, responsibility, and autonomy" (p. 177). Platt (1977) reminds us:

> The child-saving movement was not a humanistic enterprise on behalf of the working class against the established order. On the contrary, its impetus came primarily from the middle and upper classes that were instrumental in devising new forms of social control to protect their power and privilege. (p. xx)

Although there was much concern for White children, this concern did not extend to children of color. African American children had fewer options than White children. African American children were not considered for the trains because of prejudice by those in New York as well those in communities out West. Another concern was that the Children's Aid Society would be accused of practicing slavery (Cook, 1995).

Those African Americans who were not sold into slavery were excluded from orphanages for Whites (McGowan, 2010). Through the years, as African Americans were ignored by the developing child welfare system, families provided the care, nurturing, and oversight of African American children, including extended families, especially grandmothers (Hogan & Siu, 1988; Jimenez, 2006). These practices of caring for children from other families have their roots in African societies, and during slavery, contributed to "flexible kinship networks that flourished alongside the dehumanizing system created and sustained by White plantation owners" (Jimenez, 2006, p. 892). The first orphanage for African American children was established in 1822 by the Society of Friends, known as the Philadelphia Association for the Care of Colored Children (McGowan, 2005).

African American churches have a long history of providing informal social and financial assistance to families in need. In the 19th century, voluntary organizations of activist women provided for African American children. For example, the Virginia Industrial School for Colored Girls was established in 1915 (Jimenez, 2006). Efforts to assist African American children by the developing child welfare system came about because of the advocacy of the National Urban League established in 1910, the greater visibility of African Americans that resulted from their movement into cities after World War I, and a greater willingness of child welfare organizations to provide services to African Americans (McGowan, 2005). See Box 2.2 for a description of Carrie Steele, who did so much to give African American orphans a home.

In 1825, New York State had four orphan asylums that grew to over 60 institutions by 1866 (Holt, 1992). In 1868, Massachusetts began paying for foster homes. The "free" foster home placement transitioned into care supervised by agencies (Mandell, 2010). The child protection societies that evolved over time clearly intervened to assist children, but were not yet offering organized and coordinated services.

CHILD PROTECTION FROM 1875 TO 1962

The organized child protection efforts of this second era stemmed from the disturbing case, in 1874, of Mary Ellen Wilson. Mary Ellen was a 9-year-old girl whose parents had died when she was a toddler and who was abused and neglected by her guardians, the Connellys. See Box 2.3 for the story of Mary Ellen in her own words.

Much has been made of the Mary Ellen case because at that time no protective services for children existed. The religious missionary Etta Wheeler, who was committed to rescuing Mary Ellen, sought the assistance of Henry Bergh,

---

BOX 2.2 Carrie Steele (1829–1900)

Carrie Steele was born into slavery and became an orphan, like the many children she came to care for in her life. She was a cleaning person at the Atlanta railroad station, where she regularly encountered children who had been abandoned there. Carrie brought children into her own small home and then began to dream of establishing her own home for orphans. Although her own salary was just $100 a month, she managed to raise the $5,000 to build the Carrie Steele Orphan Home. African American children participated in Bible study, cultivated practical skills, and developed a strong work ethic. Her gravestone includes the words: "The Mother of Orphans. She has done what she could."

The Carrie Steele-Pitts home exists today on 26 acres in northwest Atlanta and has helped more than 20,000 children through the years.

Sources: Henson (2015); Martin (2015).

BOX 2.3 Mary Ellen 1864–1956

These are the words of Mary Ellen as she told the story of her life of abuse:

> My mother and father are both dead. I don't know how old I am. I have no recollection of a time when I did not live with the Connellys. I call Mrs. Connelly mamma. . . . I am never allowed to play with any children, or to have any company whatever. Mamma has been in the habit of whipping and beating me almost every day. She used to whip me with a twisted whip—a raw hide. The whip always left a black and blue mark on my body. I have now the black and blue marks on my head which were made by mamma, and also a cut on the left side of my forehead which was made by a pair of scissors. She struck me with the scissors and cut me; I have no recollection of ever having been kissed by anyone—have never been kissed by mamma. Whenever mamma went out I was locked up in the bedroom. I do not know for what I was whipped—mamma never said anything to me when she whipped me. I do not want to go back to live with mamma, because she beats me so. (From *The New York Times*, April 10, 1874, p. 8.)

Source: Watkins (1990).

the founder of the American Society for the Prevention of Cruelty to Animals (Watkins, 1990). It was Mr. Bergh who prevailed upon a New York Supreme Court Justice to hear the case and Mr. Bergh who contacted *The New York Times* to garner media attention for the cause. Mrs. Connelly was found guilty of assault and sentenced to a year of hard labor in a penitentiary. After an initial unsatisfactory placement in an institution, Mary Ellen joined the family of Mrs. Wheeler and then married at age 24.

The story that was of greatest interest regarding Mary Ellen was that no child protective services were available specifically for children, and thus the advocacy group for animals was forced to intervene. This myth has been debunked because history does show that parents could be held responsible for abuse before the Mary Ellen case; however, laws were not enforced in systematic ways (Watkins, 1990). Although there is disagreement on the details of the story, there is agreement that significant media attention to the case led to the development, in 1875, of the New York Society for the Prevention of Cruelty to

Children, the first organization to specifically address child protection issues (Watkins, 1990; Myers, 2008/2009). This case established the practice that children could be removed from homes and their parents prosecuted. At this time, New York became the model for other states (Watkins, 1990).

In the late 1800s and early 1900s, child protection was essentially private and then began to move toward public services. The child welfare movement in the late 19th century represented child protection as an important part of solving social problems; however, within the early 20th century, federal government funding did not focus on reducing poverty (Guggenheim, 2000). Society was content to blame families living in poverty for the variety of social problems they faced.

The development in 1899 of the juvenile court was an entrée into the realm of governmental response to difficult social problems (Myers, 2008/2009). And today, juvenile courts have much input into child protection issues. By the 20th century, the child welfare system was characterized by bureaucracy, professionalization of the field of child welfare, and increased state involvement in children's lives (McGowan, 2010).

Considered the first major development in child welfare of the 20th century, the First White House Conference on Children, held in 1909, determined that children should not be removed from their homes for poverty alone (McGowan, 2010). In 1912, the U.S. Children's Bureau was developed in response to pressure from private charitable organizations, and represented an initial recognition by Congress that the federal government had a responsibility for the welfare of children (McGowan, 2010). It was not until the White House Conference of 1930 that African American children were included in the existing child welfare system, and were considered to be entitled to the same types of care as White children (McGowan, 2010).

The Child Welfare League of America (CWLA, 2012) was founded in 1921 with 70 participating organizations. By 1922, there were approximately 300 private child protection agencies (Myers, 2008/2009). However, by 1956, only 84 societies for the prevention of cruelty to children were still operating, and by 1966, there were only ten. By 1967, the responsibility for child protection had been placed within the authority of each state (Myers, 2008/2009). CWLA (2012) has continued to address child welfare policy since its inception, and today, with more than 1,100 partner organizations, is a leader in establishing adoption standards.

It was during the Great Depression, from 1929 to 1939, that the federal government sought a stronger role in social welfare. In 1930, the White House Conference on Child Health and Protection acknowledged that children should have the right to services provided by welfare organizations (Atkinson, 1939). In the 1930s and 1940s, societies for the prevention of cruelty to children suffered from lack of charitable contributions and closed or merged with other agencies, and child protection issues came to be addressed by police and courts, or not at all (Myers, 2008/2009).

As part of the New Deal of President Franklin Roosevelt, the Social Security Act of 1935 established the Aid to Families of Dependent Children program and provided money to states to care for poor children. By the end of June 1938, services were provided by child welfare workers in 29 states (Atkinson, 1939). From the late 1930s through the late 1950s, there was agency consolidation and growth of the child welfare field, with both the Children's Bureau and the CWLA setting standards for child welfare (McGowan, 2010).

THE MODERN ERA OF CHILD PROTECTION FROM 1962 TO THE PRESENT

The 1960s and 1970s brought the expansion of state-sponsored child welfare services as the primary provider of these services. The Aid to Families with Dependent Children Foster Care Program in 1961 provided federal funding to states to support foster care (Davidson, 2008).

Much more interest in child abuse, especially among physicians, developed in the 1960s. The classic work, *The Battered Child Syndrome,* by pediatrician Henry Kempe and his colleagues, garnered considerable professional and public attention. Kempe et al. (1962) noted: "Physicians have a duty and responsibility to the child to require a full evaluation of the problem and to guarantee that no expected repetition of trauma will be permitted to occur" (p. 17). Dr. Kempe played a critical role in propelling the issue of child abuse onto the national stage, and helped to generate a great deal of research interest in child abuse issues. Dr. Kempe's efforts also contributed to the development of laws that require reporting child abuse to state agencies (Myers, 2008/2009).

The 1960s were a time of extraordinary social change that brought the Civil Rights Act of 1964 and President Johnson's War on Poverty (McGowan, 2010). In 1962 and 1967, amendments to the Social Security Law prompted child welfare professionals to seek a comprehensive public system that would bring together child welfare and family services programs to better meet the needs of poor families (McGowan, 2010). Yet politics and existing federal and state regulations stood in the way of the development of any comprehensive system. The liberal late 1960s encouraged child welfare workers to advocate for more resources and to enhance the overall quality of services to children. The 1970s proved challenging for child welfare agencies as they were criticized for allowing children to languish in foster homes, and for the failure to bring children back to their own families or place them in adoptive homes (McGowan, 2010).

Interracial adoption became more common with the civil rights movement of the 1960s (Myers, 2008/2009). A number of states such as Texas and Louisiana had banned interracial adoption practices, and in the 1960s, court cases were decided in favor of interracial adoption. Then in 1972, the National Association of Black Social Workers opposed the practice, holding the view that living in a White family would not allow healthy development of Black children (Myers, 2008/2009). These efforts resulted in fewer children of color being adopted. In the 1980s and 1990s, there was pressure to reduce the barriers to transracial adoptions. The Multiethnic Placement Act of 1994 was a national response to that pressure. It prohibited the delay of placement in foster homes or adoption based on race, but it did allow race to be considered as a factor in the appropriate placement of children (Myers, 2008/2009). The purpose was to eliminate discrimination based on race, color, and national origin of both the child and the prospective parents (Hollinger, 1998). The Multiethnic Placement Act also sought to recruit and retain foster and adoptive families.

The Interethnic Placement Act of 1996 further reduced the conditions under which race could be considered for foster care and adoption (Brooks, Barth, Bussiere, & Patterson, 1999). It established a system of financial penalties for state failure to comply with regulations. Race was not to be considered relevant except when the needs of a specific child required it, according to a determination by a social worker (Myers, 2008/2009).

The Child Abuse Prevention and Treatment Act (CAPTA) of 1974 provided states with funding and clarified the definitions of abuse and neglect, including that all children under the age of 18 should be protected from maltreatment (Davidson, 2008). The focus was on improving the reporting and investigation of child abuse and neglect (Myers, 2008/2009). CAPTA focused on child abuse and neglect without any context, defining child maltreatment as occurring within specific families without regard to the presence of poverty (Guggenheim, 2000). That is, child maltreatment was a characteristic of specific families rather than being associated with families in poverty. Importantly, many people today continue to fail to see the relationship between poverty and child maltreatment. CAPTA has had numerous reauthorizations, the most recent being in 2010. This most recent authorization sought to improve services through data collection, improve training of child welfare professionals, and encourage greater coordination among organizations that treat all forms of family violence (National Conference of State Legislators, 2015).

The Indian Child Welfare Act (ICWA) of 1978 was passed in response to concern that Native American children were placed in non-Indian foster and adoptive homes. ICWA ensures that tribes have jurisdiction over child welfare issues for children residing on reservations. Earlier, between 25% and 35% of Native children were taken from their families for alleged abuse or neglect, and the majority of them were placed in non-Native homes (Myers, 2008/2009). The Act established federal standards for the removal of children from their homes and their placements (Davidson, 2008). The ICWA of 1978 is a complex law. Under it, only tribal courts can address cases of abuse and neglect for children living on reservations (Myers, 2008/2009). The intent was to "protect the best interests of Indian children and to promote the stability and security of Indian tribes and families" (National Indian Child Welfare Association, 2015b, p. 1).

In reality, the implementation of ICWA has been slow, and funding has not been made available to provide services to children and families. However, the restrictions on termination of parental rights can support Native families staying together (Davidson, 2008). See Box 2.4 for a description of a case that received considerable media attention.

One recent effort to recruit Native American foster families has been taking place in Oklahoma. In 2015, the Wyandotte Nation developed and offered a workshop for potential Native foster families from all nine Native tribes in the state (Willis, 2015). This is a critical issue as 11,500 children in Oklahoma, many of whom are Native, were in need of foster care in 2015. The workshop included participation by current foster families who shared the rewarding experiences of offering their homes to youth in need. This kind of effort can demystify foster parenting as well as give families the opportunity to see that foster parenting can be a positive addition to their families.

BOX 2.4 ICWA Adoptive Couple v. Baby Girl

Baby Veronica's biological father was enrolled as a member of the Cherokee Nation, and her mother was Latina. The father contested the adoption of Baby Veronica by the Capobianco family because he had not been notified, as required by the rules of the ICWA. In December 2011, after Baby Veronica had lived 2 years with the Capobianco family, the South Carolina Supreme Court decided that the father should be given custody. Considerable media attention was given to the debate over the best interests of the child and the need for amendments to the ICWA law. The Capobianco family appealed to the United States Supreme Court, which decided in June 2013 by a 5-to-4 vote, that Baby Veronica should be returned to her adoptive parents. The Court determined that because the biological father never had custody of the child, and that no other Cherokee relatives or Native American families sought custody, ICWA did not apply.

The case highlights the great damage that can be done to individual children. It also illustrates the competing interests of the needs of individual children and the interests of larger groups.

Sources: Capriccioso (2013); National Indian Child Welfare Association (2015a).

By the late 1970s, the increase in the number of children in foster care had come to be a source of great national concern. Considered landmark legislation, the Adoption Assistance and Child Welfare Act (AACWA) of 1980 was a federal initiative to support family reunification and movement of children quickly out of foster care (Gainsborough, 2009; Murray & Gesiriech, 2004). AACWA was a response to the increasing numbers of children in foster care together with the extended lengths of stay in foster care that characterized the 1970s (Hines, Lemon, Wyatt, & Merdinger, 2004; Murray & Gesiriech, 2004). The Act reversed the trend toward a minimal role for the federal government in child welfare (McGowan, 2010). The AACWA provided federal funding for state foster care and subsidies to support adoption of children with special needs (Davidson, 2008). It required foster care placements to be in a family located close to the child's own family. AACWA established federal requirements to manage child welfare cases and required the state to develop a plan for how services would be provided. Funds were decreased for foster care and moved to expanding child maltreatment prevention and adoption services (McGowan, 2010). Importantly, it established a role for the court system by requiring reviews of child welfare cases on a regular basis (Murray & Gesiriech, 2004). For children who could not be reunified with their parents, financial incentives were provided for adoption.

Under President Ronald Reagan, in the 1980s, interest in children's needs and the needs of the poor declined. Reagan had campaigned on the promise to shrink the federal government. President Reagan was strongly antiwelfare and consistently repeated that the problem was government intervention in the lives of Americans. In response to President Johnson's War on Poverty, President Reagan said that poverty had won the war. In his speech on national radio on February 15, 1986, Reagan said: "Poverty won in part because instead of helping the poor, government programs ruptured the bonds holding poor families together" (Caputo, 2011, p. 30). Reagan was known to have no interest in the problems of cities, and oversaw a significant decline in federal housing subsidies, as well as a significant rise in homelessness (Dreier, 2004). The Reagan years widened the gap between rich and poor with enormous financial benefit to the rich.

In the late 1980s, the government sought to reduce reliance of families on public programs by bolstering efforts to encourage welfare recipients to obtain jobs. The Family Support Act of 1988 required states to create job training and welfare-to-work programs by 1992 (Caputo, 2011). In reality, these programs operated at a minimal level for skill acquisition and did not offer intensive educational and training services to move participants out of poverty. Between 1978 and 1985, the number of working poor increased by 50%, and the Family Support Act did not relieve the problem (Caputo, 2011).

This period set the stage for the passage of the Personal Responsibility and Work Opportunity Reconciliation Act (PRWORA) of 1996. This Act, signed into law by President Bill Clinton, had a big impact on services for children and families. It put time limits on eligibility for financial assistance, its major purpose being to reduce government spending by reducing welfare caseloads. It replaced the Aid to Families with Dependent Children (AFDC) by the Temporary Assistance for Needy Families (TANF) and "passed with no real consideration of its potential impact on families in need of child welfare" (McGowan, 2010, p. 41). Stringent work requirements extended to women with very young children (Greenberg et al., 2002). The PRWORA put in place work requirements for single mothers, and restricted total benefits to no more than 5 years (Lopoo & Raissian, 2014). The net result has been to make it even harder for single women to support their children. Other facets of PRWORA restricted assistance to immigrants, promoted marriage, and the reduction of pregnancies outside of marriage, and sought child support payments from biological fathers. The collection rates did improve, and between 1995 and 2000, there was an increase from 19% to 42% (Greenberg et al., 2002). In reality, however, welfare benefits fell more than child poverty. Overall, the Act reduced, and for some eliminated, the role of government in supporting paid work, and ensured that the poor could not move beyond low-wage jobs (Caputo, 2011). Greenberg et al. (2002) concluded: ". . . Many of the families with the most serious barriers to employment have become ineligible for assistance or have left welfare without work and have disappeared from public systems" (p. 50).

The 1990s brought increased support for family preservation and the addition of several acts to aid children. In 1993, Congress passed the Family Preservation and Support Services Program to provide services to meet the needs of troubled families without having to rely on out-of-home care. Family preservation services are brief intensive interventions to keep the child from foster care placement, and offer support services over time (McGowan, 2010). The family preservation efforts did not bring about the intended outcomes. Specifically, child abuse and neglect reports continued to rise, and research on outcomes did not show that the family preservation model was particularly successful. Additionally, "the resurgence of conservative political forces began to legitimize public attacks on families in poverty on AFDC who may have difficulty providing proper care for their children" (McGowan, 2010, p. 41).

The Adoption and Safe Families Act of 1997 was initiated as a response to the continuing trend in the high number of children in foster homes. There was a dramatic change to permanent family adoption in the Adoption and Safe Families Act. This was the first time issues of permanency were put into legislation and permanency for children was redefined (Child Welfare Information Gateway, n.d.; Gainsborough, 2009). It emphasized child safety as paramount, although efforts to preserve families continued as well (Myers, 2008/2009). This Act was designed to reduce the number of children in foster care by freeing them for adoption (Davidson, 2008). The Adoption and Safe Families Act established strict guidelines for children being returned to their parents, and if conditions were not met, parental rights could be terminated. If there was sexual abuse or long-term physical abuse, child placement and termination of parental rights could happen sooner (Myers, 2008/2009). Time limits were established for child welfare workers to assess families and provide services as well as undertake concurrent planning—the process of preparing for adoption while also seeking family reunification (Gainsborough, 2009). Each child is required to have a permanency hearing after 12 months in foster care, and every year thereafter. In situations where a child has been in a foster home for 15 of the previous 22 months, a petition must be filed, with few exceptions, for termination of parental rights (McGowan, 2010). In addition, there was the need to increase adoptions in the United States. The Act also established performance standards for states where financial penalties could be levied if they were unable to show improved outcomes (Murray & Gesiriech, 2004).

The Promoting Safe and Stable Families of 1997, reauthorized under the Adoption and Safe Families Act, was renamed the Promoting Safe and Stable Families Program. The Act required two additional services: time-limited reunification services, and the promotion of supportive adoption services (Antebi, 2002).

The Foster Care Independence Act of 1999 provided funds to assist youth and young adults who were aging out of foster care. Data from 1990 revealed that approximately 20,000 youth were aging out of the system at age 18 without appropriate preparation (Davidson, 2008). Senator Chaffee, from Rhode Island, was responsible for the Act that became known as the John H. Chaffee Foster Care Independence Program, intended to assist older youth in becoming successful adults, including allowing some to remain in foster care until the age of 21.

The Fostering Connections to Success and Increasing Adoptions Act of 2008 requires states to place siblings within the same home if possible, improve health care services for children in placement, provide incentives for adoption, support educational continuity for children in foster care, and increase services for children aging out of foster care. Further, this Act extends foster care to age 21, if needed (Center for the Study of Social Policy, 2013).

The Child and Family Services Improvement and Innovation Act of 2011 allows states to develop and test innovative approaches to child welfare by waiving some of the requirements of the Social Security Act (Center for the Study of Social Policy, 2013). Clearly, in a field dominated by bureaucracy with many laws and rules, innovation is a welcome addition to child welfare efforts.

The Preventing Sex Trafficking and Strengthening Families Act of 2014 has a variety of components. It created a National Advisory Committee on the Sex Trafficking of Children and Youth in the United States. It requires the development of procedures to identify, document, and determine the appropriate services for children at risk of sex trafficking (Children's Defense Fund, 2014).

The reporting system requires reporting to law enforcement cases of children in state custody within 24 hours. States must design and implement plans to locate children who are missing from foster homes. Importantly, it allows children aged 14 or older to participate in developing their own care plans. It includes a number of requirements for preparing older children to age out of foster care. In addition, the Act increases the financial incentives for adoption of children (Children's Defense Fund, 2014).

The modern era in child protection has brought considerable expansion and numerous changes, such as the shift away from family preservation and less tolerance for the risks with which children are confronted in abusive families (Hines et al., 2004). However, the laws requiring specific professionals to report abuse began to overwhelm the child welfare system in the United States (Myers, 2008/2009). Clearly, the child welfare system remains overwhelmed, and services continue to be disorganized and inadequate.

The racism that kept African American children from the orphan trains has not kept them from exploitative situations. African American children are over-represented in child welfare statistics (Hines et al., 2004). Children of color are more likely to be living in poverty. There is more likely to be bias in terms of race and class in initial reporting of child abuse and involvement in the system. Children of color are likely to be treated differently within the child welfare system, mirroring the harsher treatment of racial and ethnic minorities by the juvenile justice and criminal justice systems in the United States.

Into the 21st century, we still grapple with problems such as children remaining in foster care too long, inadequate resources for those who "graduate" from the child welfare system, discrimination against children and families of color, and the variety of maladies that stem from a workforce that is overworked, undereducated, and not properly trained (McGowan, 2010). Still lacking today is financial and social recognition of the importance of child welfare work. Also, reductions in public funding that support families have had a negative impact on children. As a result, the child welfare system continues to function outside of the human service organizations created to help support children and families.

SUMMARY AND CONCLUSION

As with all social policy, child welfare policies reflect the political and social interests of the time. The system began with the provision of voluntary, charitable services, and over time has been subject to more state and federal control. We have seen the financial expansion and contraction of the child welfare system, yet never reaching the point of being sufficiently strong to keep children healthy and safe. Cuts to social welfare programs invariably have a negative impact on children. The historical view illustrates our continuing lack of clarity about the best interests of the child; issues of setting standards for child welfare interventions at the local, state, and federal levels; and the degree of responsibility these levels should have. Politicians and other public policy makers may have their own agendas under the guise of helping children. Many local, state, and federal efforts have resulted in a system that still does not work very effectively to protect children and provide them with opportunities for a bright future. Although legislation can be crucial to the protection of children, the United States will not be able to legislate its way out of child maltreatment.

DISCUSSION QUESTIONS

1. What were the motives of the child savers?

2. What was the purpose of the orphan trains?

3. How were African American children treated in Colonial America?

4. Discuss the Mary Ellen case and how it helped the child welfare system develop.

5. Discuss the purpose of the Indian Child Welfare Act of 1978.

6. How did President Reagan help or hinder child welfare efforts?

7. What is meant by family preservation?

8. Discuss the pros and cons of the Personal Responsibility and Work Opportunity Reconciliation Act of 1996.

9. What impact did the Adoption and Safe Families Act of 1997 have on the child welfare system?

10. Discuss the implementation of the Preventing Sex Trafficking and Strengthening Families Act.

REFERENCES

Antebi, G. (2002, May). *Information packet: Promoting safe & stable families*. New York, NY: National Resource Center for Foster Care and Permanency Planning, Hunter College School of Social Work.

Atkinson, M. I. (1939). Child welfare services. *Annals of the American Academy of Political and Social Science, 202,* 82–87.

Brooks, D., Barth, R. P., Bussiere, A., & Patterson, G. (1999). Adoption and race: Implementing the Multiethnic Placement Act and the interethnic adoption provisions. *Social Work, 44*(2),167–178.

Capriccioso, R. (2013, June 25). Supreme Court thwarts ICWA intent in Baby Veronica case. *Indian Country Today Media Network.* Retrieved from http://indiancountrytodaymedianetwork.com/2013/06/25/supreme-court-thwarts-icwa-intent-baby-veronica-case-150103

Caputo, R. K. (2011). *U.S. social welfare reform: Policy transitions from 1981 to the present.* New York, NY: Springer.

Center for the Study of Social Policy. (2013, July). *Raising the bar: Child welfare's shift toward well-being.* Washington, DC: Author. Retrieved from https://childwelfaresparc.files.wordpress.com/2013/07/raising-the-bar-child-welfares-shift-toward-well-being-7-22.pdf

Children's Aid Society. (n.d.). *The orphan trains.* Retrieved from www.childrensaidsociety.org/about/history/orphan-trains

Children's Defense Fund. (2014, October). *Preventing Sex Trafficking and Strengthening Families Act (H.R. 4980).* Retrieved from www.childrensdefense.org/library/data/fact-sheet-on-hr-4980.pdf

Child Welfare Information Gateway. (n.d.). *Concept and history of permanency in U.S. child welfare.* Retrieved from https://www.childwelfare.gov/topics/permanency/overview/history

Child Welfare League of America. (2012, February 24). Retrieved from http://pages.uoregon.edu/adoption/people/cwla.html

Cook, J. F. (1995). A history of placing-out: The orphan trains. *Child Welfare, 74*(1), 181–197. Retrieved from http://search.proquest.com/docview/213811300?pq-origsit=gscholar

Davidson, H. (2008). Federal law and state intervention when parents fail: Has national guidance of our child welfare system been successful? *Family Law Quarterly, 42*(3), 481–510.

Dreier, P. (2004, May/June). *Reagan's legacy: Homelessness in America* (Shelterforce Online no. 135). Retrieved from www.nhi.org/online/issues/135/reagan.html

Gainsborough, J. F. (2009). Scandals, lawsuits, and politics: Child welfare policy in the U.S. states. *State Politics and Policy Quarterly, 9*(3), 325–355.

Gordon, L. (1999). *The great Arizona orphan abduction.* Cambridge, MA: Harvard University Press.

Greenberg, M. H., Levin-Epstein, J., Hutson, R. Q., Ooms, T. J., Schumacher, R. Turetsky, V., & Engstrom, D. M. (2002). The 1996 welfare law: Key elements and reauthorization issues affecting children. *The Future of Children, 12*(1), 26–57.

Grundfossen, P. D. (1965). *A study of the arguments for and against the Factory Act of 1833 used by members of Parliament in the House of Commons* (Unpublished master's thesis). Portland State University, Portland, OR.

Guggenheim, M. (2000). Somebody's children: Sustaining the family's place in child welfare policy. *Harvard Law Review, 11*(7), 1716–1750.

Henson, T. T. (2015, November 2). Carrie Steele Logan (1829–1900). *New Georgia encyclopedia*. Retrieved from www.georgiaencyclopedia.org/articles/history-archaeology/carrie-steele-logan-1829-1900

Hines, A. M., Lemon, K., Wyatt, P., & Merdinger, J. (2004). Factors related to the disproportionate involvement of children of color in the children welfare system: A review and emerging themes. *Children and Youth Services Review, 24,* 507–527.

Hogan, P. T., & Siu, S.-F. (1988). Minority children and the child welfare system: An historical perspective. *Social Work, 33*(6), 493–498. doi:10.1093/sw/33.6.493

Hollinger, J. H. (1998). *A guide to the Multiethnic Placement Act of 1994 as amended by the Interethnic Adoption Provisions of 1996.* Washington, DC: The ABA Center on Children and the Law, National Resource Center of Legal and Court Issues.

Holt, M. I. (1992). *The orphan trains: Placing out in America* (p. 49). Lincoln: University of Nebraska Press.

Jimenez, J. (2006). The history of child protection in the African American community: Implications for current child welfare policies. *Children and Youth Services Review, 28,* 888–905.

Lopoo, L. M., & Raissian, K. M. (2014). U.S. social policy and family complexity. *Annals of the American Academy of Political and Social Science, 654,* 213–230. doi:10.1177/0002716214530372

Kempe, C. H., Silverman, F. N., Steele, B. F., Droegemueller, W., Henry, K., & Silver, H. K. (1962). The battered-child syndrome. *Journal of the American Medical Association, 181*(1), 17–24. doi:10.1001/jama.1962.03050270019004

Mandell, B. R. (2010). Foster care. In B. R. Mandell (Ed.), *The crisis of caregiving: Social welfare policy in the United States* (pp. 113–144). New York, NY: Palgrave Macmillan.

Martin, D. (2015, September 2). *Carrie Steele—A mother of orphans.* Retrieved from http://worldorphans.org/blog/2015/09/carrie-steele-a-mother-of-orphans

Mason, M. A. (1994). Masters and servants: The American colonial model of child custody and control. *International Journal of Children's Rights, 2,* 317–332. Retrieved from http://scholarship.law.berkeley.edu/facpubs/2104

McGowan, B. G. (2005). Historical evolution of child welfare services. In G. P. Mallon & P. G. Hess (Eds.), *Child welfare for the twenty-first century: A handbook of practices, policies, and programs* (pp. 10–46). New York, NY: Columbia University Press.

McGowan, B. G. (2010). An historical perspective on child welfare. In S. Kamerman, S. Phipps, & A. Ben-Arieh (Eds.), *From child welfare to child well-being: An international perspective on knowledge in the service of policy making* (pp. 25–47). New York, NY: Springer.

Murray, K. O., & Gesiriech, S. (2004, November 1). *A brief legislative history of the child welfare system.* The Pew Charitable Trusts. Retrieved from www.pewtrusts.org

Myers, J. E. B. (2008/2009). A short history of child protection in America. *Family Law Quarterly, 42*(3), 449–463.

National Conference of State Legislators. (2015). *Child Abuse Prevention and Treatment Act (CAPTA) Reauthorization Act of 2010.* Retrieved from www.ncsl.org/research/ human-services/capta-reauthorization-of-2010.aspx

National Indian Child Welfare Association. (2015a). *Adoptive Couple v. Baby Girl: Information and resources.* Retrieved from www.nicwa.org/BabyVeronica

National Indian Child Welfare Association. (2015b). *Indian Child Welfare Act of 1978.* Retrieved from www.nicwa.org/Indian_Child_Welfare_Act

Platt, A. M. (1977). *The childsavers: The invention of delinquency* (2nd ed.). Chicago, IL: University of Chicago Press.

Sadler Report. (1832). *Report from the Committee on the Bill to Regulate the Labour of Children in the Mills and Factories of the United Kingdom.* London, UK: The House of Commons.

Watkins, S. A. (1990). The Mary Ellen myth: Correcting child welfare history. *Social Work, 35*(6), 500–503.

Willis, C. (2015, November 14). *Tribes recruit foster families.* KOAM TV 7. Retrieved from www.koamtv.com/story/30519846/tribes-recruit-foster-families

POVERTY AND THE CHILD WELFARE SYSTEM

W e know that the early years of a child's life can have a significant impact on the quality of life in adulthood. That is, the experiences within childhood "are decisive for later life chances" (Esping-Andersen et al., 2012, p. 576). Abused and neglected children living in poverty are likely to pay the consequences of early deprivation throughout their lives. Chapter 3 examines the relationship between poverty and child maltreatment and the increased risk of poor families coming into contact with child protection agencies. The year 2014 marked 50 years since President Lyndon Johnson declared the War on Poverty—yet the divide continues to grow between the wealthy and the poor in the United States.

The vast majority of families involved with the child welfare system in the United States live in poverty. This chapter explores the relationships among poverty, class, and race/ethnicity. Children of color are known to have higher official rates of abuse and neglect than White children. The chapter examines the "risk model" that focuses on the greater likelihood of children of color living in poverty. The "bias model" is the view that prejudice against African Americans, Hispanics, and Native Americans leads to higher rates of child abuse and neglect reporting.

Importantly, the United States does not offer or require paid sick leave, paid parental leave, or paid family leave to care for a sick relative. There is no specific child allowance benefit and no housing allowance program (Garfinkel & Zilanawala, 2015). With reduced benefits since the Personal Responsibility and Work Opportunity Reconciliation Act (PRWORA) of 1996, the United States relies on benefits provided typically by employers and inadequate programs for the poor rather than programs available to all (Garfinkel & Smeeding, 2010). As we will see, the safety net for poor families has gaping holes or may be missing entirely, with the result that the basic needs of children are unmet.

We have long known that poverty is harmful to children (Garfinkel, 1992; Garfinkel & Zilanawala, 2015; Lee & Goerge, 1999). The prevalence of all types of childhood abuse and neglect is higher among families living in poverty (Cancian, Slack, & Yang, 2010). In the mid-1990s, it was estimated that one quarter to one half of child abuse cases were "more properly considered a symptom of poverty, and . . . more appropriately handled outside the nation's child protection system" (Besharov & Laumann, 1997, pp. 5–6). However, poverty is often the critical ingredient that brings families into the child welfare system. Garfinkel and Zilanawala (2015) described as "perverse" (p. 219) that welfare state benefits are smallest during the first year of a child's life when economic needs are typically the greatest.

We continue to learn more about the negative neurocognitive impact on children suffering neglect and living in poverty. The majority of brain growth takes place from birth to age 6, and these years are especially critical to a child's physical and emotional development (Loughan & Perna, 2012). Poverty for children can result in underdeveloped parts of the brain such as the hippocampus (the center of memory, emotion, and the autonomic nervous system) and the amygdala (that processes stimuli related to eating, drinking, addictive drugs, and helps to detect fear) (Luby et al., 2013). In a sample of 65 children who experienced poverty and neglect and whose average age was 11, all exhibited behavioral/emotional disorders, in contrast to 46% of children in the general population. Children in poverty were more likely to be diagnosed with developmental delays (60% vs. 10%–20%); attention deficit hyperactivity disorder (80% vs. 3%–7%); and learning disabilities (28% vs. 5%) (Loughan & Perna, 2012). These are substantial reasons to address poverty in children sooner rather than later.

We learned in Chapter 2 that the PRWORA of 1996 had a severe impact on those in poverty, making it even more difficult for families to support their children. After the implementation of PRWORA, research showed very quickly that reduced welfare benefits and lack of employment predicted that these families were much more likely to come into contact with the child welfare system than those who were able to maintain benefits and/or obtain work (Shook, 1999). A family with two children was almost twice as likely to become involved with the child welfare system than a family with one child. A child with health problems in need of medical attention also predicted involvement with the child welfare system. Loss of benefits, unstable employment, and medical problems of children can be a recipe for intervention by child protection services.

Before the 1996 PRWORA, Aid to Families with Dependent Children (AFDC) helped more than 1 million families with children living in extreme poverty. By the middle of 2011, only 300,000 households were above the $2.00-a-day mark for individuals when receiving Temporary Assistance for Needy Families (TANF) (Edin & Shaefer, 2015). See Box 3.1 for an example of Trina's family in the aftermath of the implementation of the PRWORA.

A family's income level defines the entire day-to-day experience of children and families. Family income significantly influences children's physical and emotional comfort level within their home (if they have one). Family income also influences the community environment, the economic pressures under which families may live, the mental health of parents, the quality of childcare services, and the relationship between the parent and the child (Duncan & Brooks-Gunn, 2000). We have already learned that poverty is connected to a variety of social ills including crime, drug addiction, and lack of education. Further, recent research even links poverty to self-induced abortion (Grossman et al., 2015; Somashekhar, 2015). Living in poverty "is one of the greatest threats to healthy child development" (Annie E. Casey Foundation, 2015b, p. 20). Indeed, a family's economic circumstances can be an important predictor of cognitive outcomes for children (Adema, 2012).

Child abuse and neglect are associated with issues in adulthood of continued long-term poverty, higher unemployment rates, and reliance on Medicaid insurance coverage that can impact families over long periods of time (Eckenrode, Smith, McCarthy, & Dineen, 2014). Poverty impacts short- and long-term health, and extreme persistent poverty shows the worst outcomes (Lower-Basch, 2015). Thus, poverty must be considered one of the major risk factors for child abuse and neglect (Lanier, Maguire-Jack, Walsh, Drake, & Hubel, 2014).

Although we can argue about whether poverty causes child maltreatment, it is well known that poverty is correlated with child maltreatment (Cancian et al., 2010).

BOX 3.1 *Trina's Family Enters the Child Welfare System*

Trina was a 26-year-old mother of four. All of her children had experienced medical problems ranging from viral infections to severe asthma over the previous year. Several years earlier, Trina's oldest daughter was hit by a car and required hospitalization. As a result, Trina had not been able to work during this time. Trina gave birth to her fourth child during the same month that her AFDC grant was terminated because of the Personal Responsibility and Work Opportunity Reconciliation Act of 1996. Her landlord threatened to evict her for nonpayment of rent, and her newborn baby often went without diapers or milk. It was at this time that Trina's family was reported to child protection services, and an intact family case was opened.

Source: Shook (1999).

The association between poverty and child abuse and neglect is so strong that there is an enormous need to reduce poverty. Research evidence shows that having sufficient financial resources reduces the number of families in the child welfare system. For example, in comparing a group of mothers who received even modestly more child support income than a control group of mothers, those mothers with greater income were 10% less likely to have a child abuse or neglect report "screened in" by the child protection agency (Cancian et al., 2010).

As we have seen, children of poor families are far more likely to have contact with child welfare services than children from families that are not poor (Jonson-Reid, Drake, & Kohl, 2009). This can be related to the stress of living in poverty including difficulty paying bills and the inability to provide the basics for the family, such as lack of childcare (Jonson-Reid et al., 2009). Poor communities have higher rates of crime, including violent crime, and fewer resources to support healthy families. Jonson-Reid et al. (2009) found: "Poor children who are reported to child welfare appear to be substantially more at risk along a range of outcomes compared either to children who are reported but not poor, or children who are poor but not reported for maltreatment" (p. 426). We should also never overlook the emotional toll of living in poverty—anxiety, depression, feeling overwhelmed, and feeling helpless to provide for the basic needs of your children (Duva & Metzger, 2010).

A major issue in addressing poverty today, and throughout history in the United States, is how to help people climb out of poverty in ways that do not make them dependent on governmental support (Cook, 1995). We have notions in the United States that some people may be the "deserving" poor, whereas others are the lazy "nondeserving" poor. We have seen that the current welfare state provides very little support. These debates over images of the poor and what to do about them often occur during political campaigns for major elective offices. See Box 3.2 for the words of a woman who received the financial benefits she needed to raise her son in the 1970s, but which are no longer available today because of the PRWORA of 1996.

Yet for all that is known about the relationship, the role of poverty often goes unacknowledged in court cases and by child protection agencies, which prefer to locate problems within the specific families themselves without consideration of the social context. One review of child welfare court cases found that children have been removed from their homes specifically "for reasons of poverty" (Eamon & Kopels, 2004, p. 821). Child protection services do not focus on poverty, but narrowly seek to keep individual children from harm (Duva & Metzger, 2010). Few, if any, child welfare interventions directly address efforts to pull families out of poverty, but instead focus only on the provision of specific services. In fact, with strict eligibility criteria, some welfare policies can inhibit families from getting out of poverty. See Box 3.3 for a description of a mother with two children seeking financial assistance.

BOX 3.2 A Woman Who Received Benefits Before PRWORA

One Black woman reflected on the help she received before welfare reform. She described that during the 1970s she was a single parent who didn't have the ability to earn a good salary. She had not attended college but understood the importance of a college education to help her get a good job so she could support her son. She was eligible to receive welfare, including food stamps. She also qualified for financial aid so she could attend college. In the mid-1970s she earned her bachelor's degree and later earned her master's degree. She is grateful for the government assistance she received when it was most needed and this helped her to build a positive future for herself and her son. She feels sorry that today these benefits are not available to others who are in a situation similar to her own years ago.

_____
Adapted from Watson (2013).

The economy of the United States no longer supports a large and comfortable middle class, and increased inequality is perhaps the number one social problem in the United States today. Current views on American inequality tend to confuse two important issues: "equality of income and wealth" and "equality of opportunity and social mobility" (Putnam, 2015, p. 31). The work of the "Occupy Movement" called attention to the 1% with the money and the 99% with far less. It reminds us of the need for social policy to address and resolve the huge gap between those who have and those who do not. Today, equality of opportunity is especially challenging because poor young people have far fewer opportunities to pull themselves out of poverty and have fewer life chances for equal education, career, and family success than those with socioeconomic resources (Putnam, 2015). How can fewer opportunities for education and success not impact the fabric of American society?

OFFICIAL POVERTY

In the American household of the 1950s, one wage earner, typically the husband and father, could support a family of four or more, but today we are far from this life. After World War II, America had a booming middle class. However, during the last 30 years, most Americans have not seen an appreciable increase in wages to live on when adjusted for inflation (Reich, 2015). The working poor continue to see a decline in their wages, and by 2013 this group had grown to one of every seven Americans (Reich, 2015). The official poverty rate has not been updated since the 1960s, and measures focus on cash income, not taking into

> ### BOX 3.3 *An Employed Mother Trying To Support Her Family*
>
> A woman in her mid-40s described the difficulties of trying to support her two children, both teenagers. She applied for welfare assistance in Florida after her husband left the home. She was able to earn only $13 an hour at her job and could not make ends meet. She was eligible for only $214 a month in food stamps. In requesting additional financial assistance, she had to endure intrusive questions about the father of her children. She was also told that she could save money by moving into less expensive housing, although that was likely to result in not being able to use public transportation.
>
> _____
> Adapted from Nolan (2015).

account tax credits or things such the Supplemental Food Assistance Program (SNAP) benefits (Bailey & Danziger, 2013). Annual adjustments encompass only price changes in the Consumer Price Index (Gabe, 2015). Thus, official poverty rates use outdated methods, and do not account for the range of expenses and income within households, compounding the difficulty in determining the levels of poverty as well as who lives within them (Wimer, Fox, Garfinkel, Kaushal, & Waldfogel, 2013).

The official poverty rate according to the United States Census in 2014 was 14.8% for a total of 46.7 million Americans living in poverty (Current Population Survey, 2015). This rate has remained relatively steady since 2011. In 2011, approximately 3 million children were living in 1.5 million households where each family member lived on less than $2/day (Edin & Shaefer, 2015).

It is notable that American children under age 18 have the highest poverty rates of any other age group: 21.1% compared with 13.5% for those aged 18 to 64, and 10% for those aged 65 and older. Importantly, the lowest rate of child poverty prevailed in 1969, at 13.8% (Gabe, 2015). In 2013, the poverty line for one person living alone was $11,888/year; for a family of two, $15,142; and for a four-person family, the poverty line was $23,834 (Gabe, 2015).

Today, over 40% of children are born to unwed parents, compared with only 5% in 1960 (Child Trends, 2012). In 2014, 35% of the children in the United States lived in single-parent families (Annie E. Casey Foundation, 2015a). Single mothers are typically those who have not married, whereas single fathers are typically divorced (Kramer, Myhra, Zuiker, & Bauer, 2015). Overall, single mothers earn only about two thirds of what single fathers earn. Even when education, occupation, and number of hours worked are controlled for, the income gap does not show much of a decrease. Thus, single mothers are far more likely to live in poverty than single fathers, and continue to do so over time (Kramer et al., 2015). In fact, single women with children are the families that are most likely to be living in poverty. A child in a family headed by a single mother was five times more likely in 2013 to be poor than a child living in a family with two parents. Of single women who head a household, 45.8% were living in poverty in 2013. In Rhode Island, 25% of all children under the age of 3 were living in poverty in 2015 (Dolan, 2015; Rhode Island KIDS COUNT, 2015).

President George W. Bush (2001–2009) tried to encourage marriage as a way to reduce poverty. The Heritage Foundation, a conservative think tank, stated that if mothers of babies did not marry, approximately 55% would be poor (Rector, Johnson, Fagan, & Noyes, 2003). However, if the mothers married the biological fathers, the poverty rate would be reduced to under 17%. Rector et al. (2003) reject the criticism that it is unrealistic to expect marriage to lift women and children out of poverty because of the low wages of men. Overall, President Bush's "marriage-strengthening policy" was met with strong criticism by liberals, who considered it bizarre social policy to try to marry out of poverty.

The United States has done much more in recent years since the 1996 PRWORA to ensure that child support payments are made. The emphasis has been on law enforcement and collection of funds rather than on the effort to support economic security for children (Garfinkel & Zilanawala, 2015). Garfinkel and Zilanawala (2015) conclude: "Unfortunately, we have of late, abandoned an emphasis on enhancing economic security for an emphasis on deterring dependence. Nowhere is this more obvious than in the legislation of a life-time term limit and the implementation of work requirements in TANF" (p. 219).

High-quality childcare and educational experiences can provide significant benefits including higher educational achievement that can last throughout the life course (Esping-Andersen et al., 2012). There are long-term negative consequences when education becomes out of reach for poor students. College attendance rates dropped from 69% to 66% between 2008 and 2013. However, those students from families with the lowest 20% of income dropped 10% in college attendance rates. Some possible explanations include the fact that there are more jobs available since the recession of 2008 (even though they tend to be low paying), costs of college are increasing, and there is a lack of desire to take out student loans (Brown, 2015). For some, it means simply giving up on establishing a career and seeking work.

RACE/ETHNICITY AND POVERTY

It is both astonishing and deeply disturbing to learn how many children of color are living in poverty today. In 2013, against a national average of 22% of all children living in poverty, 39% of African American children were living in poverty, 37% of Native American children were living in poverty, and 33% of Hispanic children were living in poverty (Annie E. Casey Foundation, 2015b).

A report by the Federal Reserve in Boston found a "stunning chasm" in wealth between Whites and minority populations including African Americans, Cape Verdeans, Puerto Ricans, Dominicans, and Caribbean Blacks (Munoz et al., 2015; Woolhouse & Newsham, 2015). In the typical White household in 2015, with assets that could be quickly liquidated, for each $1 that Whites had, Caribbean Blacks had 14 cents, African Americans had 2 cents, and Puerto Ricans and Dominicans had less than 1 cent (Munoz et al., 2015).

An annual study of mortgage lending practices found that racial discrimination in mortgage lending continues in Massachusetts, with fewer applicants of color receiving mortgages even though they have the same income as Whites. In Boston, 21% of African Americans were denied mortgages along with 13% of Latinos, 7% of Asians, and 6% of Whites (Fitzgerald, 2015). In Boston, 79% of Whites own a home compared with about 50% of Caribbean Black families, 33% of African Americans, and 20% of Puerto Rican and Dominican families (Munoz et al., 2015). Overall, non-White families are less likely to own a home, and those homeowners owe more on their mortgages and are more likely to have student loans and medical debt (Munoz et al., 2015).

As we saw in Chapter 2, African Americans were historically excluded from the child welfare system; however, today we express concern that African Americans have been overincluded in the system (Pelton, 2010). Child abuse and neglect reports of African Americans are approximately twice the number of those of White children and also twice the number of cases of substantiated abuse and neglect (Drake et al., 2011). Hill's (2006) review of research found that "race is related to professionals' decision making at almost every stage of the process" (p. 5). Children of color are overrepresented at all four levels: first, in official reports of maltreatment made to child protection agencies; second, the investigations completed by child welfare workers; third, cases of substantiated abuse or neglect; and fourth, placements outside of the family home (Martin & Connelly, 2015). In the words of Lanier et al. (2014): "Exposure to risks such as poverty is an important factor driving the overrepresentation of minority groups in the child welfare system" (p. 419). To develop practice and policy solutions, it is critical to understand why children of color are overrepresented in the system.

Research studies find there are mixed results and explanations regarding the role of race and its relationship to child abuse and neglect. One explanation is that there is bias by reporters of child maltreatment and by child welfare workers that has led to so many cases. This is known as the "bias" model. Alternatively, the "risk" model is the competing explanation that children of color are more likely to live in poverty that is associated with child maltreatment.

Mumpower and McClelland (2014) found that African Americans have higher rates of reports for maltreatment than Whites and Hispanics and that the system is "less accurate" (p. 114) than for other groups. Specifically, there are high rates of false positives, where reports determine there is no maltreatment, and higher rates of false negatives, where African American children were maltreated but did not come to the attention of the child welfare system.

A number of efforts are being made to examine racial and ethnic disparities in the child welfare system to better understand decision making within the child protection system (Child Welfare Information Gateway, 2011a). Specific diagnostic tools have recently been developed that can shed light on racial disparities, including the Disproportionality Diagnostic Tool, Ecomap, and the Racial Equity Scorecard (Mumpower & McClelland, 2014; Richardson & Derezotes, 2010). The Disproportionality Diagnostic Tool can help agencies determine the social, systemic, and individual factors that set the scene for disproportionate treatment of minority children, and assists agencies to determine their strengths and weaknesses in addressing issues of disparity. The Racial Equity Scorecard organizes data on disparities in child welfare systems by race according to key points in the system from initial entrée to child outcomes. See Box 3.4 for one important project to reduce racial disparities in child welfare.

Drake et al. (2011) found that poverty is the most powerful predictor of child maltreatment, and conclude that data provides support for the risk model over the bias model. Clearly, in the United States there are historical and contemporary concerns about racism that permeate American society (Pelton, 2010; Richardson & Derezotes, 2010). And parents of children of color have had to cope with their own experiences of discrimination during their lifetimes.

Pelton (2010) concluded: "The injustices of the child welfare system pertain to class more so than to race: we have designed a system to police and paternalistically control poor families and we refuse to replace it with one designed to actually provide them with supportive aids of their choosing" (p. 275). It seems reasonable to conclude at this point that both the racial bias and the risk models are at work. Racial bias is more about prejudice and discrimination, whereas the risk model is more about class issues and poverty. Much more needs to be done to sort out the relationship. See Box 3.5 for recommendations to increase equity in the child welfare system and improve outcomes for children of color.

WORK AND POVERTY

We have long known about exploitation of American workers, as well as workers around the globe, by companies such as Walmart, that offer low wages and abusive work practices. Paid work has been the most likely way to increase the opportunity to get out of poverty (Adema, 2012), yet low-paying jobs and work alone are not necessarily sufficient to keep individuals and families above the poverty line (Johnston, 2014).

Employers of minimum-wage earners seek to hire those who have ready availability in days and times, and this is considered an important qualification. Days and

> ### BOX 3.4 The Alaska Child Welfare Disproportionality Reduction Project (2015)
>
> The Alaska Child Welfare Disproportionality Reduction Project was designed to reduce the significant number of Alaska Native children in out-of-home placement. The 4-year project represented a unique collaboration among the National Indian Child Welfare Association (NICWA), the Alaska Office of Children's Services (OCS), the Alaska Court Improvement Project (CIP), the Western and Pacific Implementation Center (WPIC), and Casey Family Programs. The goals included increasing services to avoid foster care placement and also maintaining tribal connections. This included increased efforts to recruit tribal families to provide foster care, especially so children could stay in the area. Outcomes included review and revision of policies, standards, and procedures to support Native child health and cultural connections.
>
> The collaboration was successful in reducing fear and mistrust of the child welfare system among the local Native population. To create a more trusting relationship and reduce the adversarial relationships, tribal staff members served as liaisons to families. Tribal values were integrated into the Alaska Safety Assessment model used by child protection workers. Child welfare staff members were helped to incorporate tribal cultural values into placement decision making. This resulted in the increase in recruitment of tribal foster parents and more local placement options when children must be removed from their home for safety reasons.
>
> _Sources:_ Martin and Connelly (2015); Western and Pacific Child Welfare Implementation Center (2013).

times that fluctuate often require considerable flexibility on the part of the worker. This results in an unpredictable work schedule that can mean requiring more hours or, alternately, reducing hours drastically, according to the needs of the company (Edin & Shaefer, 2015). This leaves workers with fluctuating paychecks and unstable incomes.

Irregular work schedules make it hard for parents to arrange childcare and transportation and are responsible for inconsistent incomes (Annie E. Casey Foundation, 2015b). Exploitation of workers is obvious: "Only an employer who is guaranteed a steady stream of desperate job applicants could require a worker to be on call, ready to come in if needed, with no promise of hours" (Edin & Shaefer, 2015, p. 61). One has only to hear the conversations in grocery stores between cashiers and baggers to learn about their challenging work schedules.

BOX 3.5 Strategies to Improve Equity and Outcomes for Children of Color

Several strategies can be adopted to improve racial equity in child welfare.

1. *Promote the Collection of Nuanced Data.* This addresses the importance of obtaining data for research studies that includes gender, age, race, ethnicity, and Indian Child Welfare Act (ICWA) eligibility. Data collection needs to focus on important stages of child welfare involvement including referral, assessment, substantiation of child maltreatment, and case outcomes. Data needs to be made publicly available to encourage accountability for child welfare systems.
2. *Support Families with Appropriate Services and Resources.* This includes increasing prevention and early intervention services, encouraging collaboration with other human service organizations, and developing councils to serve in the quality assurance role to review policies and practices. Evidence-based approaches that are successful need to be replicated in other areas.
3. *Ensure Policy Implementation is Supportive of Family Well-Being.* Support states should define and implement "reasonable efforts" in the Adoption and Safe Families Act of 1997 to ensure that the needs of children and families are met. This includes supporting families subject to the enforcement of immigration policies. Support foster care policies that focus on kinship care.

Source: Martin and Connelly (2015).

We assume that those who are among the poorest in the United States have not been in the workforce, but that is not necessarily the case: "Few families in $2-a-day poverty are chronically disconnected from the workforce. Rather, most of them are workers who fall into extreme poverty only when they can't manage to find or keep a job" (Edin & Shaefer, 2015, p. 42).

Again we find that children are low on the priority list. Those who work with children in childcare and preschool are low-wage earners themselves. Although the costs of childcare have doubled since 1997, childcare workers themselves have had no increase in real earnings in almost 20 years (Whitebook, Phillips, & Howes, 2014). Preschool teacher wages have increased by only 15% since 1997. In fact, childcare workers still earn less than adults who take care of animals

(Whitebook et al., 2014). In the United States, approximately 46% of families of childcare workers receive public assistance. For example, in one home childcare program located in Greenfield, Massachusetts, the director and her two assistants took care of 10 children under the age of 5. The director/owner worked a minimum of 60 hours/week and earned $17,000 a year. To provide for her three children, the director received fuel assistance, was on Medicaid, and was eligible for food stamps (Johnston, 2015).

Access to both public and private childcare programs can be successful in reducing obstacles to employment for families with young children (Adema, 2012). Quality childcare "is critical for child development, particularly for the early years" (Adema, 2012, p. 492). Yet in the United States, public funds spent on children focus on the years of legally required schooling (Adema, 2012).

Census data reveals that the rise of child poverty is associated with expensive housing and daycare, the increase in low-wage jobs, and the challenges for young parents to enter the labor market resulting from their own lack of experience (Johnston, 2014).

HOUSING AND POVERTY

The crisis in affordable housing is a national problem. It is hard to overestimate the extent of the housing crisis for poor families. The U.S. Department of Housing and Urban Development (HUD) stipulates that a family spending more than 30% of income on housing is a family that is "cost-burdened" and unlikely to have enough to cover other expenses such as food and clothing (Edin & Shaefer, 2015).

In cases of child abuse and neglect, "housing problems are a dominant theme" (Duva & Metzger, 2010). Children living in poverty are much more likely to have to move more frequently than other families. Unfortunately, they most often move to other low-income areas. We continue to learn more about the impact of living in low-income areas as compared with middle- and higher-income housing markets. A family move when children are young to a "better" community is associated with higher income in adulthood; the earlier the move in a child's life, the better (Albernaz, 2015; Chetty & Hendren, 2015). Community characteristics associated with improved upward mobility have less income inequality, less segregation by income and race, stronger school systems, fewer community crimes of violence, and a higher number of families with two parents (Albernaz, 2015).

Housing instability and homelessness are contributing factors to placing children in foster care (Eamon & Kopels, 2004; Torrico, 2009). There is a huge difference between the money low-wage earners make and the cost of housing. In reality, housing should be a top priority for safe and healthy children and families. It has been estimated that 30% of children in foster care placements could remain at home with their families if stable affordable housing was available (Courtney, McMurty, & Zinn, 2004; Torrico, 2009).

Between 1990 and 2013, rents rose faster than inflation in every state in the country. Rents rose by 65% between 2002 and 2010, yet the income of the renter decreased by 13% (Edin & Shaefer, 2015). Unfortunately, in today's housing market, even a full-time minimum-wage job cannot provide adequate housing in any state.

It is possible to manipulate the data on family income to redefine whether families are considered middle or low income. For example, Massachusetts recently revised the methodology used to define low-income families that have children attending public schools (Vaznis, 2015). For many years, "low-income students" were defined as those families that reported their incomes on applications for free school lunches. In 2015, the state changed the rules so that students are considered "economically disadvantaged" if they receive some kind of welfare benefits including food stamps. On a state level, 38.3% had previously been considered poor, but then the overall percentage was reduced to 26.3% (Vaznis, 2015). Previously in the Boston Public Schools, 77.7% of students had been considered poor; with the new calculation, 49% were considered poor in 2015. In Lawrence, Massachusetts, the percentage of poor was reduced from a whopping 95.3% to 61.7% as a result of the new methodology. Of course, this percentage does not factor in all the families that have not applied for benefits and may have no idea about their eligibility for benefits. Can we or should we redefine poverty out of existence?

Although child protection agencies cannot ensure the health of families over time, they should be accountable for referring to human service agencies and for helping families contact housing programs to locate appropriate housing (Duva & Metzger, 2010).

There is a clear need for more effective advocacy to deal with poverty. Childcare costs, unemployment, and housing costs impact poverty. Reducing inequality and poverty in our society can be the most important way to prevent child abuse and neglect (Eckenrode et al., 2014). Social Security, in reality an antipoverty program for older adults in the United States, is an example of a program that works and can be used as a model for supports for children. European countries have a much stronger and better system that provides benefits specifically for children, including pensions, housing support, and cash assistance (Horowitz, 2015).

Mandated parent training for those with young children involved in the child welfare system can be part of more effective prevention services and more efficient use of resources (Beckmann, Knitzer, Cooper, & Dicker, 2010). Yet parent training must be considered in the context of reducing the economic stress of parents (Lee & Goerge, 1999). Working to assist families out of poverty can reduce the number of child welfare cases overall by helping children remain in their homes and can lead to higher rates of reunification (Dale, 2014). Our efforts to prevent child maltreatment should not be focused exclusively on supporting parents to do better; we have much work to do to create the financial and emotional supports to assist parents (Child Welfare Information Gateway, 2011b).

When it comes to alleviating poverty in the United States, we seem to know what we need to accomplish, but despite numerous efforts over the decades, we still do not know how to do it. For many, there is a lack of will to distribute resources in ways that support the healthy development of children. Research shows policy makers and child welfare professionals must focus "primarily on situations involving deep and persistent poverty that occurs early in childhood" (Duncan & Brooks-Gunn, 2000, p. 193).

SUMMARY AND CONCLUSION

It has been obvious for many years that poverty has a negative impact on a child's physical, mental, and emotional growth. More recent research has focused on problematic brain development that ensures reduced life chances from living in poverty. As in the case of biological parents, foster parents can have few financial resources. Throughout the country, there is ambivalence about the role of federal, state, and local governments in ensuring a basic standard of living for children—an ambivalence that has a huge negative impact on the future of the United States.

It is also well known that childhood maltreatment is associated with income inequality. Yet little social policy addresses the foremost social problem facing the United States. And, as we have seen, life only gets harder for the poor. Racism persists at every level of the child welfare system. Lack of affordable housing only ensures that poverty will persist. It is unreasonable to expect child welfare workers and the child welfare system to provide for the significant needs of families to pull them out of poverty; hence, the importance of addressing overall social policy for children in the United States.

There are times when the report of child abuse or neglect results in services that help a family function better and remain together as a family unit. These services such as affordable housing, adequate food, and quality childcare should not be reserved only for those with adequate means. They should be available to all before concerns develop for child maltreatment.

DISCUSSION QUESTIONS

1. In what ways is poverty harmful to children?

2. Discuss the relationship between poverty and child maltreatment.

3. How did the Personal Responsibility and Work Opportunity Reconciliation Act of 1996 impact mothers with young children?

4. In what ways is the availability of quality childcare critical to low-income families?

5. What are the potential long-term effects of children living in poverty?

6. Compare and contrast the "bias" and "risk" models regarding the over-representation of children of color in the child protection system.

7. Discuss official poverty statistics and how well they represent families living in poverty in the United States.

8. What can be done to provide stable housing for those families in poverty?

9. Discuss the reasons it is harder for single mothers than for single fathers to raise children.

10. What are your recommendations for reducing poverty in the United States?

REFERENCES

Adema, W. (2012). Setting the scene: The mix of family policy objectives and packages across the OECD. *Children and Youth Services Review*, 34, 487–498.

Albernaz, A. (2015, June 1). Early move can lead to income rise. *The Boston Globe*, p. G2.

Annie E. Casey Foundation. (2015a, December 11). Single parents raising more than a third of U.S. kids. Baltimore, MD: Author. Retrieved from www.aecf.org/blog/single-parents-raising-more-than-a-third-of-us-kids

Annie E. Casey Foundation. (2015b). *The 2015 KIDS COUNT data book*. Baltimore, MD: Author. Retrieved from www.aecf.org/2015db

Bailey, M. J., & Danziger, S. (2013). *Legacies of the war on poverty: A review*. New York, NY: Russell Sage Foundation.

Beckmann, K. A., Knitzer, J., Cooper, J. L., & Dicker, S. (2010). *Supporting parents of young children in the child welfare system*. New York, NY: Columbia University, National Center for Children in Poverty.

Besharov, D. J., & Laumann, L. A. (1997). Don't call it child abuse if it's really poverty. *Journal of Children and Poverty*, 3(1), 5–36.

Brown, E. (2015, November 25). College enrollment on decline, especially among poorest. *The Boston Globe*, p. A7.

Cancian, M. Slack, K. S., & Yang, M. Y. (2010, August). *The effect of family income on risk of child maltreatment* (Institute for Research on Poverty, Discussion Paper No. 1385-10). Madison, WI: University of Wisconsin. Retrieved from www.irp.wisc.edu/publications/dps/pdfs/dp138510.pdf

Chetty, R., & Hendren, N. (2015, April). *The impacts of neighborhoods on intergenerational mobility: Childhood exposure effect and county-level estimates* (Working paper). Cambridge, MA: Harvard University.

Child Trends Data Bank. (2012, March). *Births to unmarried women: Indicators on children and youth*. Retrieved from www.childtrends.org/?indicators=births-to-unmarried-women

Child Welfare Information Gateway. (2011a, January). *Addressing racial disproportionality in child welfare*. Washington, DC: Administration on Children, Youth and Families, Children's Bureau.

Child Welfare Information Gateway. (2011b, July). *Child maltreatment prevention: Past, present, and future*. Washington, DC: Administration on Children, Youth and Families, Children's Bureau.

Cook, J. F. (1995). A history of placing-out: The orphan trains. *Child Welfare*, 74(1), 181–197.

Courtney, M., McMurty, S., & Zinn, A. (2004). Housing problems experienced by recipients of child welfare services. *Child Welfare*, *83*, 389–392.

Current Population Survey, 2015 Annual Social and Economic Supplement. (2014). *Income and poverty in the United States: 2014—Highlights*. Retrieved from www.census .gov/hhes/www/poverty/data/incpovhlth/2014

Dale, M. K. (2014, April 10). *Addressing the underlying issues of poverty in child-neglect cases*. American Bar Association. Retrieved from https://apps.americanbar.org/ litigation/committees/childrights/content/articles/spring2014-0414-addressing -underlying-issue-poverty-child-neglect-cases.html

Dolan, K. (2015, June 18). Report finds 25% of R.I. infants living below poverty line. *Warwick Beacon*. Retrieved from http://warwickonline.com/stories/ report-finds-25-of-ri-infants-living-below-poverty-line,103414

Drake, B., Jolley, J. M., Lanier, P., Fluke, J., Barth, R. P., & Jonson-Reid, M. (2011). Racial bias in child protection? A comparison of competing explanations using national data. *Pediatrics*, *127*(3), 471–478. doi:10.1542/peds.2010-1710

Duncan, G. J., & Brooks-Gunn, J. (2000). Family poverty, welfare reform, and child development. *Child Development*, *71*(1), 188–196.

Duva, J., & Metzger, S. (2010). Addressing poverty as a major risk factor in child neglect: Promising policy and practice. *Protecting Children*, *25*(1), 63–74.

Eamon, M. K., & Kopels, S. (2004). 'For reasons of poverty': Court challenges to child welfare practices and mandated programs. *Children and Youth Services Review*, *26*, 821–836.

Eckenrode, J., Smith, E. G., McCarthy, M. E., & Dineen, M. (2014). Income inequality and child maltreatment in the United States. *Pediatrics*, *133*, 454–461. doi:10.1542/ peds.2013-1707

Edin, K. J., & Shaefer, H. L. (2015). *$2.00 a day: Living on almost nothing in America*. New York, NY: Houghton Mifflin Harcourt.

Esping-Andersen, G., Garfinkel, I., Ham, W.-J., Magnuson, K. Wagner, S., & Waldfogel, J. (2012). Child care and school performance in Denmark and the United States. *Children and Youth Services Review*, *34*(3), 576–589.

Fitzgerald, J. (2015, December 22). Minority mortgage barriers still high: Black and Latinos rejected more often. *The Boston Globe*, pp. C1, C6.

Gabe, T. (2015, January 29). *Poverty in the United States: 2013*. Washington, DC: Congressional Research Service.

Garfinkel, I. (1992). *Assuring child support*. New York, NY: Russell Sage Foundation.

Garfinkel, I., & Smeeding, T. (2010, October). *Wealth and welfare states: What is the real story?* (Institute for Research on Poverty, Discussion Paper No. 1387-10). Madison, WI: University of Wisconsin. New York, NY: Columbia University, Institute for Research on Poverty.

Garfinkel, I., & Zilanawala, A. (2015). Fragile families in the American welfare state. *Children and Youth Services Review, 55*, 210–221.

Grossman, D., White, K., Fuentes, L., Hopkins, K., Stevenson, A., Yeatman, S., & Potter, J. E. (2015, November 17). Knowledge, opinion and experience related to abortion self-induction in Texas. *Texas Policy Evaluation Policy: Research Brief*. Retrieved from https://utexas.app.box.com/KOESelfInductionResearchBrief

Hill, R. B. (2006, October). *Synthesis of research on disproportionality in child welfare: An update* (Casey-CSSP Alliance for Racial Equity in the Child Welfare System). Retrieved from www.cssp.org/reform/child-welfare/other-resources/synthesis-of-research-on-disproportionality-robert-hill.pdf

Horowitz, E. (2015, October 29). A proven way to reduce poverty? Give poor people money. *The Boston Globe.* Retrieved from www.bostonglobe.com/business/2015/10/29/proven-way-reduce-poverty/KSMVN9DUaOILiA2I7TTOXO/story.html

Johnston, K. (2014, September 22). No easy progress on child poverty. *The Boston Globe*, pp. A1, A4.

Johnston, K. (2015, November 18). Child-care workers' pay stagnant over 20 years. *The Boston Globe*, pp. B5, B9.

Jonson-Reid, M., Drake, B., & Kohl, P. L. (2009). Is the overrepresentation of the poor in child welfare caseloads due to bias or need? *Children and Youth Services Review, 31*, 422–427.

Kramer, K. Myhra, L. L., Zuiker, V. S., & Bauer, J. W. (2015). Comparison of poverty and income disparity of single mothers and fathers across three decades: 1990–2010. *Gender Issues, 33*(1), 22–41. doi:10.13140/RG.2.1.3478.9600

Lanier, P., Maguire-Jack, K., Walsh, T., Drake, B., & Hubel, G. (2014). Race and ethnic differences in early childhood maltreatment in the United States. *Journal of Developmental & Behavioral Pediatrics, 35*(7), 419–426.

Lee, B. J., & Goerge, R. M. (1999). Poverty, early childbearing, and child maltreatment: A multinomial analysis. *Children and Youth Services Review, 21*(9/10), 755–780.

Loughan, A., & Perna, R. (2012, July). Neurocognitive impacts for children of poverty and neglect. *American Psychological Association*. Retrieved from https://apa.org/pi/families/resources/newsletter/2012/07/neurocognitive-impacts.aspx

Lower-Basch, E. (2015, December 8). Work-first welfare policies don't work for infants on TANF. *Washington Monthly*. Retrieved from www.washingtonmonthly.com/republic3-0/2015/12/workfirst_welfare_policies_don058894.php

Luby, J., Belden, A., Botteron, K., Marrus, N., Harms, M. P., Babb, C., . . . Barch, D. (2013). The effects of poverty on childhood brain development: The mediating effects of caregiving and stressful life events. *JAMA Pediatrics, 167*(12), 1135–1142. doi:10.1001/jamapediatrics.2013.3139

Martin, M., & Connelly, D. D. (2015). *Achieving racial equity: Child welfare policy strategies to improve outcomes for children of color.* Washington, DC: Center for the Study of Social Policy. Retrieved from http://www.cssp.org/publications/publicpolicy/document/Policy-RE-Paper-web.pdf

Mumpower, J. L., & McClelland, G. H. (2014). A signal detection theory analysis of racial and ethnic disproportionality in the referral and substantiation processes of the U.S. child welfare services system. *Judgment and Decision Making, 9*(2), 114–128.

Munoz, A. P., Kim, M., Chang, M., Jackson, R. O., Hamilton, D., & Darity, W. A., Jr. (2015). *The color of wealth in Boston.* Boston, MA: Federal Reserve Bank.

Nolan, H. (2015, April 21). True stories of life on the dole: Poverty from state to state. *Gawker.* Retrieved from http://gawker.com/true-stories-of-life-on-the-dole-poverty-from-state-to-1698532894

Pelton, L. (2010, Winter). Introduction: Race, class, and the child welfare system. *Journal of Health and Human Services Administration, 33*(3), 270–276.

Putnam, R. D. (2015). *Our kids: The American dream in crisis.* New York, NY: Simon & Schuster.

Rector, R., Johnson, K. A., Fagan, P. F., & Noyes, L. P. (2003, May 20). Increasing marriage would dramatically reduce child poverty. *The Heritage Foundation.* Retrieved from www.heritage.org/research/reports/2003/05/increasing-marriage-would-dramatically-reduce-child-poverty

Reich, R. B. (2015). *Saving capitalism: For the many, not the few.* New York, NY: Alfred A. Knopf.

Rhode Island KIDS COUNT. (2015). *Next steps for infants, toddlers, and their families.* Retrieved from www.rikidscount.org/Portals/0/Uploads/Documents/Special%20Publications/NextSteps-June2015-FINAL.pdf

Richardson, B., & Derezotes, D. (2010). Measuring change in disproportionality and disparities: Three diagnostic tools. *Journal of Health and Social Services Administration, 33*(3), 323–352.

Shook, K. (1999). Does the loss of welfare income increase the risk of involvement with the child welfare system? *Children and Youth Services Review, 21*(9–10), 781–814.

Somashekhar, S. (2015, November 18). Study links poverty, self-induced abortion. *The Washington Post News Service.* Retrieved from https://www.bostonglobe.com/news/nation/2015/11/17/report-nearly-percent-texas-women-say-they-tried-induce-abortion/MxkSGXn8H5W2id9szQUpKM/story.html

Torrico, R. (2009, September). From poverty to child welfare involvement: The critical role of housing in family stability. *Children, Youth & Families.* Washington, DC: National Association of Social Workers.

Vaznis, J. (2015, June 22). Fewer students found in poverty. *The Boston Globe,* pp. A1, A7.

Watson, B. (2013, June 27). My climb out of poverty wouldn't be possible today. *The Washington Post.* Retrieved from https://www.washingtonpost.com/blogs/she-the-people/wp/2013/06/27/my-climb-out-of-poverty-wouldnt-be-possible-today

Western and Pacific Child Welfare Implementation Center. (2013). *The Alaska Child Welfare Disproportionality Reduction Project*. Retrieved from www.wpicenter.org/projects-alaska.php

Whitebook, M., Phillips, D., & Howes, C. (2014). *Worthy work, STILL unlivable wages: The early childhood workforce 25 years after the National Child Care Staffing Study*. Berkeley, University of California Berkeley, Center for the Study of Child Care Employment, Institute for Research on Labor and Employment. Retrieved from www.irle.berkeley.edu/cscce/wp-content/uploads/2014/11/Executive-Summary-Final.pdf

Wimer, C., Fox, L., Garfinkel, I., Kaushal, N., & Waldfogel, J. (2013, December 5). *Trends in poverty with an anchored supplemental poverty measure* (Working paper). Retrieved from https://www.gc.cuny.edu/CUNY_GC/media/LISCenter/Readings%20for%20workshop/Madrick2.pdf

Woolhouse, M., & Newsham, J. (2015, March 27). On matters of race and wealth Boston Fed finds stunning chasm. *The Boston Globe*, pp. C1, C7.

THE EDUCATIONAL SYSTEM AND CHILD WELFARE

*T*he relationship between the educational system and the child welfare system is unsettled at best. Chapter 4 discusses the relationship among educational experiences, opportunities, and attainment and child protection issues. It examines the problems associated with educational experiences for children receiving child protection services, including the potential for lifelong negative consequences. It examines the role of teachers and educational administrators as mandated reporters in making legally required child abuse and neglect reports to state agencies. It also examines the often tense relationship between schools and child protection agencies, and recommends ways to encourage more professional collaboration.

Early deprivation as well as childhood abuse and neglect are correlated with delays in speech, cognitive development, social development, and emotional development (Casanueva, Stambaugh, Tuellar, Dolan, & Smith, 2012; Lee, Benson, Klein, & Franke, 2015). If developmental issues remain undiagnosed and/or untreated, the consequences for children can be severe. This includes lack of readiness for school and reduced chances for educational success.

As described in Chapter 3, poverty can have lifelong effects on children, and today we understand that childcare and preschool experiences can have a positive and lasting impact as well. In fact, quality childcare and early academic programs can be especially important for children living in poverty. High-quality early care and educational programs are associated with advancements in the physical and mental development of children (Lee et al., 2015). Yet child welfare workers can lack an understanding of the importance of high-quality early academic programs, which often results in settling for custodial childcare (Lee et al., 2015).

Today, access to quality education is a challenge throughout the United States. Not long ago we thought of access to education as the great equalizer in American society. Unfortunately, that premise is changing because fewer children have access to quality education owing to inability to pay. Those families with money can pay for private schooling or pay the high housing prices and property taxes associated with high-quality public schooling. We also know that families living in poverty do not have the same access and often must settle for deeply troubled public school systems. With some exceptions, the schools a child attends from the elementary level through high school can directly impact their college opportunities. Although high standardized test scores and excellent grades open college doors, these are the exceptions rather than the rule for poor children. See Box 4.1 for an example of families who cannot pay for early childcare learning programs.

Herbert (2014) provides a picture of the challenges of a child living in poverty trying to get an education:

> A child who is chronically hungry is not likely to be a first-rate student. A child with undiagnosed vision or hearing problems will have trouble keeping up with classmates. A child whose mother was just beaten up by a drug-addicted live-in boyfriend will have all kinds of trouble concentrating on math and reading. A child who is worried about dodging bullets or negotiating the terrain of rival street gangs when going to and from school will have a very hard time acing a fourth-grade reading test. Children who are homeless, neglected, anxious, depressed, tired, or dealing with any of the other endless agonies associated with poverty will

BOX 4.1 Families Unable to Pay for Childcare and Preschool

One provider of childcare/early learning programs addressed the problem of financial cutbacks:

> So now because of the budget cuts everybody got affected. A lot of children stopped coming to school because the parents couldn't afford it. We just had one parent sign up their child. . .they thought that we were giving free services to them, but she was going to be paying $70 a week. Seventy dollars to us is like really nothing, but to her, I don't know, maybe that is a meal on a plate for her children for dinnertime. I don't know. But a lot of parents, yeah, I have to agree with her, a lot of our parents are backing out from taking their children to school because [of] money. (p. 175)

Source: Lee, Benson, Klein, and Franke (2015).

typically—although not always—have a much tougher time learning than their more affluent and environmentally fortunate peers. (pp. 157–158)

A report on education reform in Massachusetts concluded: "There is no way to eliminate the opportunity gaps in our schools without addressing poverty and our state's increasing income inequality" (French, Guisbond, Jehlen, & Shapiro, p. 8). The very same is true in all states.

High-quality education is needed at all levels, but is perhaps most important early in a child's life. Although we talk about the importance of high-quality daycare and early childhood education, less attention is given to defining what that means. High-quality early childcare and education are defined by having a sufficient number of teachers and other staff, well-structured programs that are accredited, and appropriate teacher credentials and licensing (Lee et al., 2015). Teachers and staff also need to display personal characteristics such as sensitivity and warmth toward the children, and they need to establish relationships with parents to cultivate parental involvement in their child's education.

Although the literature touts the importance of early childcare and educational experiences, little research exists to address the educational experiences of children receiving child protection services (Lee et al., 2015). In one study of low-income children in educational programs before the kindergarten year, children in child protective services continued to struggle both academically and socially, despite attending high-quality programs (Kovan, Mishra, Susman-Stillman, Piescher, & LaLiberte, 2014). These children exhibited differences that included lower vocabulary and math-reasoning abilities when compared with children not involved with child welfare services. Teachers rated children involved with child welfare services as having higher rates of anger, aggression, and anxiety (Kovan et al., 2014).

Access to early educational programs is a critical issue. In 2011 within the general population, approximately 65% of 3- to 6-year-old children from low-income families were enrolled in childcare/educational centers (ChildStats, 2011). However, only 41% of eligible children within the child welfare system attended these programs (Casanueva et al., 2012). Children in the foster care system can access free Head Start and Early Head Start programs, but in 2008 to 2009, less than 10% of eligible children ages under 1 to 5 years old participated in these programs (Administration of Children and Families, 2010; Lee et al., 2015). Head Start is a national program funded by the federal government to assist low-income preschoolers to prepare for entry into school. The inability to access available services is a major problem—although we often bemoan the lack of resources in child protection cases, here is an example of important resources that are underutilized. Clearly, a much better job must be done to inform child welfare workers and foster parents of available childcare and educational resources.

In a sample of 253 children in foster care attending Head Start programs, there were "modest direct short-term and indirect longer-term impacts of Head Start on school readiness outcomes" (Lipscomb, Pratt, Schmitt, Pears, & Kim, 2013, p. 28). These gains included improvements in relationships between teachers and children, improved preacademic skills, and fewer behavioral problems.

Head Start is not without challenges. In the most recent review of effectiveness, Head Start had "potentially positive effects on general reading achievement and no discernible effects on mathematics achievement and social-emotional development for 3- and 4-year-old children" (U.S. Department of Education, 2015, p. 1).

On the basis of evidence that some early learning programs can improve outcomes for children in child protection, some policy makers have requested greater participation for low-income children receiving child protection services. In a study of over 1,600 children, after receiving services for 18 months, the children had modestly improved language outcomes (Merritt & Klein, 2015). It is not surprising that some children with developmental deficits, trauma-related learning issues, and behavioral issues may have an especially hard time benefiting from early childhood interventions. See Box 4.2 for recommendations for early childhood educational programs and child protection agencies.

It is clear that children involved in the child welfare system suffer educational disruption at all levels of schooling. The effects of educational disruption can reduce future opportunities such as achieving a high school diploma or attending college, and can last throughout their lifetimes. Educators and child welfare professionals must work to reduce school absences to provide greater stability (Rubin et al., 2013). In addition to the academics, it is important to remember that school can be a stabilizing force for children known to child protective services including those in foster care. This fact strongly supports the need for positive educational experiences for children (Moore, 2007).

Increased attention to preparing students for high-stakes testing as required by No Child Left Behind of 2001 siphons time and resources from real educational programming and academic experiences for students. With all the emphasis on standardized testing, and linking teacher pay to career stability and advancement to test scores, it is hardly surprising if low-income children receive even less academic attention. The hard-grinding focus on standardized testing is "narrowing of school curricula" in elementary and high schools, and has been especially noted in low-income schools (French et al., 2013, p. 5). The intense pressure results in educators choosing to "teach to the test" and in some cases, cheating in the hope of achieving higher test scores. Teachers and administrators have been caught cheating in a number of states. In Atlanta, Georgia, initially 178 educators were charged with cheating to raise standardized test scores, 80 reached deals to avoid criminal prosecution, and 35 were charged (Jarvie, 2015a). Of these, 11 were sentenced to up to several years in

BOX 4.2 Recommendations for Early Childhood Education

High-quality early childhood education holds some promise in bolstering a child's future academic success. The following recommendations support improvements in the professional relationships between educators and child protection agencies:

1. Develop and revise early childhood policies to support practice guidelines that facilitate use of educational and other services for children in the child welfare system.
2. Expedite and simplify communication between early educational programs and child welfare agencies.
3. Develop healthy organizational environments in both educational and child welfare systems that include agreed-upon expectations of workers in both environments.
4. Address the child placement issues that make it difficult to maintain consistency in early foster home placement with the goal of reducing successive placements.
5. Encourage child welfare workers to locate and enroll children in strong early educational learning environments rather than child-care programs that emphasize supervision and custodial care of children.

Source: Lee, Benson, Klein, and Franke (2015).

prison; ultimately, three had their sentences reduced from 7 to 3 years when the judge had second thoughts about the harshness of the initial sentences (Ellis & Lopez, 2015; Jarvie, 2015b). The ripple effects of high-stakes testing abound, with some teachers and administrators violating ethical principles against cheating and also violating the law.

TEACHERS AND OTHER SCHOOL PERSONNEL AS MANDATED REPORTERS

All teachers, school counselors, and school administrators are mandated reporters of child abuse and neglect, and therefore must contact the state's child protection agency to report suspected child maltreatment. Teachers and other school personnel can be reticent to report suspicion of abuse, yet reporting can make a significant difference in early intervention with maltreated students (Goebbels, Nicholson, Walsh, & De Vries, 2008). School personnel face a variety of barriers to reporting child abuse. These barriers include lack of recognition of the problem, lack of understanding of reporting requirements, poor training on reporting requirements, concern that they lack proof, and concern that greater harm will come to the child (Bryant, 2009; Kesner & Robinson, 2002). Inexperienced teachers, with fewer academic credentials and little confidence in their own abilities to recognize abuse, are less likely to report suspicions of child maltreatment (Goebbels et al., 2008). One study of child abuse reporting found that school counselors, rather than teachers or administrators, reported the majority of cases to the child protection agency (Bryant, 2009).

A study of school personnel found that on average over their careers, educators will suspect 92 cases of child maltreatment (VanBergeijk & Sarmiento, 2006). This speaks to the importance of mandated reporters having the knowledge, training, and support to fulfill their legal and ethical obligation to report child maltreatment. Varying degrees of assistance are available to ensure that mandated reporters in the education field are aware of their responsibilities and act accordingly. The U.S. Department of Health and Human Services has put out a helpful manual titled *The Role of Educators in Preventing and Responding to Child Abuse and Neglect* (Crosson-Tower, 2003). Each state offers differing degrees of training for school personnel. For example, in Texas, the Department of Family and Protective Services offers a 1-hour certificate training program for school staff that focuses on definitions of child abuse and neglect, reviews of case vignettes, and a web-based e-reporting system (Texas Department of Family and Protective Services, 2014). In Florida, a child abuse and neglect manual is available to school personnel to assist them with making mandatory reports, and includes a resource guide to assist in locating services for children (Florida Department of Education, 2011).

In part, the uneasy relationship between schools and child protection agencies results from schools feeling that child protection agencies do not take their reports of suspected maltreatment as seriously as they should, and fail to respond quickly. See Box 4.3 for a description of a teacher reporting abuse to a child welfare agency.

FOSTER CARE AND EDUCATION

The relationship between foster care placement and education is complex, and academic success is a far greater challenge for this group of children. Children in foster care are more likely to have to change schools owing to foster placements than children not in foster care (Conger & Finkelstein, 2003). There are often delays in placements caused by the required paperwork and the need for coordination among biological parents, foster parents, schools, and the child protection agency. There can be numerous barriers to academic success for children in foster care including changes in schools, lack

BOX 4.3 A Teacher Makes a Report of Child Abuse

One teacher with 20 years of experience teaching all elementary school grades filed a child abuse report on behalf of Colleen, a 9-year-old girl. She had been reported several times previously, but had received no intervention. The child protection agency investigated after Colleen was found performing oral sex on boys on school grounds. The teacher had this to say about child protective services:

> I was screaming, and they weren't listening, you know, in essence. And I don't want to condemn them; I've never worked for them! I don't know. . .but what seemed mighty frustrating is that, you know, I had what I considered to be something severe. And I'm on the phone, and they're saying well you have to wait; someone will get back to you. And it's not that the child was in any immediate danger, but it was. . .something that I wanted dealt with at this moment! And I think that might come from the fact that. . .that's day to day for them. And maybe what I was sharing with them was. . .not as severe as what. . .they see on a case-by-case basis. . . . (p. 89)

Source: VanBergeijk and Sarmiento (2006).

of transportation, time to enroll in a new school, credit transfer issues, lack of identified advocates, tracking into vocational programs, and unmet remedial educational needs (Daehlen, 2015; National Working Group on Foster Care and Education, 2014b).

There is a huge gap between school-aged children in foster care and those who are not in foster homes, with those in foster care most likely to be older than non–foster care students (National Working Group on Foster Care and Education, 2014a). Other characteristics include lower standardized test scores, fewer foster children who graduate from high school, and fewer foster children who attend college. In 2012, only 50% of high school students in foster care graduated, and only 20% went on to college. The average reading level for foster children aged 17 to 18 in 2012 was at a seventh-grade level, a most disturbing finding (National Working Group on Foster Care and Education, 2014a).

Children in foster care are more likely to be attending public schools rather than private schools and can have fewer academic supports (Altshuler, 2003). Foster children with special learning needs may have an even more difficult time in school, especially if the services do not fit the individual child's needs.

Children in foster care are also far more likely to be diagnosed with learning issues (Courtney, Roderick, Smithgall, Gladden & Nagaoka, 2004). However, children in foster care may be offered special education services to address low achievement, although these services may not address the child's specific learning issues. Special education services also cannot be expected to solve the problem of behavioral issues in school (Wulczyn, Smithgall, & Chen, 2009). This calls for services geared to the specific learning needs of children, and for those with behavioral problems, the opportunity for psychotherapy.

As we have seen, children in foster care are likely to suffer academically, but can also suffer socially in the school environment (Altshuler, 2003; Courtney et al., 2004). Frequent changes in schools can make it very difficult to access already established peer groups. Foster children can also seem to be marked by others such as teachers and other students for having a difficult time in school, a kind of labeling that becomes a self-fulfilling prophecy. That is, this kind of expectation for difficulties in school adjustment can result in just that. In focus groups, there was the belief by the child protection workers and the students themselves that foster children would, overall, have a harder time than other children (Altshuler, 2003).

Challenges to child welfare workers abound in working with children in foster care. Regarding academics, workers may have to search for the most appropriate school for a child's needs, and help motivate the child to stay in and perform well in school (Courtney et al., 2004). Child protection workers also have an important role in preparing children for life after high school, including completing college applications.

The Fostering Connections to Success and Increasing Adoptions Act of 2008 requires child protection agencies to ensure that children in foster care are provided with "educational stability" (National Working Group on Foster Care and Education, 2014a). Children fortunate enough to be in a stable foster care placement have a greater opportunity to achieve educational stability (Rubin et al., 2013). Importantly, children in foster care who attended early childcare programs were less likely to have disrupted foster care placements than children whose foster parents did not utilize childcare services (Meloy & Phillips, 2012). Children in foster care can be better supported to succeed academically when foster parents notify the school about the foster care arrangement, and when foster parents maintain contact with school professionals (Altshuler, 2003). They can also benefit from individual tutoring services.

THE NATIVE AMERICAN BOARDING SCHOOL EXPERIENCE

There are times when education of children, especially poor children of ethnic minority status, serves to exploit children and their families. For Native Americans, placement in boarding schools for "education" was a tool of oppression and abuse. Starting in the 1870s and continuing into the 1900s, approximately 150,000 Native American children were forcibly taken from their families in Canada and parts of the United States and placed in Indian residential schools (Bedrosian, 2013). The "reformers" that conceived these ideas "waged cultural, psychological and intellectual warfare on Native students as part of a concerted effort to turn Indians into 'Americans'" (Davis, 2001, p. 20). Stripped of their identities, language, and traditions, they were to be made "civilized" (Bear, 2008; Davis, 2001). A report in 1928 titled *The Problem of Indian Administration* found "children at federal boarding schools were malnourished, overworked, harshly punished and poorly educated" (Bear, 2008, p. 11). See Box 4.4 for the experience of one Native woman taken from her mother as a newborn.

With the terrible behavior Whites have inflicted upon Native American families and children through boarding school experiences, there has been some acknowledgement of abuse. In 2008, the Canadian Prime Minister issued an apology for forcing Native children into boarding schools, and established a Truth and Reconciliation Commission to find out what happened to the children, provided compensation to victims, and provided healing gatherings across Canada (Bedrosian, 2013). For poor children currently living on reservations in the United States, there are 183 Indian schools in 23 states overseen by the Interior Department's Bureau of Indian Education, most in significant disrepair (Hefling, 2014). The Little Singer Community School for Navajo children in Arizona is "verging on decrepit. The school. . .consists of a cluster of rundown classroom buildings containing asbestos, radon, mice, mold, and flimsy outside door locks" (Hefling, 2014, p. A11). Again, we see that educational challenges continue, especially for poor ethnic minorities. Although severe abuses of the past are over, poverty and educational neglect remain major issues for Native Americans living on reservations.

HOMELESSNESS AND EDUCATION

For homeless children, educational experiences can be much worse than what is typically offered to poor children involved with child protection services. As we will discuss in the next chapter, homelessness itself can lead to child protection involvement.

The McKinney-Vento Homeless Assistance Act of 1987 requires states to provide a number of services to homeless individuals and families. It is considered landmark legislation in that it requires the provision of educational services to homeless children not in foster care so that they are able to meet the academic standards that are set for all children (National Coalition for the Homeless, 2006). The Fostering Connection to Success and Increasing Adoptions Act of 1980, as mentioned previously, provides services for children in foster care who are not eligible for McKinney-Vento homelessness services. The overlap in the two Acts provides for children who are awaiting placement in a foster home, children who

BOX 4.4 A Native American Child in a Boarding School

With no explanation, Mary-Catherine, of the Sisseton Wahpeton Oyate, was just three months old when she was taken from her mother to Tekakwitha Orphanage.

At the age of 65, here are her words:

All I remember of my earliest years at Tekakwitha was being hungry and a punishment that consisted of being placed in a dark crawl space. When I was 6, they moved me from the Papoose House for babies to the main building so I could start school. The nuns there would take us to their private quarters and do things to our bodies that even at that young age I knew were not right. . . . When I was 8 or 9, Father Pohlen placed me with a Michigan family. I understood it was a tryout for being adopted by them. I have a memory of being told to go get Vaseline, then returning to the room to find the boys and men in the family waiting for me. This lasted for a summer. . . . I didn't know where to turn or who to tell. Father Pohlen had placed me with the family, so I couldn't confide in him, and the nuns were so cold—they didn't care about our feelings and showed us no affection. . . . When I was about 10, Father Pohlen placed me with a Spanish-speaking dentist, who wanted to teach me his language so I could speak it once he and his wife adopted me and took me to their country. Instead, he raped me and said he wanted to continue his 'affair' with me, though I mustn't tell his wife. After several weeks, I was returned to the orphanage. Again, I never said anything to Father Pohlen or the nuns, other than that I didn't want to learn Spanish or live with that man. I'd learned that to protect myself I shouldn't say much.

Source: Woodward (2011).

are runaways from foster placements, and foster children living in emergency shelters or transitional housing (Legal Center for Foster Care and Education, 2010). Appropriate educational services for homeless children is one more of the many needs of these children and their families.

EDUCATOR AND CHILD PROTECTION WORKER RELATIONSHIPS

The relationship between the child welfare system and schools is often character-ized by ineffective communication, mistrust, and misunderstanding, and at times even appears to be adversarial (Altshuler, 2003; Conger & Finkelstein, 2003; Rubin et al., 2013). In focus groups with caseworkers and educators, a caseworker stated: ". . . even though we would all deny that there's an adversarial relationship between the schools and [child welfare], I think there is" (Altshuler, 2003, p. 55). One educator said: "It just kind of seems like we're just fighting back and forth" (p. 55).

Challenges to the child welfare–school relationship can focus on confidentiality requirements that limit child welfare information permitted to be shared with teachers and school administrators. Similarly, educators can be restricted from sharing information under the Family Educational Rights and Privacy Act (FERPA), which requires states to keep records confidential unless there is parental consent, although in some cases the child welfare agency may act in this role (Feierman, 2012). Educators can also be dissatisfied with child protection workers who do not share educational information soon enough to allow for better educational planning for children.

Child welfare workers at times feel that the questions regarding the children's background are intrusive and go beyond what is needed to develop the educational plan. They complain that schools are not particularly concerned with helping students in foster care, especially those children with behavioral problems (Altshuler, 2003). One caseworker stated about her experiences working with teachers: "It's negative, negative, negative about the kid. 'Oh, this child is receiving D's but that's okay because we understand where this child is coming from.' That's all they expect from this child" (Altshuler, 2003, p. 57).

To address school stability for foster children, schools can choose to have more flexible rules regarding residency requirements that can allow children to remain in their original school environment. If foster care involves kinship care, it is more likely that students can stay in their own communities and schools. For example, one study in New York City found that of children placed in kinship foster care, 26% were able to remain in the same school. In contrast, only 14% of children placed in regular foster care remained in the same community and school (Conger & Finkelstein, 2003).

Historically, there have not been many efforts to support collaboration between public schools and child protection agencies, and in some circumstances, children do not receive adequate services from either (Altshuler, 2003). Obstacles to collaboration include difficulty in achieving agreement on which students/ clients need services, and which services they need. Other obstacles are the differing goals of programs providing services, the location and delivery of services, and the approaches to evaluating programs (Altshuler, 2003).

In recent years, the need for improved collaborative efforts has garnered more attention because there are growing concerns for accountability from both schools and child welfare organizations. As we have seen, in public education, the No Child Left Behind laws required greater attention to meet federal standards through the complex system of state testing (Wulczyn et al., 2009). Within the child welfare system, greater attention is paid to overall child well-being, using school success as an indicator of overall success of the child protection intervention.

The importance of child welfare and schools working together is reflected by the following statement: "Failure to do the hard work of collaboration will inevitably leave us with the uncomfortable feeling that we have not done enough to reduce the perils facing at-risk children. Indeed, we may discover that we have only added to the perils, despite our best intentions" (Wulczyn et al., 2009, p. 58).

RECOMMENDATIONS FOR COLLABORATION

As discussed, the need for collaboration between educational and child welfare organizations is critical (Lee et al., 2015). Many kinds of activities can foster greater collaboration and continuity to the provision of services to children. To promote collaborative efforts, caseworkers can shadow teachers to acquire a deeper understanding of their work and challenges (Altshuler, 2003). Educators and child protection workers can be trained at the same time. Children in foster care can be assigned a teacher who will also serve as a mentor (Altshuler, 2003). Routine case review meetings between child protection workers and educators can bolster professional relationships, and improve understanding and respect for the work of other professionals. It can also lead to better decision making regarding a child's future.

The integration of educational, child welfare, and behavioral health services benefits the children as well as the professionals who come to support one another (Rubin et al., 2013). For example, the child protection agency in Fresno County in California, the Department of Social Services, and the Office of Education have established integrated services for children in foster care, including mental health services. Child protection workers have a place in schools that have a large number of children in foster care, and they visit those schools several times weekly. The Department of Social Services has educational liaisons assigned to preschools, elementary schools, middle schools, and high schools. The liaisons provide training and case management support, and serve as consultants to both the school and the child protection staff (Rubin et al., 2013).

In Philadelphia, educational professionals and child protection workers established a protocol to address how school stability decisions are to be made for children in foster care (Legal Center for Foster Care & Education, 2011). To minimize confusion, the protocol addresses who must initiate transportation requests to schools, and provides guidelines for the use of transportation services for children. See Box 4.5 for a template on how to develop greater collaboration between schools and child protection organizations, recommendations that are very similar to those made for early educational programs and child protection agencies.

BOX 4.5 *Cultivating Collaboration Between Child Welfare Organizations and Schools*

Recommendations for how child welfare staff and educators can better collaborate on behalf of their clients/students:

STEP 1. CREATE A COMMON KNOWLEDGE BASE.

Child welfare and school personnel must first know and understand their own laws, policies, and practices regarding the provision of services to children. They must address barriers to completing their own work and successfully advocating for children before the process of collaboration can begin. Then each organization must understand the laws, policies, and practices of the other organization. Each organization must identify one leader to advance the collaboration.

STEP 2. SET A PROCESS AND GOALS FOR THE COLLABORATION.

Each organization must recognize the value in the partnership and together establish goals for the partnership. Staff must determine the process by which existing structures, including other stakeholders, can facilitate the developing partnership. They must identify obstacles to collaboration and seek solutions. They should start with small projects that can serve as pilots and that can be expanded if proven successful. They must determine how progress will be measured and evaluated. Goals must include maintaining children in the same schools if at all possible; providing assistance for necessary transitions to a new school; ensuring that children are academically prepared to enter school and have opportunities to participate in nonacademic programs, such as hobby clubs and sports; providing supports to deter behavioral problems and prevent dropping out; ensuring that the children themselves actively participate in setting goals, providing mentors for children in foster care; and ensuring that children and youth have access to college.

STEP 3. KEEP THE CONVERSATION GOING AND MAINTAIN MOMENTUM.

Staff must be provided with the resources needed by both organizations to ensure that collaboration strengthens and continues. Both organizations must stay up-to-date by looking for "best practices" that can help them

(continued)

> ## BOX 4.5 Cultivating Collaboration Between Child Welfare Organizations and Schools (continued)
>
> respond to the challenges they face. A high level of commitment from the leadership of the organizations must be cemented. Although laws and policies regarding confidentiality must be complied with, data must be shared on the progress of the work. Ongoing communication and shared trainings can solidify the work as well as ensure that it continues.
>
> _____
>
> *Source:* Legal Center for Foster Care and Education (2011).

SUMMARY AND CONCLUSION

Poor children have a harder time performing well in school and face more academic and behavioral challenges than children who are not poor. The school environment is likely to be even more difficult for children known to child protective services. Children placed in foster care due to maltreatment can have the most difficult time, especially if they are compelled to change schools. They face greater difficulty in keeping up academically, are more likely to drop out of school, and are less likely to continue their education even if they do graduate from high school. For homeless children, educational experiences can be extremely challenging.

Although child safety rather than education is the highest priority for child welfare workers, much more can be done. The relationship between child welfare workers and school personnel needs to be improved to eliminate ineffective communication and basic mistrust. To strengthen collaboration between educators and child welfare professionals, both systems can create a common knowledge base, establish a process and goals for collaboration, and ensure that resources and relationships are strengthened over time. All of these strategies can significantly improve the services on which maltreated children must rely.

DISCUSSION QUESTIONS

1. What is the relationship among educational attainment, poverty, and child welfare?

2. How can poverty affect a child's ability to learn?

3. Discuss the role of Head Start in low-income families with very young children.

4. What are the special educational challenges of children living in foster homes?

5. Why is it important to maintain foster children in the same schools they attended before placement?

6. Discuss the experiences of Native American children taken from their homes and placed in residential schools.

7. Why have educator and child protection worker relationships been characterized by mistrust?

8. What are the educational challenges of homeless children living in emergency shelters and transitional housing?

9. In what ways can schools and child welfare organizations become more collaborative?

10. Why is it necessary to have the support of the leadership of schools and child welfare organizations?

REFERENCES

Administration of Children and Families. (2010). *The AFCARS report: Preliminary FY 2009 estimates as of July 2010*. Washington, DC: U.S. Department of Health and Human Services, Children's Bureau. Retrieved from www.acf.hhs.gov/sites/default/files/cb/afcarsreport17.pdf

Altshuler, S. J. (2003). From barriers to successful collaboration: Public schools and child welfare working together. *Social Work, 48*(1), 52–63.

Bear, C. (2008, May 19). American Indian boarding schools haunt many. *National Public Radio*. Retrieved from www.npr.org/templates/story/story.php?storyId=16516865

Bedrosian, C. (2013, Winter). They came for our children. *Spirit of Change Magazine*, pp. 40–43.

Bryant, J. K. (2009). School counselors and child abuse reporting: A national survey. *Professional School Counseling, 12*(5), 333–342.

Casanueva, C., Stambaugh, L., Tuellar, S., Dolan, M., & Smith, K. (2012). *NSCAW II wave 2 report: Children's services* (OPRE report No. 2012-59). Washington, DC: Office of Planning, Research and Evaluation, Administration for Children and Families, U.S. Department of Health and Human Services.

Childstats.gov Forum on Child & Family Statistics (ChildStats). (2011). American's children: Key national indicators of well-being. Retrieved from www.childstats.gov/americaschildren

Conger, D., & Finkelstein, M. J. (2003). Foster care and school mobility. *Journal of Negro Education, 72*(1), 97–103.

Courtney, M. E., Roderick, M., Smithgall, C., Gladden, R. M., & Nagaoka, J. (2004, December). *The educational status of foster children* (Issue Brief No. 102). Chicago, IL: Chapin

Hall Center for Children at the University of Chicago. Retrieved from http://www
.chapinhall.org/sites/default/files/publications/152.pdf

Crosson-Tower, C. (2003). *The role of educators in preventing and responding to child abuse and neglect.*
Washington, DC: U.S. Department of Health and Human Services, Children's Bureau.

Daehlen, M. (2015). Child welfare clients and educational transitions. *Child & Family Social Work.* Retrieved from http://onlinelibrary.wiley.com/doi/10.1111/cfs.12243

Davis, J. (2001). American Indian boarding school experiences: Recent studies from native perspectives. *Organization of American Historians Magazine of History, 15*(2), 20–22.

Ellis, R., & Lopez, E. (2015, April 30). Judge reduces sentences for three convicted in Atlanta cheating scandal. *Cable News Network.* Retrieved from www.cnn.com/2015/04/30/us/atlanta-schools-cheating-scandal

Feierman, J. (2012). Information education agencies can share with child welfare under the Family Educational Rights and Privacy Act (FERPA). *Trends in State Courts.* Retrieved from www.ncsc.org/sitecore/content/microsites/future-trends-2012/home/Privacy-and-Technology/Information-Education-Agencies.aspx

Florida Department of Education. (2011). *Child abuse prevention sourcebook for Florida school personnel: A tool for reporting abuse and supporting the child.* Tallahassee, FL: Student Support Services Project, Bureau of Exceptional Education and Student Services.

French, D., Guisbond, L., Jehlen, A., & Shapiro, N. (2013, June). *Twenty years after education reform: Choosing a path forward to equity and excellence for all.* Boston, MA: Citizens for Public Schools.

Goebbels, A. F. G., Nicholson, J. M., Walsh, K., & De Vries, H. (2008). Teachers' reporting of suspected child abuse and neglect: Behavior and determinants. *Health Education Research, 23*(6), 941–951.

Hefling, K. (2014, October 19). Indian schools housed in run-down buildings. *The Boston Globe,* p. A11.

Herbert, B. (2014). *Losing our way: An intimate portrait of a troubled America.* New York, NY: Doubleday.

Jarvie, J. (2015a, April 1). Atlanta schools cheating scandal: 11 educators convicted of racketeering. *The Los Angeles Times.* Retrieved from www.latimes.com/nation/la-na-atlanta-school-cheating-convictions-20150401-story.html

Jarvie, J. (2015b, April 30). Judge in Atlanta school cheating case reduces stiff prison sentences. *The Los Angeles Times.* Retrieved from www.latimes.com/nation/la-na-atlanta-teacher-sentence-20150430-story.html

Kesner, J. E., & Robinson, M. (2002). Teachers as mandated reporters of child maltreatment: Comparison with legal, medical, and social services reporters. *Children & Schools, 24*(4), 222–231.

Kovan, N., Mishra, S., Susman-Stillman, A., Piescher, K. N., & LaLiberte, T. (2014). Differences in the early care and education needs of young children involved in child protection. *Children and Youth Services Review, 46,* 139–145.

Lee, S.-Y., Benson, S. M., Klein, S. M., & Franke, T. M. (2015). Accessing quality early care and education for children in child welfare: Stakeholders' perspectives on barriers and opportunities for interagency collaboration. *Children and Youth Services Review*, *55*, 170–181.

Legal Center for Foster Care and Education. (2010). How fostering connections and McKinny-Vento can support school success for all children in out-of-home care. *Foster Care & Education Q & A*. Retrieved from www.americanbar.org/content/dam/aba/migrated/child/education/publications/qa_fc_and_mv_overlap_final.authcheckdam.pdf

Legal Center for Foster Care and Education. (2011). Making it work: Child welfare and education agencies collaborating to ensure school stability for children in foster care. *Foster Care & Education Issue Brief*. Retrieved from www.americanbar.org/content/dam/aba/publications/center_on_children_and_the_law/education/making_it_work_final.authcheckdam.pdf

Lipscomb, S. T., Pratt, M., Schmitt, S. A., Pears, K. C., & Kim, H. K. (2013). School readiness in children living in non-parental care: Impacts of Head Start. *Journal of Applied Developmental Psychology*, *34*(1), 28–37.

Meloy, M. E., & Phillips, D. (2012). Rethinking the role of early care and education in foster care. *Children and Youth Services Review, 34*, 882–890.

Merritt, D. M., & Klein, S. (2015). Do early care and education services improve language development for maltreated children? Evidence from a national child welfare sample. *Child Abuse & Neglect*, *39*, 185–196.

Moore, J. (2007, Fall). *A look at child welfare from a homeless education perspective*. Greensboro, NC: National Center for Homeless Education at the SERVE Center.

National Coalition for the Homeless. (2006, June). *McKinney-Vento Act* (NCH Fact Sheet No. 18). Washington, DC: Author.

National Working Group on Foster Care and Education. (2014a, January). Fostering success in education: National factsheet on the educational outcomes of children in foster care. *Research highlights on education and foster care*. Retrieved from www.fostercareandeducation.org/OurWork/NationalWorkGroup.aspx

National Working Group on Foster Care and Education. (2014b). *Congressional briefings: Improving educational outcomes for children in foster care*. Retrieved from www.fostercareandeducation.org/DesktopModules/Bring2mind/DMX/Download.aspx?EntryId=1940&Command=Core_Download&method=inline&PortalId=0&TabId=1167

Rubin, D., O'Reilly, A., Zlotnick, S., Hendricks, T., Zorc, C., Matone, M., & Noonan, K. (2013, Spring). Improving education outcomes for children in child welfare. *PolicyLab Center to Bridge Research, Practice, & Policy*. Retrieved from http://policylab.chop.edu/sites/default/files/pdf/publications/PolicyLab_EtoA_%20Improving_Education_Outcomes_for_Children_in_Child%20Welfare_2013.pdf

Texas Department of Family and Protective Services. (2014). *Training objectives*. Retrieved from https://www.dfps.state.tx.us/Training/Reporting

U.S. Department of Education. (2015, July). Head Start. *What Works Clearinghouse (WWD) Intervention Report*. Retrieved from https://ies.ed.gov/ncee/wwc/pdf/intervention_reports/wwc_headstart_072815.pdf

VanBergeijk, E. O., & Sarmiento, T. L. L. (2006). The consequences of reporting child maltreatment: Are school personnel at risk of secondary traumatic stress? *Brief Treatment and Crisis Intervention, 6*(1), 79–98.

Woodward, S. (2011, July 28). South Dakota boarding school survivors detail their abuse. *Indian Country Today*. Retrieved from http://indiancountrytodaymedianetwork.com/2011/07/28/south-dakota-boarding-school-survivors-detail-sexual-abuse-42420

Wulczyn, F., Smithgall, C., & Chen, L. (2009). Child well-being: The intersection of schools and child welfare. *Review of Research in Education, 33*, 35–62. doi:10.3102/0091732X08327208

HEALTH, HOMELESSNESS, AND CHILD WELFARE

*T*here are numerous concerns regarding the physical and mental health issues of children in the child welfare system. Health issues become even more pronounced when children and their families are homeless. Chapter 5 examines the health issues of families known to child protection agencies. The children can have health problems, as can their parents. The substance abuse and mental health problems of parents can be significant contributors for children to become known to child protection agencies. This chapter reviews the mental health problems of children and the greater likelihood that they will be prescribed psychotropic medications. It also examines substance abuse issues of parents and children.

Homeless children face unique challenges in maintaining their health. Few things are as challenging as trying to maintain any kind of family life within a shelter environment, if it is even available. This chapter examines the relationship between homelessness and contact with child protection agencies. It examines the challenges of children living in shelters with numerous rules, outside of their own communities, which can contribute to a sense of rootlessness. It also examines the efforts to reduce homelessness for children receiving child welfare services.

Children in the child protective services system are at greater risk of developing physical problems such as asthma, and mental health issues such as anxiety and depression than children not in the system (Gonzalez, 2014; Merrick & Latzman, 2014). These children also face greater difficulty in accessing the care they need to address their multiple health problems. Unfortunately, childhood health and mental health issues often continue into adulthood. Adult survivors of maltreatment have more health problems and more painful symptoms associated with health problems than adults who did not endure maltreatment (Sachs-Ericsson, Cromer, & Hernandez, 2009). For some types of abuse, consequences can be lifelong, especially for childhood sexual abuse (Mignon, Larson, & Holmes, 2002).

For adults, medical problems associated with childhood maltreatment include headaches, back pain, irritable bowel syndrome, gastrointestinal illnesses, gynecological problems, arthritis, and higher rates of mental health problems. Depression in adults is highly correlated with childhood abuse and neglect. Smoking, substance abuse, suicidality, and risky sexual behaviors are all associated with a history of childhood maltreatment (Merrick & Latzman, 2014). It is important that when adults seek health care they are screened for a history of childhood maltreatment (Sachs-Ericsson et al., 2009).

ACCESS TO MEDICAL CARE AND HEALTH INSURANCE

For children as well as adults, access to health care is largely determined by health insurance coverage and ability to pay. Medicaid, a combined federal and state health insurance program for eligible low-income individuals, has served as the primary insurance for children in the child protection system since the 1980s. Children in foster care are more likely to have Medicaid coverage than children who do not receive child protection services (Raghavan, Shi, James, et al., 2009).

Children who have been abused and/or neglected have higher rates of use of health services, and Medicaid expenditures are significantly higher for this group. Medical needs can be greater, requiring assessment and treatment from several providers, for example, both a primary care physician and a mental health practitioner (Bai, Wells, & Hillemeier, 2009). In a time of fiscal austerity, more attention gets paid to how public funds are used for health care. Although preventing and treating the medical problems of maltreated children should be the paramount concern, saving money can easily become the dominant concern. Children known to child protective services have greater utilization of health services and receive more expensive outpatient and inpatient care (Florence, Brown, Fang, & Thompson, 2013). The first systematic study of Medicaid payments for children investigated for maltreatment found that the average Medicaid expenditure was $2,600 more per child than for children on Medicaid who had not been investigated for maltreatment (Florence et al., 2013).

Foster children are a medically vulnerable group and have even higher rates of chronic health problems (Schneiderman, Smith, Arnold, Fuentes & Duan, 2013). The biggest obstacle to providing appropriate and continuous health care for foster children is successive foster home placements (Mekonnen, Noonan, & Rubin, 2009). Medicaid coverage can be disrupted when children are moved to a succession of foster homes in areas where there may be different eligibility requirements for Medicaid (Raghavan, Shi, James, et al., 2009). Improvements in health care for foster children cannot be made when there are multiple placements. Behavioral and health challenges can become worse when children are expected to adjust to new surroundings and a different family and, of course, make it even harder to access needed health services (Mekonnen et al., 2009). With changes in foster placements comes the need for a change in health providers as well, contributing to the lack of access to a child's medical history. It also interferes with the establishment of a strong patient and medical provider relationship. One study of foster children found that 75% of trips to a hospital emergency room occurred within 3 weeks of a new foster placement, typically immediately after the new placement (Mekonnen et al., 2009). The benefits of receiving continuous health care services from the same providers cannot be overstated.

For adolescents transitioning out of foster care, it can be very difficult to obtain health insurance. Most adolescents in the United States receive health insurance coverage as dependents on the health plans of their parents; such coverage is often unavailable to foster children (Raghavan, Shi, Aarons, Roesch, & McMillen, 2009). A study of 206 adolescents found 67% without health insurance within a 3-month period (Raghavan, Shi, Aarons, et al., 2009). Only 17% were able to get insurance again, and that was after an average of 8 months without coverage. Health insurance coverage is often a benefit with employment; however, only about half of the adolescents were able to obtain a job.

Of course, Medicaid should be extended to foster children up to the age of 21. The Foster Care Independence Act of 1999 provided the option of extending Medicaid, but has been implemented slowly. Today, under the Affordable Health Care Act, more youth are eligible for insurance coverage, some up to age 26, but they may not be aware of their eligibility (Glier, 2015). Some states require paperwork that can present another obstacle for those leaving foster care, but other states do not. For example, youth leaving foster care in California and New York are automatically enrolled in Medicaid. Removing this barrier in all states will assist these youth in continuing their insurance coverage.

Recent innovations seek to improve the quality of health care provided to children in the child protection system. The Fostering Success Act of 2008 created a "medical home" model to ensure that one health practitioner coordinates care with specialists needed by the child (Mekonnen et al., 2009). One study of a medical home model in Illinois found that it worked well for children in foster care who utilized more primary care services, needed fewer specialty services, and fewer trips to hospital emergency rooms (Jaudes, Champagne, Harden, Masterson, & Bilaver, 2012). Another model is to have child welfare systems take on the responsibility to coordinate medical care with case management funds available through Medicaid. More than 38 states have used this targeted case management funding. Some child protection agencies have established their own "health care coordination units" (Mekonnen et al, 2009, p. 409). And some regions have devised a system of "health passports" to grant children greater continuity in health care and ensure that multiple providers have access to medical records. In Philadelphia, mental health professionals work closely with child protection intake workers to provide assessments for children with mental health and behavioral problems. It should be a priority for child welfare workers to ensure that children have continuous health insurance coverage, even after they leave foster care (Raghavan, Shi, James, et al., 2009).

NUTRITION

Lack of food, also known as "food insecurity," can be a major problem for all poor families. It is a mistake to assume that the Supplemental Nutrition Assistance Program (SNAP) benefits address all the needs of hungry families in the United States. In fact, SNAP benefits were reduced in 2013 from $1.70/meal to $1.40/meal (Pace, 2016). More states are now adding drug testing for illicit substances to their requirements, designed to further reduce food stamp eligibility.

Recent research establishes that nutrition plays an important role in the functioning of the brain and a person's overall physical and mental health (Pace, 2016). Children in families that do not have nutritious food are more likely to become ill, be hospitalized, and have developmental delays than children who have sufficient healthy foods. Those with inadequate nutrition can experience higher levels of stress that, in turn, can develop into depression, a factor in hyperactivity and chronic health problems (Pace, 2016). One study found that 28% of children entering foster care were overweight or obese, although they tended not to gain more weight while in care (Schneiderman et al., 2013). Child welfare workers need to be attuned to weight issues as part of the overall health of children.

MENTAL HEALTH ISSUES AND TREATMENT

It is not surprising that children who have been victims of abuse and neglect have greater mental health needs than children not subjected to maltreatment. Children with a history of abuse and/or neglect are more likely to experience the internalizing behaviors of anxiety and depression, and more likely to exhibit externalizing behaviors such as aggression (Merrick & Latzman, 2014). Yet existing mental health services tend to be inadequate for the needs of children in child protection systems (Bai et al., 2009).

In a national study of 3,803 children aged 2 to 14 who had been the subject of child welfare investigation for abuse or neglect, 47.9% were determined to have "significant emotional or behavioral problems" (Burns et al., 2004, p. 960). Yet only one quarter of these children received any mental health services within the year prior to the study, a huge gap that must be addressed. African American children have less Medicaid funding spent on their psychiatric needs, which can reflect decreased opportunities for psychiatric care for this group (Raghavan et al., 2014).

Children in foster care use mental health services 8 to 11 times more often than other poor children covered by Medicaid who are not in foster care (Mekonnen et al., 2009). Foster children utilize between 25% and 41% of money for mental health services covered by Medicaid but represent just 3% of those on Medicaid. With a lack of screening for mental health problems, and a lack of prevention and early intervention mental health services, Medicaid payments are more likely to be used to pay for psychiatric hospitals, residential treatment programs, and group homes—the most intensive and expensive kinds of care.

A study of 659 adults who had been in foster care between 1988 and 1998 in Washington and Oregon provides a picture of the challenges of mental health problems in this population (Pecora et al., 2005). Respondents were on average 24 years of age at the time of participation in the study and had been in foster care an average of 6 years, averaging 1.4 placements each year. Within the year prior to participation in the study, 54.4% had one or more mental health disorders. Twenty-five percent had a diagnosis of posttraumatic stress disorder, and 20% had been diagnosed with major depression (Pecora et al., 2005). Again we see the critical importance of placement stability to the overall physical and mental health of foster children as they become adults.

PSYCHIATRIC CARE AND PSYCHOTROPIC MEDICATIONS

Children in the child welfare system are more likely to report psychological stress, make more frequent visits to physicians and other providers for mental health problems, and to be on psychotropic medications (Hamilton, Paglia-Boak, Wekerle, Danielson, & Mann, 2011). Psychotropic medications, defined as medicines that affect the mind, emotions, and behavior, are increasingly prescribed to children receiving child protection services. Children in the child welfare system are two to three times more likely to be put on psychotropic medication than those not in the system (Raghavan et al., 2014; Zito et al., 2008). Clients in child protection systems are less likely to be involved in the decision to begin taking medications (Moses, 2008). For years, concerns have been raised about the overuse of psychotropic medications for these children, and research shows great variability among geographic locations in their use (Leslie et al., 2011).

There can be several motivations for prescribing psychotropic medications to children. Psychotropic medications may be necessary to treat mental health problems, and they may be given to reduce behavioral challenges and impacts on others or as part of an effort to make families eligible for disability benefits. Overuse of psychotropic medications can be related to short and inadequate assessments, psychiatric hospitalizations that are not sufficiently long to stabilize children, lack of communication between prescribers and child protection workers, and legal liability concerns of professionals (McMillen, Fedoravicius, Rowe, Zima, & Ware, 2007). It can be very difficult to sort out the numerous health issues, and competing interests, to establish an appropriate treatment plan. See Box 5.1 for the case of a child who started on psychotropic medications at the age of 2.

The increased use of psychotropic medications in foster care "can be linked directly to the fragmented system of care for these children and the inadequate resources for assessment and treatment" (Mekonnen et al., 2009, p. 407). Other factors include successive placements and lack of mental health knowledge

BOX 5.1 The Case of Rebecca Riley

Rebecca Riley was born on April 11, 2002, and died on December 13, 2006, at age 4 on her parents' bedroom floor in Hull, Massachusetts. Tragically, Rebecca died from an overdose of prescribed psychotropic drugs she had taken since she was two, specifically, Depakote for bipolar disorder, Seroquel, an antipsychotic medication, and clonidine, a blood pressure medication prescribed to calm and put a child to sleep. Rebecca had been diagnosed with bipolar disorder and attention deficit hyperactivity disorder at age two by a psychiatrist at Tufts-New England Medical Center in Boston. The medical examiner's office determined that Rebecca died from "intoxication due to the combined effects" of several drugs and that "this occurred as a result of the intentional overdose . . . ." Two older children, a sister age 6, and a brother age 11, were also on psychotropic medications, and the Department of Social Services removed them from the home after Rebecca's death, placing them in foster homes. Both siblings also had diagnoses of bipolar disorder and attention deficit hyperactivity disorder and were on psychotropic medications.

The Department of Social Services had been involved with the family since the year of Rebecca's birth after a complaint of neglect was filed regarding the oldest child. There were many complaints including

(continued)

> ### BOX 5.1 The Case of Rebecca Riley (continued)
>
> physical abuse to the son, sexual abuse of the mother's daughter by another relationship, and a restraining order against the father.
>
> Prosecutors suggested that the mother made up Rebecca's symptoms so that she could qualify for Supplemental Security Income (SSI) from the Social Security Administration and receive monthly financial benefits, as did the family on behalf of her two older siblings. In February 2010, Rebecca's mother was found guilty of second-degree murder that in Massachusetts brings the possibility of parole in 15 years. Rebecca's father was found guilty of first-degree murder in September 2010 and received a sentence of life in prison with no possibility of parole. Tufts-New England Medical Center paid $2.5 million to the estate, from which the older siblings are expected to benefit.
>
> Numerous issues are raised by this case. Is it appropriate to diagnose a 2-year-old child with bipolar disorder? With attention deficit hyperactivity disorder? If any, what are the appropriate dosage levels of psychotropic medication that should be given to very young children? Who or what is to blame for Rebecca's tragic death?
>
> _____
> *Sources:* Abel (2007); Associated Press (2007); Wen (2011).

and training of foster parents and child welfare workers. Lack of coordination among the health care, mental health, and the child welfare systems can have a significant negative impact. For example, placement disruptions can lead to medications being abruptly terminated if no prescription or access to the medication is available.

Routine screening of child welfare populations for mental health problems should be provided, as should greater access to mental health care (Burns et al., 2004). Collaboration between mental health and child welfare professionals is essential. There must also be evaluations of the quality of services to ensure that referrals for mental health treatment are appropriate, that evidence-based clinical care is provided, and that professionals are up-to-date on standards of mental health care (Burns et al., 2004).

There are recent innovations to curb the overprescription of psychotropic drugs. For example, to combat the overmedication of children in foster care, California has passed laws to strengthen the oversight of prescriptions for foster children, to require increased evidence to support the use of medications, and to provide medical oversight to group homes, especially those with a history of overprescribing (Kardish, 2015).

Some cases of reported child maltreatment involving physical and mental health are so complex that they do not lend themselves to easy resolution, and perhaps no resolution. See Box 5.2 for the case of Justina Pelletier whose physicians, child welfare professionals, and parents could not agree on her diagnosis and treatment.

Mental health care should play an important part in the overall goals of child protection systems—safety, permanence, and well-being of the children (Landsverk, Hurlburt, & Leslie, 2007). Coordination between mental health agencies and child protective services must take place not only on an individual case basis, but also on programmatic and resource levels (Bai et al., 2009). Improved access is important, but better outcomes cannot be achieved without high-quality services (Landsverk et al., 2007). A "comprehensive screening

---

BOX 5.2 The Case of Justina Pelletier

In a most unusual child welfare case, the parents of Justina Pelletier were accused of medical child abuse. The case involved disagreements regarding diagnoses by well-known medical professionals at Tufts Medical Center and Boston Children's Hospital as well as threats to child protection workers, the judge, and Justina's physicians. The considerable media attention led to public calls to "Free Justina."

Justina, age 15, was taken to the emergency room at Boston's Children's Hospital in February 2013, and within a few days Children's staff filed a child abuse and neglect report stating that the parents had ignored their daughter's mental health problems and sought medical interventions that were not appropriate for her needs. The parents insisted Justina suffered from a metabolic disorder called mitochondrial disease that resulted in gastrointestinal problems and difficulty walking, and that she had been treated for the disease at Tufts Medical Center for over 1 year. The parents rejected the Children's Hospital diagnosis of "somatoform disorder," which describes those who have physical symptoms that have no organic cause. Over the 16-month period in medical treatment and psychiatric care, including 11 months as an inpatient at Children's Hospital, Justina's condition did not improve and deteriorated to the extent that she needed to use a wheelchair.

The Department of Children and Families took legal custody in February 2013, and in May 2014 arranged for Justina to be admitted to

(continued)

BOX 5.2 The Case of Justina Pelletier (continued)

a residential treatment center in Connecticut, closer to her home. The judge in the case hoped the child protection agency in Connecticut would agree to monitor Justina, but the agency refused because "they wanted nothing to do with the contentious case involving parental rights and the controversial new field of medical child abuse" (Wen & Swidey, 2014a, p. A11). Massachusetts officials sought to terminate involvement in the hope that the Connecticut agency would then have to handle the case. Perhaps part of the reason that Massachusetts officials sought to terminate involvement was that they had spent over $400,000, based on Medicaid rates up to June 2014.

In June 2014, Justina was allowed by a Massachusetts juvenile court judge to return to her home in Connecticut with her parents, who planned to continue Justina's treatment for mitochrondrial disease at Tufts Medical Center. In February 2016, Justina's parents filed a suit against Children's Hospital and four physicians, accusing them of "gross negligence and civil rights violations" (Levenson, 2016, p. A8). The family is seeking an unspecified amount in monetary damages.

Sources: Levenson (2016); Wen and Swidey (2014a, 2014b).

protocol is needed," and referral for a full assessment should be provided for those children who screen positive for mental health problems (Landsverk et al., 2007, p. 148). This improved provision of service must include ongoing monitoring, follow-up, and evaluation. The use of screening protocols can assist in predicting the needs of children and can also better help to plan for Medicaid spending (Raghavan et al., 2012).

SUBSTANCE ABUSE

The relationship between substance abuse and child maltreatment is very complex (Mignon, Larson, & Holmes, 2002). Although it is not necessarily the case, substance abuse by a parent with young children can interfere with the ability to provide appropriate structure and supervision. Children whose parents are substance abusers are at increased risk themselves of becoming substance abusers. Adults who have been victimized as children can also be at much higher risk of substance abuse than those who have not had a history of child maltreatment (Mignon et al., 2002). The relationship between substance abuse and child maltreatment, or any kind of family abuse, is further complicated by an association with mental health problems. Overall, families where substance abuse is present are more likely to come into contact with child protection agencies.

Women are less likely to enter substance abuse treatment than men, and part of the reason can be that there is no one to care for their children (Mignon, 2015; Mignon, Faiia, Myers, & Rubington, 2009). In Washington, DC, new programs such as Samaritan Inns have been developed to allow women with substance abuse problems to enter residential treatment with their children for stays of up to 6 months (Fenston, 2015). Because substance abuse problems can worsen over time, this use of Medicaid funding can best be availed of earlier rather than later.

In an early survey of 254 managers of child welfare services, considerable concern was expressed about the impact of substance abuse in the family on the delivery of child protection services (Curtis & McCullough, 1993). The impact of substance abuse on service delivery "is profound and adversely affects the system by compounding problems, such as personnel shortage and shortages in the availability of foster homes" (Curtis & McCullough, 1993, p. 533). Both professionals and foster families can feel unprepared to deal with substance abuse issues. Those families with substance abuse problems are likely to have extended child protection agency intervention and longer stays in foster care. Further, they are likely to make family preservation and reunification more challenging (Curtis & McCullough, 1993; Ryan, Marsh, Testa, & Louderman, 2006).

The Project Connect program offers intensive in-home supports to substance-abusing families in the child welfare system (Olsen, Laprade, & Holmes, 2015). This model provides comprehensive services, including home visits and parenting groups, which are matched to client and family needs, with an emphasis on the quality of the relationship between the family and the provider. The program begins with a service plan tailored to the specific family including financial and employment concerns, and can even address transportation needs. Parents receive referrals for some type of substance abuse treatment including outpatient, day treatment, or inpatient treatment. Those parents who were most highly involved in the Project Connect program reduced their substance use, improved their own mental health, improved their parenting skills, and had healthier parent–child relationships (Olsen et al., 2015).

Because physical health, mental health, and substance abuse treatment services are typically offered by different agencies, the need for collaboration is especially crucial. Professionals within each field must understand the child's and family's needs and must cultivate effective communication practices within the limits of confidentiality (Coates, 2015).

HOMELESSNESS

There are few things in life more dreadful than trying to survive without a home. Homelessness of children known to child protection agencies defies all we know about the need for consistency and appropriate structure for children. Housing instability can be a major factor in why families become known to child welfare agencies; it is estimated that about 30% of children come into foster care because of unstable housing (Harburger & White, 2004; Partners for Our Children, 2011). Part of the definition of child neglect has to do with failure to provide adequate shelter for children. Therefore, housing instability can easily precipitate child protection issues. Housing instability creates considerable stress for parents and children, and can also serve as a barrier to family reunification for children in foster care.

In January 2014, approximately 578,424 people were homeless across the United States (National Alliance to End Homelessness, 2015). About 216,261 individuals in families were homeless, which is about 37% of the homeless population. About 45,205 "unaccompanied" children and youth were homeless, or 7.8% of the homeless population. Overall, homelessness decreased by 2.3% from 2013 to 2014. Since 2007, veterans have seen a 33% decrease in homelessness, and those experiencing chronic homelessness decreased by 30%. In 2015, federal funding totalling $4.5 billion was provided to a variety of agencies to address homelessness, which, however, was insufficient to meet the need (National Alliance to End Homelessness, 2015). Positive gains in recent years can be attributed to improvements in services, increased resources, and a shift in orientation to provide permanent supportive housing. Not all have reaped the benefits of more resources for the homeless. See Box 5.3 for the story of Jayden, a boy living in a homeless shelter with his mother and siblings.

The prelude to homelessness for children often includes living in poverty, hunger, and more health problems than other children with homes (Child Trends Databank, 2015). Homelessnes of families most often results from lack of affordable housing, poverty, and family violence. At least one quarter has witnessed violence. Ten percent of children under the age of 1 were living in shelters in 2013, 39% were aged 1 to 5, 33% were aged 6 to 12, and 18% were aged 13 to 17 (Child Trends Databank, 2015). For children on their own, staying in shelters, referred to as "unaccompanied youth," 87% were aged 13 to 17, with 7% between the ages of 6 to 12. For unaccompanied youth, homelessness most often results from lack of affordable housing, mental health problems, and substance abuse (Child Trends Databank, 2015).

It is very difficult to obtain an accurate count of homeless children, but using data from children enrolled in schools and those living in shelters, it is estimated that 1.4 million children were homeless at the beginning of the 2013 to 2014 school year (Child Trends Databank, 2015). At that time, 75% of students were living

---

BOX 5.3 Jayden's Story of Homelessness

For Jayden's family, his mother and two siblings, homelessness started with the physical abuse of his mother by his father. After 6 years of abuse and concern for her children's safety, Jayden's mother took him and his siblings to a domestic violence shelter and then arranged to leave the state. Living in an emergency shelter, the family had to share one room. Shortly after, Jayden made several trips to the emergency room for his hacking cough that was eventually diagnosed as asthma. Jayden's breathing difficulties made it difficult for him to function and sleep. Homelessness made it even more difficult to cope with asthma, and Jayden also suffered from depression. He felt guilty he could not protect his mother from the abuse of his father, and suffered nightmares. His health issues contributed to his lack of school attendance as well as his inability to complete his school work. Emotional isolation made it more difficult for him to cultivate friends. The story concludes: "Jayden hopes his family will find a better life. His future depends in part on legislators and public leaders far from the little room where he coughs his way through the night."

Source: The National Center on Family Homelessness (2014).

---

with other families; 15% were in shelters; 6% lived in motels or hotels; and 3% were living in cars, abandoned buildings, or on the streets. Not surprisingly, there are differences in homelessness according to race and ethnicity. In 2013, of the families living in shelters, African Americans formed 48%; Hispanic families, 23%; White families, 23%; and Native Americans, 3% (Child Trends Databank, 2015).

Massachusetts is the only state that is required to provide shelter to all eligible residents (Miller, 2015). This means that if the 3,400 shelter beds are filled, the Commonwealth of Massachusetts is obligated to pay for homeless families to stay in a hotel or motel at the cost of approximately $106/night. Housing advocates point to the numbers of homeless people who have jobs but are unable to afford an apartment. In Massachusetts, a person making the mandated minimum wage of $10/hour, working 50 hours/week, made $26,000 annually in 2015. The average apartment rental in the Boston area in 2015 was $24,000/year (Miller, 2015). This means there is virtually no chance of obtaining housing in Boston for the individual minimum wage earner.

One study of homeless youth in Denver found that over one third had a history of foster care placement and were "generally living in precarious situations" (Bender, Yang, Ferguson, & Thompson, 2015, p. 227). The vast majority had suffered some kind of trauma in the streets (83%), had sought money from panhandling (45%), stealing (25%), and selling drugs (21%).

A study of homeless youth in three midwestern states who aged out of foster care found that between 31% and 46% of study respondents had been homeless by the age of 26 (Dworsky, Napolitano, & Courtney, 2013). Increases in homelessness were associated with male clients, a physical abuse history, multiple foster care placements, running away from placement, delinquent behaviors, and mental health problems.

Although this population is clearly in need of many resources—stable housing, education, employment opportunities, and mental health and substance abuse treatment—we have little research on the effectiveness of these services (Bender et al., 2015). Safe housing for independent underage children is needed. See Box 5.4 for a description of the important work of the National Center for Housing and Child Welfare to address the needs of homeless maltreated children.

BOX 5.4 The National Center for Housing and Child Welfare

The National Center for Housing and Child Welfare (NCHCW) focuses on developing partnerships to address housing and homelessness policy; supports housing and child welfare systems to collaborate at the local, regional, and national levels; and provides training and other resources to improve the services for homeless children in the child welfare system. The NCHCW provides resources for older children in foster care to achieve stable housing. The NCHCW also works with legislators and policy makers at the federal level including the U.S. Department of Health and Human Services, Housing and Urban Development, and the U.S. Interagency Council on Homelessness, to provide funding to reduce homelessness among the child welfare population. Their website gives the example that in 2008 to 2009, NCHCW was successful in the lobbying efforts to obtain $50 million for Section 8 housing vouchers for families with children in the child welfare system. The NCHCW also provides training for public housing authority staff, shelter workers, and child welfare staff. Participants have found these to be worthwhile trainings that increase awareness of community resources and eligibility requirements, as well as improving their own professional confidence in assisting families and children in need.

Source: National Center for Housing and Child Welfare (2015).

Independent living under the Foster Care Independence Act of 1999, known as the "Chafee Act," has not proven to be especially effective in assisting youth (Dworsky & Courtney, 2009; Freundlich, 2010). The services have not been sufficiently specific and practical. In a review of research over a 10-year period found that programs have not been effective in addressing educational needs, employment needs, housing, pregnancy prevention, or diversion from juvenile and adult justice systems (Freundlich, 2010). It is unrealistic to expect 18-year-olds to achieve independence at that early age, and the more recent Connected by 25 approach improves upon the Foster Care Independence Act by providing more educational, training, employment opportunities, and social supports (Youth Transition Funders Group, 2010).

Child welfare workers must know whether clients are in danger of losing their homes, and therefore, housing stability should be an integral part of a family assessment (Partners for Our Children, 2011). Child welfare workers need more information on housing resources, increased professional connections, and more flexibility in using them (Partners for Our Children, 2011; Shadaimah, 2009). Better collection of data and dissemination of information on housing and child welfare is needed (Shadaimah, 2009). Although child welfare systems and professionals should not be held accountable for the provision of housing, they can join other professionals in advocating increased appropriate housing options for maltreated children. See Box 5.5 for a description of the success of the Building Changes program in reducing homelessness in Washington State.

SUMMARY AND CONCLUSION

Children in the child welfare system are more likely to experience physical and mental health problems and much more likely to be prescribed psychotropic medications. To improve the provision of health services that address all the medical needs of children, there are critical roles for biological parents, foster parents, health care professionals, and child protection professionals. Physical and mental health assessments of all children coming into the child protection system provide the opportunity for early intervention to prevent problems from becoming worse. Health care professionals can do much more to ensure that children's basic health needs are met, and must increasingly engage with child welfare professionals to deliver improved care. It is time for child protection agencies to make health issues and the integration of health services, as well as insurance coverage, a central theme of their work.

Homelessness and child protection issues are deeply intertwined. In view of their numerous responsibilities, it is unreasonable to expect child welfare workers to solve the problem of homelessness for their clients. To ensure an

---

BOX 5.5 Building Changes in Washington State

Building Changes is a nonprofit organization based in Seattle, Washington, designed to achieve stable housing for families, including those within the child welfare system. Since 2014, Building Changes has reduced family homelessness in Washington State by a whopping 35%. It has brought together numerous agencies such as schools, public housing authorities, community colleges, and health care organizations to work toward housing stability, and to develop innovative collaborations to redesign the housing system. Building Changes accomplishes this by providing a coordinated system of entry and assessment, fast rehousing placement, specialized services to address the unique needs of each homeless family, and economic opportunities including workforce development. The diversion program focuses on settling families very quickly into stable housing by addressing financial problems, performing an active housing search, providing mediation services, and paying the first and last months' rent, all at a lower cost than traditional housing advocacy services.

In addition, Building Changes has collaborated with public housing authorities to provide rental subsidies to support reunification of foster children with their families. This type of program increases the numbers of children who reunify with their families in stable housing units, reduces the number of children who return to foster placement, and saves foster care expenditures and time by reunifying families more quickly.

Sources: Building Changes (2015); Partners for Our Children (2011).

---

adequate supply of appropriate housing, child welfare workers must be knowledgeable about existing housing resources and the responsibilities of local, state, and federal governments and policy makers. There is much to be learned from recent innovative housing models.

DISCUSSION QUESTIONS

1. What kinds of health problems are children in the child welfare system likely to develop?

2. What impact does access to health insurance have on children in the child welfare system?

3. Discuss the mental health problems of children who have been victims of abuse and neglect.

4. What lessons should be learned from the tragic death of Rebecca Riley?

5. Discuss the relationship between substance abuse and child maltreatment.

6. What are some alternatives for parents with addiction problems who need to take care of their children?

7. What could have been done by medical professionals and child welfare professionals to bring the case of Justina Pelletier to an earlier and more successful resolution?

8. What kinds of difficulties are homeless children likely to endure?

9. What do you know about homelessness and resources to combat it in your own community?

10. What are your own suggestions for reducing homelessness for the child welfare population in the United States?

REFERENCES

Abel, D. (2007, February 6). Hull parents arrested in girl's poisoning death. *The Boston Globe*. Retrieved from www.astraeasweb.net/politics/riley.html

Associated Press. (2007, September 28). *Mom charged in child's drug overdose says bipolar diagnosis wrong*. Retrieved from www.astraeasweb.net/politics/riley.html

Bai, Y., Wells, R., & Hillemeier, M. M. (2009). Coordination between child welfare agencies and mental health service providers, children's service use, and outcomes. *Child Abuse & Neglect*, 33, 372–381.

Bender, K., Yang, J., Ferguson, K., & Thompson, S. (2015). Experiences and needs of homeless youth with a history of foster care. *Children and Youth Services Review*, 55, 222–231.

Building Changes. (2015). *Approach*. Retrieved from www.buildingchanges.org/approach

Burns, B. J., Phillips, S. D., Wagner, H. R., Barth, R. P., Kolko, D. J., Campbell, Y., & Landsverk, J. (2004). Mental health need and access to mental health services by youths involved with child welfare: A national survey. *Journal of the American Academy of Child and Adolescent Psychiatry*, 43(8), 960–970.

Child Trends Databank. (2015). *Homeless children and youth*. Retrieved from www .childtrends.org/?indicators=homeless-children-and-youth

Coates, D. (2015). Working with families with parental mental health and/or drug and alcohol issues where there are child protection concerns: Inter-agency collaboration. *Child and Family Social Work*. Retrieved from http://onlinelibrary.wiley .com/doi/10.1111/cfs.12238/abstract

Curtis, P. A., & McCullough, C. (1993). The impact of alcohol and other drugs on the child welfare system. *Child Welfare*, 72(6), 533–542.

Dworsky, A., & Courtney, M. E. (2009). Homelessness and the transition from foster care to adulthood. *Child Welfare, 88*(4), 23–56.

Dworsky, A., Napolitano, L., & Courtney, M. (2013). Homelessness during the transition from foster care to adulthood. *American Journal of Public Health, 103*(Suppl. 2), S318–S323.

Fenston, J. (2015, June 19). *When mom needs rehab, what about the kids? New D.C. programs offer solutions.* WAMU. Retrieved from http://wamu.org/programs/metro_connection/15/06/19/when_mom_needs_rehab_what_happens_to_her_kids_new_dc_programs_seek_to_offer_solutions

Florence, C., Brown, D. S., Fang, X., & Thompson, H. F. (2013). Health care costs associated with child maltreatment: Impact on Medicaid. *Pediatrics, 132*(2). Retrieved from www.pediatrics.org/cgi/doi/10.1542/peds.2012-2212

Freundlich, M. (2010, April). *Chafee plus ten: A vision for the next decade.* St. Louis, MO: Jim Casey Youth Opportunities Initiative.

Glier, R. (2015, October 1; updated December 22). *Many former foster youths don't know they have health care.* National Public Radio. Retrieved from www.npr.org/sections/health-shots/2015/10/01/444779762/many-former-foster-youths-don't-know-they-have-health-care

Gonzalez, M. J. (2014). Mental health care of families affected by the child welfare system. *Child Welfare, 93*(1), 7–57.

Hamilton, H. A., Paglia-Boak, A., Wekerle, C., Danielson, A. M., & Mann, R. E. (2011). Psychological distress, service utilization, and prescribed medications among youth with and without histories of involvement with child protective services. *International Journal of Mental Health and Addiction, 9*, 398–409.

Harburger, D. S., & White, R. A. (2004). Reunifying families, cutting costs: Housing-child welfare partnerships for permanent supportive housing. *Child Welfare, 83*(5), 493–508.

Jaudes, K. P., Champagne, V., Harden, A., Masterson, J., & Bilaver, L. A. (2012). Expanded medical home model works for children in foster care. *Child Welfare, 91*(1), 9–33.

Kardish, C. (2015, June 16). California's plan to curb America's overmedication of foster kids. *Governing.* Retrieved from www.governing.com/topics/health-human-services/gov-california-psychotropics-foster-kids.html

Landsverk, J. A., Hurlburt, M. S., & Leslie, L. K. (2007). Systems integration and access to mental health care. In R. Haskins, F. Wulczyn, & M. B. Webb (Eds.), *Child protection: Using research to improve policy and practice.* Washington, DC: Brookings Institution Press.

Leslie, L. K., Raghavan, R., Hurley, M., Zhang, J., Landsverk, J., & Aarons, G. (2011). Investigating geographic variation in use of psychotropic medications among youth in child welfare. *Child Abuse & Neglect, 35*, 333–342.

Levenson, M. (2016, Feburary 26). 'I'm very angry,' teen says of ordeal: Pelletiers sue Children's Hospital, cite misdeeds. *The Boston Globe*, pp. A1, A8.

McMillen, J. C., Fedoravicius, N., Rowe, J., Zima, B. T., & Ware, N. (2007). A crisis of credibility: Professionals' concerns about the psychiatric care provided to clients of the child welfare system. *Administration Policy and Mental Health, 34*(3), 203–212.

Mekonnen, R., Noonan, K., & Rubin, D. (2009). Achieving better health care outcomes for children in foster care. *Pediatric Clinics of North America, 56*(2), 405–415. doi:10.1016/j.pcl.2009.01.005

Merrick, M. T., & Latzman, N. E. (2014). Child maltreatment: A public health overview and prevention considerations. *The Online Journal of Issues in Nursing, 19*(1). Retrieved from www.nursingworld.org/MainMenuCategories/ANAMarketplace/ANAPeriodicals/OJIN/TableofContents/Vol-19-2014/No1-Jan-2014/Child-Maltreatment.html

Mignon, S. I. (2015). *Substance abuse treatment: Options, challenges, and effectiveness.* New York, NY: Springer Publishing Company.

Mignon, S. I., Faiia, M. M., Myers, P. L., & Rubington, E. (2009). *Substance use & abuse: Exploring alcohol & drug issues.* Boulder, CO: Lynne Rienner.

Mignon, S. I., Larson, C. J., & Holmes, W. M. (2002). *Family abuse: Consequences, theories and responses.* Boston, MA: Allyn & Bacon.

Miller, J. (2015, January 9). Fewer homeless families sheltered in hotels, motels. *The Boston Globe*, p. B4.

Moses, T. (2008). Psychotropic medication practices for youth in systems of care. *Journal of Child and Family Studies, 17*(4), 567–581.

National Alliance to End Homelessness. (2015). *The state of homelessness in America.* Washington, DC: Author.

National Center for Housing and Child Welfare. (2015). *Welcome to the National Center for Housing and Child Welfare.* Retrieved from www.nchcw.org

Olsen, L. J., Laprade, V., & Holmes, W. M. (2015). Supports for families affected by substance abuse. *Journal of Public Child Welfare, 9*(5), 55–570.

Pace, P. R. (2016, January). Nutrition plays role in mental well-being. *NASW News*, pp. 7, 9.

Partners for Our Children. (2011, August 11). *Poverty and housing instability: The implications for families involved in the child welfare system.* Retrieved from http://partnersforourchildren.org

Pecora, P. J., Kessler, R. C., Williams, J., O'Brien, K., Downs, A. C., English, D., . . . Holmes, K. (2005). *Improving family foster care: Findings from the Northwest Foster Care Alumni Study.* Seattle, WA: Casey Family Programs. Retrieved from http://www.casey.org/northwest-alumni-study

Raghavan, R., Brown, D. S., Allaire, B. T., Garfield, L. D., Ross, R. E., & Snowden, L. R. (2014). Racial/ethnic differences in Medicaid expenditures on psychotropic medications among maltreated children. *Child Abuse & Neglect, 38*, 1002–1010.

Raghavan, R., Brown, D. S., Thompson, H., Ettner, S. L., Clements, L. M., & Key, W. (2012). Medicaid expenditures on psychotropic medications for children in the child welfare system. *Journal of Child and Adolescent Psychopharmacology*, 22(3), 182–189.

Raghavan, R., Shi, P., Aarons, G. A., Roesch, S. C., & McMillen, J. C. (2009). Health insurance discontinuities among adolescents leaving foster care. *Journal of Adolescent Health*, 44(1), 41–47. doi:10.1016/j.jadohealth.2008.08.008

Raghavan, R., Shi, P., James, S., Aarons, G. A., Roesch, S. C., & Leslie, L. K. (2009). Effects of placement changes on health insurance stability among a national sample of children in the child welfare system. *Journal of Social Science Research*, 35, 352–363.

Ryan, J. P., Marsh, J. C., Testa, M. F., & Louderman, R. (2006). Integrating substance abuse treatment and child welfare services: Findings from the Illinois Alcohol and Other Drug Abuse Waiver Demonstration. *Social Work Research*, 30(2), 95–107.

Sachs-Ericsson, N., Cromer, K., & Hernandez, A. (2009). A review of childhood abuse, health, and pain-related problems: The role of psychiatric disorders and current life stress. *Journal of Trauma & Dissociation*, 10, 170–188.

Schneiderman, J. U., Smith, C., Arnold, J. S., Fuentes, J., & Duan, L. (2013). Weight changes in children in foster care for 1 year. *Child Abuse & Neglect*, 37(10), 832–840.

Shadaimah, C. C. (2009). "CPS is not a housing agency"; housing is not a CPS problem: Toward a definition and typology of housing problems in child welfare cases. *Child and Family Services Review*, 31, 211–218.

The National Center on Family Homelessness. (2014). *America's youngest outcasts: State report card on child homelessness.* Newton, MA: Author.

Wen, P. (2011, January 25). Tufts settles suit against doctor in girl's death for $2.5m. *The Boston Globe*. Retrieved from www.boston.com/news/local/massachusetts/articles/2011/01/25/tufts_settles_suit_against_doctor_in_girls_death_for_25m

Wen, P., & Swidey, N. (2014a, June 19). Pressures mounted to end fight on custody. *The Boston Globe*, pp. A1, A11.

Wen, P., & Swidey, N. (2014b, December 7). A difficult return to hospital for Justina Pelletier. *The Boston Globe*. Retrieved from https://www.bostonglobe.com/metro/2014/12/07/difficult-return-hospital-for-justina-pelletieru4JXzmt5YsmWhYk95za2aK/story.html

Youth Transition Funders Group. (2010, Spring). *Connected by 25: Effective policy solutions for vulnerable youth.* Retrieved from www.ytfgconnectedby25.org/YTFGConnectedby25FullIssueBriefApril2010.pdf

Zito, J. M., Safer, D. J., Sai, D., Gardner, J. F., Thomas, D., Coombes, P., ... Mendez-Lewis, M. (2008). Psychotropic medication patterns among youth in foster care. *Pediatrics*, 121(1), e157–e163. doi:10.1542/peds.2007-0212

THE JUVENILE JUSTICE SYSTEM
AND CHILD WELFARE

*T*hroughout U.S. history, it has been a consistent concern that child abuse and neglect lead to juvenile delinquency and adult criminal activity (Barth, Duncan, Hodorowicz, & Kum, 2010). As we discussed in Chapter 2, this concern provided the impetus for the "child saving" activities of the 19th century, an effort to care for children in ways that would make them law-abiding adults. Chapter 6 examines the strong relationship between child maltreatment and child and adolescent delinquent behaviors. The chapter addresses parental incarceration and how it impacts children, propelling some toward illegal activity. The chapter then examines children in both the child welfare system and the juvenile justice system referred to as "crossover" or "dual status" youth.

Much of the advocacy work on behalf of maltreated children is rendered to help them avoid the juvenile justice system and the adult criminal justice system (Barth et al., 2010). Overall, we have fallen short, and involvement in the child protection system is strongly associated with coming into contact with the juvenile justice system. The vast majority of children involved with child protective services are poor and are likely to commit more delinquent acts, have more arrests, and commit more crimes than other poor children who are unknown to child protective services (Barth et al., 2010).

It can be difficult to sort out and compare findings from research studies to understand more clearly the relationship between involvement with child protective services and the juvenile justice system. These research challenges include reliance on self-reports of those committing crimes, with no mechanism to verify the information, no standardized definitions and classifications of crimes among states, and outcome studies that follow youth for varying lengths of time (Barth et al., 2010). The professional backgrounds, orientations, and biases of the researchers themselves can also impact research results.

Involvement in the criminal justice system by a parent is a major contributor to family instability, perhaps taking away the family breadwinner and main emotional support for children (Sykes & Pettit, 2014). Yet correctional policy in the United States does not often take into consideration the effects on children (Murphey & Cooper, 2015). The negative impact on children stems not only from having a parent in prison, but also from parental involvement in other parts of the criminal justice system. For example, for parents on probation or parole, negative effects can spread to children and other family members (Phillips & Dettlaff, 2009). The children of adults who have been arrested are subject to a higher number of risk factors for their own involvement in the juvenile justice system and the adult criminal justice system.

THE IMPACT OF PARENTAL INCARCERATION ON CHILDREN

More than 5 million children in the United States have a parent with whom they resided who is currently or was formerly incarcerated (Murphey & Cooper, 2015). In 2007, 2.3% of all children in the United States had an incarcerated parent. The numbers of children with a parent in prison increased by 80% between 1991 and mid-2007 (Glaze & Maruschak, 2008). During the same period, the number of children with an incarcerated mother grew by 131%, and children with an incarcerated father grew by 77%. African American children were 7.5 times more likely than White children, and Hispanic children were more than 2.5 times more likely than White children to have an incarcerated parent (Glaze & Maruschak, 2008).

Children and their families have much to cope with when a parent is incarcerated. All family members share the stigma of incarceration, and that may encourage social isolation. The concerns for the well-being of children are even greater when the mother is incarcerated. Children are much more likely to need a placement when the mother is incarcerated than when the father is incarcerated (Johnson, & Waldfogel, 2002; Mignon & Ransford, 2012).

The number of women in prison in the United States has risen in the late 20th and early 21st centuries and then began to decrease, only to rise again. In 2006, the number of women in prison increased by 4.5% over the previous 5 years for a total of 112,498 prisoners (Sabol, Couture, & Harrison, 2007). Most recently, women in state and federal prisons who received sentences of more than 1 year increased by 2% in 2014, from 104,300 in 2013 to 106,200 in 2014 (Carson, 2015).

For children, the experience of having an incarcerated parent is associated with a significantly greater risk of homelessness, food insecurity, traumatic experiences, health problems, depression and anxiety, difficulties in school, and behavioral and emotional problems (Murphey & Cooper, 2015; Mignon & Ransford, 2012; Sykes & Pettit, 2014). Certainly, there is the personality of the child that determines the child's response; one child's reaction to a parent's incarceration can be aggression and behavioral problems, yet another child's reaction can be anxiety, sadness, withdrawal, and even depression (Hairston, 2009).

There are many risk factors for children associated with parental incarceration, making it difficult to tease out the causes and impacts of these difficulties. We have already seen that incarceration rates are significantly higher for those living in poverty, and prison inmates are disproportionately racial and ethnic minorities (Murphey & Cooper, 2015). Children living in poverty have experienced parental incarceration at three times the rate of those not living in poverty. When a parent is incarcerated, children have about a 50% chance of living with someone with a substance abuse problem (Murphey & Cooper, 2015). More than 25% have lived with someone with mental illness, including adults who have made suicide attempts.

The criminal justice system is rife with discrimination. Incarceration and every kind of involvement in the criminal justice system disproportionately affect poor families of color (Alexander, 2010; Hairston, 2009). African American men with low levels of education are more likely to become known to the criminal justice system as are their children (Murphey & Cooper, 2015). Adolescent African American males with a history of child maltreatment are more likely to be involved in the juvenile justice system than those who do not have a history of abuse or neglect (Williams, Van Dorn, Bright, Jonson-Reid, & Nebbitt, 2010).

As we have seen, Black children are overrepresented in the child welfare system—they are more likely to grow up in poor areas that have heavy involvement with the child welfare system (Honore'-Collins, 2005; Roberts, 2012). Both the child welfare and criminal justice systems have a very strong impact on African American mothers: "The simultaneous buildup and operation of the prison and foster care systems rely on the punishment of black mothers, who suffer greatly from the systems' intersection" (Roberts, 2012, p. 1476). Roberts (2012) continues: "As a result of the political choice to fund punitive instead of supportive programs, criminal justice and child welfare supervision of mothers is pervasive in poor black communities" (p. 1491). See Box 6.1 for the story of Dave, a young man whose mother was arrested and taken from the home when he was 9.

Police and correctional programs typically do not ask about parenthood and whether children left behind are in need of assistance. Much more needs to be done to ensure that these inquiries are made (Christian, 2009). For example, since 2007, Hawaii has required parents to be placed in correctional facilities based on the

BOX 6.1 Story of Dave Whose Mother Was Arrested and Taken From Their Home When He Was 9

The story of Dave who was left behind with his 1-year-old brother when their mother was arrested, in his own words:

I was 9 when my mom got arrested. The police came and took her. I was trying to ask them what was going on and they wouldn't say, and then everything went so fast. I guess they thought someone else was in the house. I don't know. But nobody else was in the house. They arrested her and just left us there. For 2 or 3 weeks I took care of my 1-year-old brother and myself. I knew how to change diapers and feed him and stuff. . . . I wasn't really afraid. I was just trying to take care of my brother. . . . Sometimes he would cry because he probably would want to see my mom. When my mom was there, every day we used to take my little brother for a walk in the stroller. I still did that every day, even though my mom wasn't there. Her friend across the street saw us and I guess she figured out something was wrong. She called Child Protective Services and they came and took us.

My mom did come back eventually, but by that time we were already gone. All I know is that they just rushed me in the system and that was that. They didn't tell me why I can't go back with my mom. I was sent to a temporary foster home and my brother was in a different foster home. Then I got placed in the foster home where I live now. I've been here for about 8 years. I feel bad about being separated from my brother. I should have had visits with my brother, to at least know exactly where he was. I just prayed that he was doing OK. During the time we were split up, my mom died. So then I was really mad because my brother was the only person I had left of my family and I didn't know where he was. I think when the police first arrested my mom, they should have looked around the house and seen that we were there by ourselves. Then I wouldn't have had to take care of my brother for that long. The police should sit down and talk with you. Explain the situation.

Source: San Francisco Children of Incarcerated Parents Partnership (2005).

location and needs of the family, rather than on economic or administrative concerns. Colorado requires correctional programs to determine whether inmates are parents and, if so, to offer information on community resources that could be helpful to the children (Christian, 2009). The San Francisco Children of Incarcerated Parents Partnership developed a bill of rights for children who have an incarcerated parent to ensure that their needs are addressed. See Box 6.2 for the Bill of Rights for Children of Incarcerated Parents.

The rise in the number of incarcerated women over time brought with it an increase in children in foster care placement (Halperin & Harris, 2004). When mothers are incarcerated, there is a greater likelihood that children must move to other homes, whether with families or in state foster care placements. A study of family relationships of incarcerated mothers in Massachusetts found that 50% of children were living with their mothers before the mothers entered prison (Kates, Mignon, & Ransford, 2008). Fifteen percent were living with grandparents, over 7% were in foster care, almost 5% were living with their fathers, and almost 5% had been adopted. After the mothers' incarceration, 39% were living with grandparents, 17% in foster care, 14% with fathers, and 12% had been adopted (Kates et al., 2008). Foster care placements more than doubled, as did the number of adoptions after the mothers' incarceration.

BOX 6.2 *The Bill of Rights for Children of Incarcerated Parents*

This Bill of Rights for Children of Incarcerated Parents was first published in 2003 and revised in 2005. In March 2012, the United Nations Human Rights Council passed a resolution on the rights of the child, incorporating substantial parts of the Bill of Rights for Children of Incarcerated Parents.

1. I have the right to be kept safe and informed at the time of my parent's arrest.
2. I have the right to be heard when decisions are made about me.
3. I have the right to be considered when decisions are made about my parent.
4. I have the right to be well cared for in my parent's absence.
5. I have the right to speak with, see, and touch my parent.
6. I have the right to support as I face my parent's incarceration.
7. I have the right not to be judged, blamed, or labeled because my parent is incarcerated.
8. I have the right to a lifelong relationship with my parent.

Source: San Francisco Children of Incarcerated Parents Partnership (2005).

In a review of national surveys, Hairston (2009) found that approximately 2% of children with incarcerated parents are in the child welfare system. There are several reasons why this figure seems to be so low. One reason is that parents may not know that their children are in state custody. This can be the case especially for fathers who have had limited contact with their children. Parents may not understand that if their children are in kinship care (living with family members), this can mean that they are in state custody. It can also be difficult to obtain accurate data from the juvenile justice and child welfare systems, and some important data may not be collected at all. For example, estimates of children in foster care who have an incarcerated parent vary widely from 6% to 70% (Hairston, 2009). This wide variation in estimates points to the need for further research to more accurately determine how many children in foster care have an incarcerated parent.

The purpose of the correctional environment is to ensure public safety, and thus it is not surprising that the typical correctional facility does little to support the connections between parents and children. Children tend to do better when they can maintain contact with their parent who is in prison (Hairston, 2009). However, it is very difficult to remove the obstacles to communication and visitation. There are expenses associated with communicating with incarcerated parents. If prison inmates do not have family or friends to deposit money into their prison accounts, they may not be able to purchase stamps and paper to write letters. Phone calls can be exorbitant and typically require collect calls paid for by the family member. There are significant transportation obstacles as well, and the parent may be in a prison hours away from where the child is living (Kates et al., 2008; Roberts, 2012).

In one sample of jailed women, only 20% of their children were able to visit, and 50% had no phone contact with their mothers (Lawrence, Stepteau-Watson, & Honore'-Collins, 2007). In a sample of women in a state prison, mothers were much more likely to have mail and telephone contacts with their children; however, almost one half of the mothers never received a visit from a child (Mignon & Ransford, 2012). Movements have been afoot to reduce the barriers to telephone contact between family members and prison inmates. For example, to combat excessive costs of telephone calls, New York State requires their state correctional agency to seek the lowest costs and bars the agency from receiving excessive profits (Christian, 2009).

Child welfare workers may not do enough to help children and caregivers stay in touch with their incarcerated parents. For child welfare workers, lack of time is a major issue owing to high caseloads, and arranging visits can be labor intensive in view of all visitation requirements and restrictions of correctional facilities that need to be met. In some Massachusetts prisons today, drug-sniffing dogs are used regularly to screen prison visitors, which adds to the overall stress and discomfort of prison visitation.

Trauma to children can be reduced by supporting communication between parents and children, including child-friendly visits to correctional institutions. Yet few services are in place to strengthen the bonds and maintain relationships between incarcerated mothers and their children (Mignon & Ransford, 2012).

Factors that support a child's well-being are the quality of the relationship with the caregiver and the quality of the home environment while a parent is incarcerated. Kinship care and other foster care placements for caregivers are especially difficult because they must follow the regulations of the child welfare system and the criminal justice system (Hairston, 2009). If the incarcerated parent can maintain a positive relationship with the foster parent, this can help to ensure a smoother experience for the children. Incarcerated mothers with children in foster care should be able to participate in planning for and maintaining contact with their children, but this is not necessarily the case. When children are not in kinship foster care, the child welfare worker may be the one responsible for arranging transportation for the children, which is a difficult task (Halperin & Harris, 2004).

Termination of parental rights can result from long prison sentences, especially for a mother (Halperin & Harris, 2004). The Adoption and Safe Families Act (ASFA) of 1997 has been problematic for incarcerated parents (Johnson & Waldfogel, 2002). As discussed in Chapter 3, ASFA requires states to terminate the rights of parents when the child has been abandoned or placed in foster care for 15 of the most recent 22 months (Christian, 2009; Rosado, 2015). Although ASFA does not require the termination of parental rights for incarcerated adults, this can be the result for parents who have been in jail or prison for more than 15 months. Not surprisingly, the parents of children in foster care are at especially high risk of having their parental rights terminated. ASFA also offers financial incentives to states to increase the number of foster children moving into adoptive families, and can thereby encourage termination of parental rights (Roberts, 2012). The opportunities for families to reunify can be undercut by ASFA, which requires child protection agencies to seek adoptive families for those in foster care yet simultaneously work to preserve the family (Roberts, 2012). Overall, children in foster care with an incarcerated parent are much less likely to be able to reunite with their families (Hayward & DePanfilis, 2007). And those who are aging out of foster care are at higher risk of entering the criminal justice system themselves (Ryan, Hernandez, & Herz, 2007).

More action needs to be taken to reinforce the importance of parent–child relationships during parental incarceration. An in-depth needs assessment for incoming prison inmates should include obtaining information on where the children are living and who is caring for them (Kates et al., 2008). Correctional facilities and child protection agencies can do much more to enhance parent–child contacts and to increase facilitation of visits. Cyber-visiting via Skype or another method of video chatting could also be important ways to maintain contact (Kates et al., 2008). The addition of an outreach program coordinator position within correctional facilities can identify community resources and support services for caregivers and children. Child protection agencies can also develop a closer relationship with correctional programs, including placing child protection workers in facilities to coordinate all cases where child protection issues are involved (Kates et al., 2008).

At this time, there are no well-proven models and interventions to assist children with incarcerated parents, and it is very difficult to determine whether interventions in the home, in the school, or at the community level are best (Sykes & Pettit, 2014). Of course, data collection and research studies are required to evaluate the quality of services and move the field toward more definitive best-practice interventions (Hairston, 2009). The research arm of each state department of corrections can be instrumental in developing this. Research findings can help with efforts to evaluate the positive and negative consequences of correctional practices on the state and federal levels, and serve as the basis for policy change.

CROSSOVER OR DUAL STATUS YOUTH

Children can intersect with both the child welfare and juvenile justice systems in a variety of ways. For example, a child can be known to child welfare services and can then get arrested and enter the juvenile justice system. A second example is when a child who has a closed child welfare case is arrested and is referred back to the child welfare agency. A third example is when a child is arrested and then it is learned for the first time that she or he has been abused and/or neglected; the child is then referred to the child welfare system. Finally, a child may be arrested and placed in a correctional facility, and then upon release, there may be no home to which to return, so the child is referred to child welfare services for foster care placement.

Out-of-home placement typically refers to different things for children in the child welfare and the juvenile justice systems. Children in the child welfare system are removed from their homes because of safety issues such as maltreatment (Kolivoski, Barnett, & Abbott, 2015). These children may be placed in kinship care, in a state foster care placement, or in a group setting. Youth in the juvenile justice system may be placed in detention facilities for a short stay after arrest, in longer-term residential facilities run by the state, or in correctional group homes. In fact, youth may move between the systems and placements but do not necessarily move from less restrictive to more restrictive placements according to the child's behavior and needs (Kolivoski et al., 2015). As discussed in Chapter 4, barriers to the educational needs of crossover youth include placement instability and frequent moves; difficulty in accessing educational records by a new school; enrollment obstacles; lack of communication, coordination, and understanding between agencies; and lack of a designated advocate (Leone & Weinberg, 2010).

There is evidence that a history of involvement in the child welfare system puts children at greater risk of deeper involvement in juvenile justice programs, known as the "child welfare bias" (Kolivoski et al., 2015). Judges and others may think the history of an unstable home environment calls for a more intensive juvenile justice response. For example, one study compared first offenders with and without a child welfare history. Those youth without a child welfare history were more likely to be placed on probation, whereas those in the child welfare system were more likely to be sentenced to a juvenile correctional placement (Ryan, Herz, Hernandez, & Marshall, 2007). See Box 6.3 for an example of what can go wrong in a residential correctional program for delinquent boys.

It is difficult to estimate how many children are crossover youth, mainly because separate records are kept by child welfare and juvenile justice systems.

BOX 6.3 Abuse of Youth at the Casa Isla Short-Term Treatment and Revocation Center

Children in institutions in the juvenile justice system are not necessarily safe from harm. In 2015, eight staff members of the Casa Isla Short-Term Treatment and Revocation Center in Boston were charged with assault and battery and other serious charges stemming from their physically abusive treatment of juveniles remanded to the residential correctional program by a juvenile court judge. As a result, Casa Isla closed. It had been run by Volunteers of America Massachusetts since 1991, and had been contracted to provide services to adolescent boys through the Massachusetts Department of Youth Services, the state juvenile correctional agency. The charges stemmed from the severely abusive practice referred to as the "orange chicken," in which boys were stripped below the waist and an orange sandal was used to hit them on their bare buttocks. One father described the trauma his son endured: "He thought he was going to be raped. . . . He was dealt with [sic] such force and intimidated in such a way he thought he was going to die." (p. A13)

Source: Herndon, Allen, and Cramer (2015).

Some research examines how many youth in the child welfare system enter the juvenile justice system. Other research looks at youth in the juvenile justice system who have received child welfare services. Research findings also vary according to the age groups studied (Herz et al., 2012). Overall, research shows that between 9% and 29% of children in child protective services commit delinquent acts (Leone & Weinberg, 2010).

Crossover youth are more likely to enter the juvenile justice system earlier and for more serious offenses than those not in the child welfare system (Leone & Weinberg, 2010). Youth in the juvenile justice system with extensive involvement with child protection services are more likely to be female, African American, and Native American (Wiig & Tuell, 2013). One study of 99 women in jail (typically much shorter stays than prison) with daughters at an average age of 13 found their daughters had poorer outcomes than daughters of incarcerated women not in the child welfare system (Lawrence, Stepteau-Watson, & Honore'-Collins, 2007). Daughters with dual involvement were more likely to experience multiple foster care placements within a short time and poor academic performance. In addition, they were more likely to commit delinquent behaviors.

Overall, placement instability is associated with increases in delinquent behaviors. One study found that adolescent males with three placements were 1.54 times more likely to have been charged with a delinquent act (Ryan & Testa, 2005). Those with four or more placements were 2.13 times more likely to have been charged with a delinquent act than youth who had only one placement. Those with substantiated cases of child abuse or neglect had delinquency rates 47% higher than children who were not victims of maltreatment. Approximately 16% of children in placement had at least one delinquency charge compared with 7% of all abuse victims still living with their families (Ryan & Testa, 2005). Youth in correctional group home placements are more than twice as likely to commit delinquent acts as those in foster home placement (Ryan, Marshall, Herz, & Hernandez, 2008). One reason could be that group placements tend to be reserved for those youth with an extensive delinquent history who may not have been successful in foster home placements.

PROMISING PRACTICES AND RECOMMENDATIONS

The Crossover Youth Practice Model (CYPM) developed by the Center for Juvenile Justice Reform (CJJR) at Georgetown University seeks to assist and improve outcomes for youth involved in the child protective system and the juvenile justice system. By supporting collaborative efforts between juvenile justice and child protection agencies, the model aims to reduce the number of children entering both systems as well as the time youth spend in foster care.

In San Antonio, Texas, Crossover Court was developed for this purpose and requires child welfare and court professionals to hold case conferences before detention hearings and devise mutually agreeable recommendations that are presented to the judge (Kolivoski et al., 2015). In Crossover Courts, typically probation officers and child protection staff have reduced caseloads to work on these labor-intensive crossover cases.

Behavioral health issues are correlated with crossover youth, although a causal relationship has not been proven. Specifically, children can be traumatized as a result of abuse and/or neglect that can then be associated with mental health problems, substance abuse, and juvenile delinquency (Abbott & Barnett, 2015). Providing treatment for mental health and substance abuse problems can prevent youth from crossing over, and holds the potential to reduce recidivism. See Box 6.4 for an example of the Crossover Youth Program Model.

Evidence-based practices or those considered "best" or "promising" practices are critical to the success of future crossover programs (Herz et al., 2012). Trauma-informed care must be provided that acknowledges a relationship between the child's background and experiences and current behavior.

BOX 6.4 The New York Mental Health Work Group

The Crossover Youth Program Model has been developed for all five boroughs in New York City to ensure mental health screening for crossover youth. The Mental Health Work Group consists of professionals from Children's Services, Probation, the Family Court, the state office of Mental Health, and other community organizations. A guiding principle is that youth need to receive the mental health services likely to be most effective for their specific mental health problems. The screening protocol was named "Life Experience" to reduce the stigma associated with mental illness. The protocol includes screening for depression, posttraumatic stress disorder, substance abuse, and a strengths-based tool known as the Behavioral and Emotional Rating Scale. The screening is provided at no charge. Names of youth are cross-referenced between the juvenile justice and child welfare systems, and then the youth are offered the opportunity for screening. Implementation of the CYPM has resulted in earlier intervention for youth to get them the mental health and substance abuse treatment they need, and to provide continuity of care.

Source: Abbott and Barnett (2015).

Greater efforts must be made to reduce disparities in treatment for children of color in both the juvenile justice and the child welfare systems (Herz et al., 2012). We need stronger efforts to uncover the ways these systems can work together to prevent child abuse and neglect and delinquency and many opportunities to develop better outcomes for children and families (Wiig & Tuell, 2013).

There are a number of specific practices that can assist individual crossover youth. There need to be individualized client-centered goals for the youth within the family and the community (Wiig & Tuell, 2013). Crossover youth need to be identified early in their entry into the child welfare and juvenile justice systems. Screening and assessment tools can enhance the opportunity to access the appropriate services. Alternatives to official processing, such as diversion programs, should be considered at an early point. Case procedures need to be established to ensure ongoing involvement of child protection workers and probation officers. Family members need to be engaged in any decision-making process that affects these dual status youth (Wiig & Tuell, 2013).

Juvenile justice and child welfare systems also must agree on the improved outcomes they seek in working with youth. The systems must work toward reduced child maltreatment at the same time that they work toward fewer delinquent behaviors (Wiig & Tuell, 2013). They must seek appropriate screening and assessment of mental illness, substance abuse, and academic performance of youth. They must ensure that youth are residing with supportive adults where community support is available. It is no small task to find an environment where all of the many needs of dual status youth can be addressed. To bring about this kind of success for youth, the child welfare and juvenile justice systems must enter a true partnership. See Box 6.5 for the recommendations of the CJJR to establish this kind of partnership.

BOX 6.5 *Imperatives of the Center for Juvenile Justice Reform*

To bring about improvements in services for crossover youth, the CJJR recommends adopting six imperatives for the future:

1. *Develop leadership and establish governance and management structures.* The juvenile justice and child welfare systems must become mobilized and seek the support of other agencies such as mental health and substance abuse programs, housing agencies, other community services. They must develop the foundations that will support the integration of systems.

(continued)

> ### BOX 6.5 *Imperatives of the Center for Juvenile Justice Reform (continued)*
>
> 2. *Study and analyze data.* Data must be collected on the characteristics of crossover youth and their outcomes. Technology needs to be utilized that will allow clients to be matched in both systems. An inventory of the screening and assessment tools and resources used by child welfare and juvenile justice agencies can ensure there is no overlap. From this effort a resource manual can be developed so that all will be aware of available services.
> 3. *Create culture change across systems.* Culture change among staff can best occur when staff from both systems are in the same location, which encourages collaborative relationships. A comprehensive training plan to include child welfare and juvenile justice professionals can support collaborative work.
> 4. *Prevent youth from crossing over.* The staff members work together to prevent arrests and initial entry into the juvenile justice system by engaging with law enforcement and school officials. Police officers in schools can be engaged in these efforts. Diversion programs to keep youth from entering the juvenile justice system can be useful in providing services and avoiding the stigma associated with juvenile delinquency.
> 5. *Engage the family and the community.* A family strengths–based perspective is needed in which family members are involved in all aspects of planning for crossover youth. Case reviews by the professionals involved and family members can go a long way to developing appropriate and specific interventions for youth.
> 6. *Develop policies, procedures, and practices for agencies to work collaboratively.* Resource and information sharing can contribute to planning for positive youth development. Case planning and reviews and coordinated case supervision can contribute to the positive development of practices that help children be more successful.
>
> *Source:* Herz et al. (2012).

SUMMARY AND CONCLUSION

Children of mothers and fathers in the criminal justice system have more problems than children whose parents are not in the criminal justice system.

The children are themselves at greater risk of physical health, mental health, and juvenile justice problems. It is difficult to tease out specific impacts of the child welfare and criminal justice systems on children. It is clear that crossover or dual status children can have greater challenges than children in only one system. What resources are needed to assist children in both systems? We do not have good answers at this time, yet the quest for a deeper understanding continues.

As with the educational and health care systems, the juvenile justice and criminal justice systems require better coordination and collaboration to serve maltreated and delinquent children. Strategies for better coordination and integration of services between the juvenile justice and child welfare systems include sharing funds, training professionals from each system together, routinely identifying dual status children, and developing specific policies for both systems. The CYPM holds promise in seeking increased collaboration of juvenile justice and child welfare professionals. Programs specifically designed for dual status youth can make positive contributions to a more successful future.

DISCUSSION QUESTIONS

1. Why are children of incarcerated parents at great risk of being involved in the juvenile justice and criminal justice systems?

2. Discuss the challenges children face when trying to maintain contact with their incarcerated parent.

3. Describe the characteristics of crossover or dual status youth.

4. In what ways do we see racial discrimination in the criminal justice system?

5. Discuss the evidence for children in child protective services being more likely to be in the juvenile justice system than children not receiving protective services.

6. Discuss the impact of the Adoption and Safe Families Act of 1997 on parents serving long prison terms.

7. What are some appropriate punishments for correctional staff that abuse children in their care?

8. Describe the Crossover Youth Practice Model and the benefits for children.

9. Discuss the potential outcomes for youth when child protection and juvenile justice systems collaborate on the provision of services.

10. What are your own suggestions for helping maltreated children stay out of the juvenile justice system?

REFERENCES

Abbott, S., & Barnett, E. (2015). *The Crossover Youth Practice Model (CYPM). CYPM in brief. Behavioral health and crossover youth.* Washington, DC: Center for Juvenile Justice Reform, McCourt School of Public Policy, Georgetown University.

Alexander, M. (2010). *The new Jim Crowe: Mass incarceration in the time of colorblindness.* New York, NY: The New Press.

Barth, R. P., Duncan, D. F., Hodorowicz, M. T., & Kum, H.-C. (2010). Felonious arrests of former foster care and TANF-involved youth. *Journal of the Society for Social Work and Research, 1*(2), 104–123.

Carson, E. A. (2015, September). *Prisoners in 2014* (NCJ 248995). Washington, DC: U.S. Department of Justice, Office of Justice Programs, Bureau of Justice Statistics. Retrieved from www.bjs.gov/content/pub/pdf/p14.pdf

Christian, S. (2009). *Children of incarcerated parents.* Washington, DC: National Conference of State Legislatures. Retrieved from www.ncsl.org/documents/cyf/childrenofincarceratedparents.pdf

Glaze, L. E., & Maruschak, L. M. (2008, August). *Parents in prison and their minor children.* Washington, DC: U.S. Department of Justice, Office of Justice Programs, Bureau of Justice Statistics. (Revised January 8, 2009)

Hairston, C. F. (2009, May). *Kinship care when parents are incarcerated: What we know, what we can do.* Baltimore, MD: The Annie E. Casey Foundation.

Halperin, R., & Harris, J. L. (2004). Parental rights of incarcerated mothers with children in foster care: A policy vacuum. *Feminist Studies, 30*(2), 339–352.

Hayward, R. A., & DePanfilis, D. (2007). Foster children with an incarcerated parent: Predictions of reunification. *Children and Youth Services Review, 29*(10), 1320–1334.

Herndon, A. W., Allen, E., & Cramer, M. (2015, July 23). Eight accused of abuse at DYS site. *The Boston Globe,* pp. A1, A13.

Herz, D., Lee, P., Lutz, L., Stewart, M., Tuell, J., & Wiig, J. (2012, March). *Addressing the needs of multi-system youth: Strengthening the connection between child welfare and juvenile justice.* Washington, DC: Georgetown University, Center for Juvenile Justice Reform.

Honore'-Collins, C. P. (2005). The impact of African American incarceration on African American children in the child welfare system. *Race, Gender, & Class, 12*(3–4), 107–118.

Johnson, E. I., & Waldfogel, J. (2002). Parental incarceration: Recent trends and implications for child welfare. *Social Service Review, 76*(3), 460–479.

Kates, E., Mignon, S., & Ransford, P. (2008, June). *Parenting from prison: Family relationships of incarcerated women in Massachusetts.* Boston, MA: University of Massachusetts Boston, Center for Women in Politics & Public Policy.

Kolivoski, K. M., Barnett, E., & Abbott, S. (2015). *The Crossover Youth Practice Model (CYPM). CYPM in brief: Out-of-home placements and crossover youth.* Washington, DC: Georgetown University, McCourt School of Public Policy, Center for Juvenile Justice Reform.

Lawrence, S. K., Stepteau-Watson, D., & Honore'-Collins, C. (2007). An exploratory study: Incarcerated mothers with daughter involved in child welfare. *Race, Gender & Class, 14*(1–2), 227–235.

Leone, P., & Weinberg, L. (2010). *Addressing the unmet educational needs of children and youth in the juvenile justice and child welfare systems*. Washington, DC: Georgetown University, Center for Juvenile Justice Reform.

Mignon, S. I., & Ransford, P. (2012). Mothers in prison: Maintaining connections with children. *Social Work in Public Health, 27*, 69–88.

Murphey, D., & Cooper, P. M. (2015, October). Parents behind bars: What happens to their children? *Child Trends*. Retrieved from http://www.childtrends.org/?publications=parents-behind-bars-what-happens-to-their-children

Phillips, S. D., & Dettlaff, A. J. (2009). More than parents in prison: The broader overlap between the criminal justice and child welfare systems. *Journal of Public Child Welfare, 3*(1), 3–22. doi:10.1080/15548730802690718

Roberts, D. E. (2012, August 1). Prison, foster care, and the systemic punishment of Black mothers (Paper No. 432). *Faculty Scholarship*. Retrieved from http://scholarhsip.law.upenn.edu/faculty_scholarship/432

Rosado, S. (2015, May). *Impact of parental incarceration and child welfare*. New York, NY: Hunter College, National Center for Child Welfare Excellence at the Silberman School of Social Work.

Ryan, J. P., Hernandez, P. M., & Herz, D. (2007). Developmental trajectories of offending for male adolescents leaving foster care. *Social Work Research, 31*(2), 83–93.

Ryan, J. P., Herz, D., Hernandez, P. M., & Marshall, J. M. (2007). Maltreatment and delinquency: Investigating child welfare bias in juvenile justice processing. *Children and Youth Services Review, 29*, 1035–1050.

Ryan, J. P., Marshall, J. M., Herz, D., & Hernandez, P. M. (2008). Juvenile delinquency in child welfare: Investigating group home effects. *Children and Youth Services Review, 30*, 1088–1099.

Ryan, J. P., & Testa, M. F. (2005). Child maltreatment and juvenile delinquency: Investigating the role of placement and placement instability. *Children and Youth Services Review, 27*, 227–249.

Sabol, W. J., Couture, H., & Harrison, P. M. (2007). *Prisoners in 2006*. Washington, DC: U.S. Department of Justice, Office of Justice Programs, Bureau of Justice Statistics.

San Francisco Children of Incarcerated Parents Partnership. (2005). *Children of incarcerated parents: A bill of rights*. Retrieved from www.sfcipp.org/images/brochure.pdf

Sykes, B. L., & Pettit, B. (2014). Mass incarceration, family complexity, and the reproduction of childhood disadvantage. *Annals of the American Academy of Political and Social Science, 654*, 127–149.

Wiig, J. K., & Tuell, J. A. (with Heldman, J. K.). (2013). *Guidebook for juvenile justice and child welfare system coordination and integration: A framework for improved outcomes* (3rd ed.). Boston, MA: Robert F. Kennedy Children's Action Corps.

Williams, J. H., Van Dorn, R. A., Bright, C. L., Jonson-Reid, M., & Nebbitt, V. E. (2010). Child maltreatment and delinquency onset among African American adolescent males. *Research on Social Work Practice, 20*(3), 253–259.

FOSTER CARE

7

What are the ramifications when children are forced to leave their homes and families because of maltreatment? Chapter 7 examines the many facets of foster care and describes what happens to children when their biological parents are deemed abusive and/or incapable of providing for them, and they are placed in other homes. When children have numerous unsuccessful foster care placements, the consequences include long-term negative impacts. Placement with family members, known as kinship care, provides connectedness to family and can have better outcomes for children. The plight of older children is examined as they age out of foster care, specifically the difficulties they can experience transitioning into independent adulthood.

Foster care for children is typically depicted as a short-term intervention for abused and/or neglected children based on a substantiated report of abuse, and such children are considered unsafe in their own homes (Bass, Shields, & Behrman, 2004). Children also enter foster care when parents become physically or mentally incapacitated, when parents are incarcerated, or when the family is homeless (Swann & Sylvester, 2006). Further, when children with behavioral or emotional problems cannot be handled at home, they may be placed in specialized therapeutic foster care.

Foster care placement can be viewed as a temporary fix for family problems with the hopes of quickly reuniting. However, the average stay in foster care has been 24 months to 33 months (Bass et al., 2004; Doyle, 2007). The most recent data estimates that children in the United States are in foster care for an average of 20.8 months (Children's Bureau, 2015). Infants are those most likely to experience their first foster care placement at the time they are most vulnerable and unable to protect themselves (Perlman & Fantuzzo, 2013). Determining when it is appropriate to return children to their birth families is extremely challenging (Rzepnicki, 1987).

There are an inherent number of contradictions in foster care placement for children. At its most basic, the message of foster care represents that parents are unable or unwilling to provide appropriate care for their children, and parents are to blame. Despite poverty, homelessness, disability, mental illness, or addiction, parents are expected to care for their children. And when they cannot or do not, judgment is swift and harsh. The implicit message to children is "You have a bad parent. We need to place you with good parents." Although these are not the spoken words, clearly, they are the unspoken messages. The birth family is not necessarily valued in the foster care placement process: "The importance of the birth family to the child has not been sufficiently appreciated in the child welfare system. A deep antifamily bias often exists, growing out of our anger at parents who do not provide adequate nurturing for their children" (Beyer & Mlyniec, 1986, p. 239).

Between 2002 and 2012, foster care placement in the United States declined by 23.7%, from 523,616 children to 399,546 children in care (United States Department of Health and Human Services, 2013). African American children in foster care declined by 47%, Native Americans declined by 33.9%, Whites by 17.7%, and Hispanics by 2.5%. The most recent data available shows that on September 30, 2014, 415,129 children were in foster care (Children's Bureau, 2015). Overall, 45% of foster children are White, 23% are African American, and 21% are Hispanic.

By the late 1970s, it became clear that the foster care system was not working well. Children taken from their parents could be languishing for months or even years in foster homes without a clear plan for reunification with biological parents, or termination of parental rights followed by adoption (Beyer & Mlyniec, 1986). In fact, termination of parental rights did not provide any guarantee that the child would be adopted.

In the 1980s and 1990s, legislation was passed to reduce the number of children moving among foster homes. The Adoption Assistance and Child Welfare Act of 1980 pressed state child protection agencies to make a "reasonable effort" to keep children within their families with services, and to work to reunify families where foster care placement had already taken place (Rzepnicki, 1987; Swann & Sylvester, 2006). The Act provided funding to states to develop alternatives for children in long-term foster care (Beyer & Mlyniec, 1986). It was also an effort by Congress to help children achieve permanency.

In 1985, there were 276,000 children in foster care. And by 1999, that number more than doubled to 568,000 children (Swann & Sylvester, 2006). The mid-1980s

saw a considerable rise in the number of children in foster care, largely attributed to the rise in both the crack cocaine and HIV/AIDS epidemics. However,
Swann and Sylvester (2006) concluded that the most direct causes of the rise
in foster care were the increases in incarceration of women and the decline in
welfare benefits. The Anti-Drug Abuse Act of 1986 resulted in more women in
prison and longer prison sentences. The analysis concluded that incarceration
of mothers was the largest factor, accounting for a 23% increase in foster care
caseloads between 1985 and 2000. The reduction in welfare benefits accounted
for an 11% increase in foster care (Swann & Sylvester, 2006).

The Family Preservation and Family Support Program of 1993 was an
additional effort to overcome the insufficient progress made to keep families
together, and doubled the amount of federal funding to support families (Swann
& Sylvester, 2006). The year 1997 marked the highest number of children in
foster care nationally (Havlicek, 2010).

As discussed in previous chapters, the Adoption and Safe Families Act (ASFA)
of 1997 promoted child safety and well-being as of paramount importance. The
Act identified conditions where waivers could be given to the "reasonable efforts" requirement, yet simultaneously promoting reunification, termination of
parental rights, and adoption (Swann & Sylvester, 2006). From the perspective
of the child welfare system, workers were expected to reconcile two opposing
points of view regarding child protection and family preservation. Thus, workers were expected to devise two plans: one to reunify the child with the family,
and the other to prepare children for adoption.

CHARACTERISTICS OF CHILDREN AND THEIR FAMILIES ENTERING FOSTER CARE

It has long been known that foster care placement puts children at risk for a
variety of problems including mental health and substance abuse problems as
well as entrée into the juvenile justice and criminal justice systems. As discussed
in Chapter 4, multiple foster home placements are typically very disruptive to a
child's education (Stone, D'Andrade, & Austin, 2006). Consequences of multiple
placements can be unstable relationships between children and adults, and can
impact the child's ability to have healthy relationships in the future (Duncan &
Argys, 2007).

Children in foster care have less access to health care, with 30% to 80% having untreated medical conditions, leading the American Academy of Pediatrics
(2015) to call on pediatricians to do more to assist foster children. Research on
foster care placements finds a direct relationship between multiple placements
and negative outcomes for children that can persist into adulthood (Connell

et al., 2006). Therefore, we must move beyond simply counting the number of foster placements of children and do more to determine the reasons placement changes are made (Usher, Randolph, & Gogan, 1999).

The majority of foster children come from families that receive welfare benefits (Geen, Kortenkamp, & Stagner, 2002). Reduced welfare benefits in the form of Aid to Families of Dependent Children (AFDC), now the Temporary Assistance for Needy Families (TANF) program, account for a substantial increase in foster care placements in several ways. Lower levels of cash assistance to families result in less family income, which increases the likelihood of child maltreatment as well as the likelihood of reports to child protection agencies (Swann & Sylvester, 2006). Less income may encourage family members to become official foster parents, or to provide kinship care, to qualify for financial benefits. Because the majority of families from which children enter foster care are poor welfare beneficiaries, foster placement can also serve as a substitute for welfare benefits (Swann & Sylvester, 2006). Child protection services and TANF offices must coordinate efforts to provide resources to actually help families stay together.

What motivates people to become foster parents? In a study of foster parents of 10- and 11-year-old children in Sweden, four different motivations emerged in interviews with them (Andersson, 2001). Relatives were motivated to become foster parents because they felt some responsibility for a specific child. Some couples were motivated to become foster parents because they were unable to have children. For some families, the mother was at home caring for her biological children and found foster care preferable to seeking low-paying work outside the house. Other families with grown children were motivated by wanting to continue in a parenting role.

Economic incentives have been successful in reducing the number of placements children in foster care have to endure. In the first study to examine financial incentives in foster care settings, increased monthly payments reduced the probability of moving a child (Duncan & Argys, 2007). In the early to mid-2000s, increasing monthly payments by just $100 resulted in a 28.7% reduction in children moving from foster care to group homes. This same $100 reduced the average number of placements by 20% (Duncan & Argys, 2007).

There are the few adults who are scamming the system by becoming foster parents, which further exploits the children. One deeply troubling case involved a husband and wife in Texas who had served as foster parents for 36 children since 2000 (Martinez, 2015). Through foster parenting arrangements with a variety of agencies, they were able to be paid a whopping $1.6 million! Within this home, foster children were forced to engage in sex acts with both the foster father and the foster mother. At this writing, both foster parents have pending charges of sexual assault on a child (Yee, 2015).

Today, payments vary by state, and Massachusetts pays only $21 to $26 a day for a foster child depending on the child's age (Levenson, 2016). Clearly, increased compensation for foster parents should be part of an overall effort to improve the quality of foster care, and to reduce placement instability for children.

What about the relationship between the child and the biological parent when the child is in foster care? For an infant, the closer relationship is likely to develop with the foster parent (Haight, Kagle, & Black, 2003). For older children, visits with biological parents can be a mixed bag. There may be considerable anxiety on the part of the child as well as the parent. The visit is likely to be in a child welfare office rather than in a home-like environment, and that can add to the stress.

Visits with biological parents are especially important if there is a reasonable chance of family reunification. Child welfare professionals typically recommend weekly visitation (Haight et al., 2003). It is not unusual for children to exhibit behavioral issues in the foster home after a visit with a biological parent, and this is to be expected. Both children and parents should be receiving emotional support from child welfare workers before and after visits. The Connections Project in Washington State served as an excellent example of what can happen when professionals work toward cultivating deeper relationships between children and birth parents, as well as between parents and professionals. An evaluation of the Connections Project found a high level of success in weekly visits by birth parents to children in foster care, considerable contact between the birth families and the foster families, and overall stronger relationships between parents and child protection workers (Gerring, Kemp, & Marcenko, 2008).

THE COURTS AND FOSTER CARE

The court system plays a critical role in foster care. Judges review the status of children in foster care and promote permanency of placements for children; however, they should do so in a more timely manner (Allen & Bissell, 2004). Courts have played the role of defining the rights of birth parents, the rights of children in foster care, and the rights of those involved in kinship care. The courts have also been called upon to make important decisions regarding the quality of care children receive from state agencies, including improved service delivery. Owing to deaths of children in foster care, the system has come under increased scrutiny by lawsuits against state child welfare agencies and related media attention. A number of lawsuits have been filed not only to address the inadequacies of the foster care system but also to cast light on the damage done to children under the guise of helping them. Children's Rights, a child welfare advocacy group, has filed numerous lawsuits against states for failure to provide placement stability and appropriate services to children. See Box 7.1 for a successful lawsuit that led to a court finding against the Texas child protection agency.

In 2004 in Mississippi, a lawsuit was filed for violating the constitutional rights of children in foster care by failing to adequately protect them, and for failing to provide necessary services. This lawsuit sought court-ordered changes in the system, which were agreed upon in 2008. The state of Mississippi recently acknowledged that it had failed to improve the system. The suit was based on underfunding, inadequate staffing of child protection workers, an extremely high number of cases, and lack of appropriate investigations of abuse and neglect (Palmer & Robertson, 2016). Some of the cases in Mississippi included a child placed in the home of a convicted rapist, a foster mother who threw a toddler to angry dogs, and the failure to protect a 14-year-old girl that resulted in her rape and subsequent pregnancy. The state of Mississippi has

---

BOX 7.1 Children's Rights Texas Case

On December 17, 2015, federal judge Janis Jack ruled that the state of Texas violated the constitutional rights of children in foster care by placing them at "reasonable risk of harm" where youth are compelled to move often and where they can be living in institutions with poor supervision and oversight. The judge found that the state Department of Family and Protective Services child protective workers had "impossible workloads." A special master was ordered to oversee the required substantial improvement to the child protection system, including finding the least restrictive and most appropriate placements for children in foster care. The court required that each child be provided with a Court Appointed Special Advocate to protect his or her interests.

The class-action lawsuit had been filed in 2011 by Children's Rights, a national advocacy organization, and took over 4 years to resolve. The founder and former executive director of Children's Rights and a lead attorney in the case, Marcia Robinson Lowry, stated: "Texas has one of the worst foster care systems in the country." She lauded the judge's decision as "stunning."

Sources: Byrne (2016); Garrett (2016); Walters and Ramshaw (2015).

been ordered back to court for its continuing failure to improve its foster care system (Wade, 2015).

In 2015, New York City and New York State had a federal class-action lawsuit filed against them, alleging that mismanagement, incompetence, and delays resulted in very long foster placements (Yee, 2015). In fact, children in New York City spent double the time in foster care as children in other states, and New York agencies have taken the most time to reunite children with biological parents. Also, for children moving into adoptive homes, New York City has taken longer than any other city or state to place children (Yee, 2015).

In April 2010, Children's Rights filed a lawsuit against the Massachusetts child protection agency, the Department of Children and Families, for "causing physical and psychological harm" to the children they are mandated to protect. The lawsuit ended in a 2014 U.S. Federal Court of Appeals decision affirming the lower court decision to dismiss the lawsuit on the grounds of lack of jurisdiction. The Chief Justice stated: "Improvements must come from the normal state political processes. The problems are now for the Governor and the legislature to resolve" (McKim, 2014). To date, these problems remain to be resolved, and as a result, conditions for children in Massachusetts have been worse.

The Massachusetts Department of Children and Families has been struggling with locating appropriate foster care placements for an increasing number of children who have been maltreated. Between fiscal years 2013 and 2015, the number of children in Massachusetts removed from their families increased 28%, from 2,655 to 3,383 (Levenson, 2016). The increase is attributed to responses to the high number of deaths of children in the custody of the Department of Children and Families as well as to the increase in opioid overdoses and deaths in the state.

Because the Massachusetts Department of Children and Families has been overwhelmed with cases, it has been granting waivers to extend the number of children allowed in foster homes. Between October 2014 and October 2015, 172 waivers were granted to foster homes to accept more children, an increase from the 118 waivers granted in the previous year (Levenson, 2016). Existing rules allow four foster children in a home and up to a maximum of six children in the home, typically including the biological children of the foster parents. With the waivers, six foster children can be placed in a home up to a maximum of eight children. Eight children in a home? Is this even remotely adequate care for foster children? The results can be disastrous, and indeed they have been. In 2015, the Department of Children and Families approved a waiver for a mother to care for three foster children, in addition to her own three children, one of whom had special needs. During the summer of 2015, the mother responsible for the care of six children, including two foster children, aged 22 months and 2 years, forgot them in their car seats. As a result, both children suffered heat stroke, and the 2-year-old girl died (Levenson, 2016).

Agency instructions to child protection workers reaffirm that their decisions should focus on the best interests of the children, and that it is important to keep siblings together. Still the question remains: Are too many children being placed in foster care? An attorney at the Massachusetts Law Reform Institute commented, "It raises the question: do we really need to be investing more in keeping kids out of foster care rather than becoming more lenient in our safety requirements for foster homes?" (Levenson, 2016, p. 12).

Nationally, 12 states have some form of court monitoring or other monitors to oversee foster care. Seven states have unresolved class-action lawsuits (Palmer & Robertson, 2016). As compelling as it is to have a legal judgment against a child protection agency, there is no guarantee that conditions under which foster children live will improve.

KINSHIP FOSTER CARE

Kinship care, the placement of a child with a relative, can be formal or informal. Formal kinship care means that the state child protection agency has been involved and made the arrangements. Informal kinship care occurs when relatives come together and make decisions about where a child will live without child welfare system involvement. Kinship care began to grow in the mid-1980s. This growth is attributed to less availability of traditional foster homes, an increase in the number of children deemed to need placement, changing attitudes about services the government should offer, and seeking extended family as an important support for children (Berrick, 1998). See Box 7.2 for an example of informal kinship care that works very well.

Although kinship care can provide continuity not available in traditional foster care, it presents a number of issues. Kinship foster parents are typically older and less healthy than traditional foster parents, and they are more likely to have a lower level of education and income (Geen, 2004). In addition, kinship foster parents receive fewer financial and emotional supports than traditional foster parents.

Most recently, children in formal kinship foster care represent 29% of the total number of children in foster care (Children's Bureau, 2015). Research supports the fact that kinship foster care is more stable than traditional foster care (Strijker, Knorth, & Knot-Dickscheit, 2008). Not surprisingly, kinship foster care is less likely to achieve legal permanence for children (Berrick, 1998).

BOX 7.2 Native American Grandparents Raising Grandchildren

The North American Indian Center of Boston and the Institute of New England Native American Studies at the University of Massachusetts Boston partnered to study and provide supports to Native American grandparents raising their grandchildren, including the development of a resource manual. In a sample of 50 respondents, 86% of caregiving grandparents were women, and 14% were men. Thirty-six percent of families had substance abuse within their families. Substance abuse by parents was the most common reason grandparents were raising their grandchildren. The resource manual was especially helpful in locating substance abuse and mental health treatment programs, as well as transportation options.

This example of informal kinship care worked well despite the lack of financial support from family members and from state and federal entitlement programs. Although the grandparents faced many challenges, they described the joys of seeing their grand-children thrive in the healthy environment they worked hard to provide. An additional positive outcome was that the focus groups conducted for the study developed into an ongoing support group for grandparents.

Source: Mignon and Holmes (2013).

One study found that children more likely to go to kinship care are African American or Latino, have been neglected rather than abused, are older children, and are from families not receiving welfare benefits (Grogan-Kaylor, 2000). Another study found that African American fathers of children in kinship foster care were rarely sought out by child welfare workers to assist in planning for the child's present and future needs (O'Donnell, 1999). Clearly, much more must be done to engage fathers in the support of their children in kinship care and to support them in their parenting role.

Kinship foster care is not without challenges. Tension can exist between birth parents and kinship foster parents that can be difficult to manage, putting children between birth and kinship care parents. Assumptions should not be made that policies and practices applicable to traditional foster care will be effective for kinship care families (Geen, 2004).

A study of children in kinship care found that the children appreciated the opportunity to stay within the family, and that they felt less trauma and stigma in not living with their parents (Messing, 2005). They did not feel that transitioning into the home of a relative was especially difficult, and expressed a desire to avoid traditional foster care. Although the children voiced disappointment in their parents, especially regarding lack of parental visits, overall, they remained hopeful about returning to live with a parent in the future (Messing, 2005).

AGING OUT OF FOSTER CARE

The Foster Care Independence Act of 1999 provided an extension of transition assistance from age 18 to age 21 as well as greater funding for the services older children need such as housing, education, employment, financial assistance, and counseling services. However, as we have seen, states still struggle to provide assistance, resulting in youth left without the support they need.

One study examined outcomes for 294 adolescents aged 16 to 18 leaving foster care (Ryan, Hernandez, & Herz, 2007). Of the sample, 46% were African American, 43% were White, and 11% were Latino. The average age was 16.8. Forty-eight percent were involved in the criminal justice or juvenile justice system, 21% were those with few offenses, and 27% were considered chronic offenders at their youthful ages. Overall, 28% had identified substance abuse problems, and 25% had dropped out of high school. Importantly, when their time in foster care ended, fully one third (33%) returned to live with a biological parent (Ryan et al., 2007). It is unclear whether these youth had no option but to return to live with a biological parent or whether they saw it as a positive choice for themselves.

Four studies over time with a large sample of adults who had aged out of foster care concluded they did worse than their peers on almost every measure. They were studied at age 19, age 21, ages 23 and 24, and finally at age 26. The first study determined that at age 19 those who transitioned out of foster care were doing more poorly than their peers in terms of educational level, ability to earn a living, employment status, mental health, and substance abuse problems. Further, these former foster children had a greater likelihood of involvement in the criminal justice system (Courtney et al., 2005). The second study, at age 21, revealed that the Foster Care Independence Act did not ensure for them any follow-up services. This second study showed that the former foster children were not learning life skills necessary to become independent and successful adults (Courtney et al., 2007). Twenty-five percent of those aged 21 lived with a parent or other relative. Over one third had lived in at least three different places since leaving foster care, and 23% had neither a high school diploma nor had passed a General Educational Development (GED) test. In the third study, respondents at ages 23 and 24 continued the pattern of economic hardships, and fewer than half were employed (Courtney, Dworsky, Lee, & Raap, 2010). Surprisingly, 53% thought their lives were much better than when they left foster care. In the fourth study, at age 26, this group of foster care graduates continued to do poorly, with much lower educational and employment attainment than others, and significantly greater chances of incarceration (Courtney et al., 2011). Overall, these studies confirmed that insufficient progress is being made to help youth age out of foster care. Further research is required to more fully evaluate the services received by those aging out of foster care (Courtney et al., 2011).

The risk of involvement in the juvenile justice and criminal justice systems can be reduced by strong family support and job security (Vaughn, Shook & McMillen, 2008). Not surprisingly, living in a poor unstable neighborhood among peers involved in the justice system increases the risk to youth aging out of foster care. See Box 7.3 for an extreme case of aging out of an 18-year-old pregnant adolescent deported back to El Salvador.

BOX 7.3 Pregnant 18-Year-Old Is Deported

Gabriella Portillo came to the United States in a cargo truck with 10 other children to escape her childhood as a sex worker in El Salvador. She was charged by immigration officials as an unaccompanied minor. Gabriella spent 5 years in the foster care system in Oklahoma after the state took custody of her amid allegations that she was again a victim of sexual abuse. Gabriella had significant behavior problems and was sent to group homes and even juvenile detention. While in a treatment program, she was charged with arson and assault for spitting on a staff member. She pleaded guilty and received a suspended sentence of 10 years. Gabriella was unaware that a guilty plea could have a negative impact on becoming a legal resident of Oklahoma. Within a few months of aging out of the foster care system at age 18, Gabriella was deported back to El Salvador by immigration officials—back to the home of her grandmother who initiated her into the world of sexual victimization.

Source: Graham (2015).

RECOMMENDATIONS AND PROMISING PRACTICES

It is not difficult to develop recommendations to improve services with the aim of reducing the number of children in foster care, and better serving those children for whom there is no reasonable alternative. The challenging part is to formulate a specific strategic plan to improve the lives of children including the development of additional funding and resources. Consistent efforts must be made within a context of political and social will, both of which seem to be lacking. The recommendations of a long-time child welfare professional and foster and adoptive mother remind us of both the importance and the difficulty of these efforts (Badeau, 2004):

1. **Do no harm.** This is a clear statement that interventions should not make the life of a foster child worse, although that can happen when policies and practices fail to provide the services needed by children and their parents.
2. **Focus on the whole child, in context.** Incentives must be provided to bring all necessary services together, especially health and mental health services. This underscores the need for improved coordination and collaboration among child welfare agencies, health organizations, and educational institutions.
3. **Uphold connections to family and other significant relationships.** If possible, children must be allowed to maintain connections with parents, and especially with siblings. Foster care and adoptions should be open, and extended family members can be potential foster parents or provide support.
4. **Consider the child's developmental needs, timetable, and lifetime needs.** Case plans for foster children often look very similar regardless of individual circumstances. Plans should be tailored to the specific needs of each child; especially consider the children's ages—the needs of an adolescent are not the needs of an infant. Although immediate needs should take precedence, a child's ongoing needs must not be ignored, and there must be a long view into adulthood and building a healthy and bright future.
5. **Culturally respectful approaches, not unequal treatment, must be utilized.** Race and ethnicity have a significant impact on how children and their families are treated within the child welfare foster care system, courts, and educational systems. It is imperative that policies in child protection services address and support respect for cultural differences.
6. **Outcomes-based approaches should not eliminate innovation.** Evidence-based practices and research that examines foster care outcomes are critical, but do not provide a complete picture. Child protection workers must look beyond traditional foster care resources for innovative opportunities to support children such as interested aunts and uncles, cousins, and perhaps even teachers.

In focus groups with those who had been in foster care, respondents described positive as well as negative experiences (Mariscal, Akin, Lieberman, & Washington, 2015). The youth encourage greater efforts to match families and children, better preparation for foster parents, allowing children to participate in the placement process, and a more coordinated system of care. See Box 7.4 for a description of an innovative approach, the LINKS program in North Carolina.

The use of the recently developed Child Placement Questionnaire holds promise for making better decisions on behalf of foster children (Meiksans, Iannos, & Arney, 2015). Piloted with a sample of 53 child protection professionals in Australia, the Child Placement Questionnaire, through a series of case vignettes and questions, assists in measuring factors that help determine the most appropriate decisions. The questionnaire measures the attitude of child protection workers about placement, the social norms about placement decisions, the worker's perceived control over placement decisions, and the worker's intention about where the child will be placed (Meiksans et al., 2015). Further research is needed on the Child Placement Questionnaire.

Some recent innovations include better outreach and services for lesbian, gay, bisexual, transgender, and questioning (LGBTQ) youth in foster care (Crary, 2015). LGBTQ youth can be subject to prejudice and rejection because of their sexual orientation. In 2012, New York City established within its child welfare agency

BOX 7.4 The LINKS Program in North Carolina

The LINKS program is the North Carolina Foster Care Independence Program for youth and young adults who have been in foster care for a long time and need assistance in transitioning to adulthood. Services include an assessment of the youths' strengths and needs to support them to become successful adults. Then a plan is devised based on individual goals, and youth must accept the responsibility for fulfilling the plan. Services are then matched to help the youth achieve positive outcomes, including a stable home environment, a vocational plan to match the interests and abilities of each youth, adequate income, access to health care, and a supportive network of adults. Youth can remain in their placements after the age of 18 if they are in a placement licensed by the state and are enrolled as full-time students. Youth can also enroll in federally funded programs that contribute toward college tuition.

Sources: North Carolina Department of Health and Human Services (2012); WakeGOV Human Services (2014).

the Office of LGBTQ Policy and Practice to improve care for these children and provided staff training on LGBTQ issues. Significantly, New York City now requires all licensed foster care providers to accept LGBTQ youth into their homes.

Although abuse and neglect are traumatic for children, removal from the home can also traumatize children (Doyle, 2007). We must continually ask what is in the best interests of the children and how to best meet their needs. Of course, these are highly debatable topics, and the answers depend on who is asked. Children who are close to being placed by child protective workers tend to do better if they remain with their own families, especially children who are older (Doyle, 2007). Of course, meeting the financial needs of families with additional supportive resources can help ensure the needs of the children are met.

More efforts need to be made to reduce foster care placements and to support the development of innovative programs and approaches. Although the public can be very critical of foster care, especially in view of negative media attention, in fact the public has little knowledge of the actual workings of foster care (Bass et al., 2004). Badeau (2004) concludes: "Unfortunately, lack of public will remains a serious barrier to making genuine improvements in the care of vulnerable children in our society" (p. 177). For reform of the foster care system in the United States to be achieved, it must critically evaluate outcomes and practices, thoroughly examine and update child welfare organizations, and diligently provide oversight of child protection services (Bass et al., 2004).

SUMMARY AND CONCLUSION

Children are placed in foster care when biological parents are unable or unwilling to care for them. It can be a difficult adjustment for children, especially older children. Negative experiences and frequent changes in foster care placement are associated with behavioral problems that can have lifelong negative consequences. Every effort must be made to ensure families and children have their basic needs met before children are removed from their birth parents. In the case of child sexual abuse and violence, it is more evident that removal of children is necessary.

Formal and informal kinship care can be less traumatic for children although relatives are likely to receive fewer financial and social supports than traditional foster care parents. Many lawsuits have been filed that reveal the inadequacies of foster care for children in the United States. Despite many court judgments against foster care systems, improvements are sorely lacking. Youth aging out of foster care can have an especially difficult time transitioning into adulthood. The LINKS program in North Carolina is an example of an innovative approach to help youth succeed while aging out of foster care.

DISCUSSION QUESTIONS

1. Discuss the purpose foster care serves within the child welfare system.

2. Discuss the philosophy behind placing children in foster care.

3. What are the characteristics of children and their families that are in the foster care system?

4. Discuss possible motivations for becoming a foster parent.

5. How important do you think it is for children in foster care to keep in touch with their birth parents?

6. Discuss why states have had lawsuits filed against them regarding foster care services.

7. Define kinship care and how it may be preferable to regular foster care.

8. What are the problems associated with aging out of foster care?

9. Describe several innovative practices in foster care.

10. What are your own recommendations for improving the foster care system in the United States?

REFERENCES

Allen, M. L., & Bissell, M. (2004). Safety and stability for foster children: The policy context. *The Future of Children, 14*(1), 48–73. Retrieved from http://www.future ofchildren.org/publications/journals/article/index.xml?journalid=40&articleid= 134&sectionid=882

American Academy of Pediatrics, Committee on Adolescence, and Council on Early Childhood, Council on Foster Care, Adoption, & Kinship Care. (2015, September). Health care issues for children and adolescents in foster care and kinship care. *Pediatrics*. Retrieved from http://pediatrics.aappublications.org/content/early/2015/09/22/ peds.2015-2655

Andersson, G. (2001). The motives of foster parents, their family and work circumstances. *British Journal of Social Work, 31*, 235–248.

Badeau, S. H. (2004). Five commentaries: Looking to the future (Commentary 1). *The Future of Children, 14*(1), 175–177. Retrieved from http://futureofchildren.org/ futureofchildren/publications/journals/article/index.xml?journalid=40&articlei d=140&sectionid=920&submit

Bass, S., Shields, M. K., & Behrman, R. E. (2004). Children, families, and foster care: Analysis and recommendations. *The Future of Children, 14*(1), 5–29. Retrieved from http://www .futureofchildren.org/publications/journals/article/index.xml?journalid=40&articleid=132

Berrick, J. D. (1998). When children cannot remain home: Foster family care and kinship care. *The Future of Children, 8*(1), 72–87.

Beyer, M., & Mlyniec, W. J. (1986). Lifelines to biological parents: Their effects on termination of parental rights and permanence. *Family Law Quarterly, 20*(2), 233–254.

Byrne, D. (2016, January 8). Court decision shows Texas needs stronger safety net for foster children. *The Texas Tribune*. Retrieved from http://www.star-telegram.com/opinion/opn-columns-blogs/other-voices/article53816575.html

Children's Bureau. (2015, July). *The AFCARS Report. Adoption and Foster Care Analysis and Reporting System (No. 22)*. Washington, DC: U.S. Department of Health and Human Services, Administration for Children and Families, Administration on Children Youth, and Families. Retrieved from http://www.acf.hhs.gov/sites/default/files/cb/afcarsreport22.pdf

Connell, C. M., Vanderploeg, J. J., Flaspohler, P., Katz, K. H., Saunders, L., & Tebes, J. K. (2006). Changes in placement among children in foster care: A longitudinal study of child and case influences. *Social Service Review, 80*(3), 398–418.

Courtney, M. E., Dworsky, A., Brown, A., Cary, C., Love, K., & Vorhies, V. (2011). *Midwest evaluation of the adult functioning of former foster youth: Outcomes at age 26*. Chicago, IL: Chapin Hall at the University of Chicago.

Courtney, M. E., Dworsky, A., Cusick, G. R., Havlicek, J., Perez, A., & Keller, T. (2007). *Midwest evaluation of the adult functioning of former foster youth: Outcomes at age 21*. Chicago, IL: Chapin Hall at the University of Chicago.

Courtney, M. E., Dworsky, A., Lee, J. S., & Raap, M. (2009). *Midwest evaluation of the adult functioning of former foster youth: Outcomes at ages 23 and 24*. Chicago, IL: Chapin Hall at the University of Chicago.

Courtney, M. E., Dworsky, A., Ruth, G., Keller, T., Havlicek, J., & Bost, N. (2005). *Midwest evaluation of the adult functioning of former foster youth: Outcomes at age 19*. Chicago, IL: Chapin Hall at the University of Chicago.

Crary, D. (2015, October 30). Foster-care agencies expand efforts to help LGBTQ youths. *EdgeMediaNetwork*. Retrieved from www.edgeboston.com/news/national/news//187984/foster-care_agencies_expand_efforts_to_help_lgbtrq_youths

Doyle, J. J., Jr. (2007). Child protection and child outcomes: Measuring the effects of foster care. *The American Economic Review, 97*(5), 1583–1610.

Duncan, B., & Argys, L. (2007). Economic incentives and foster care placement. *Southern Economic Journal, 74*(1), 114–142.

Garrett, R. T. (2016, January 21). Federal judge finds Texas has "broken" foster care system, says she'll order changes. *The Dallas Morning News*. Retrieved from http://trailblazersblog.dallasnews.com.2015/12/federal-judge-finds-texas-has-broken-foster-care-system-says-shell-order-changes.html

Geen, R. (2004). The evolution of kinship care policy and practice. *The Future of Children, 14*(1), 130–149. Retrieved from http://www.futureofchildren.org/publications/journals/article/index.xml?journalid=40&articleid=138&sectionid=906

Geen, R., Kortenkamp, K., & Stagner, M. (2002). Foster care experiences of long-term welfare recipients in California. *Social Service Review, 76*(4), 552–574.

Gerring, C. E., Kemp, S. P., & Marcenko, M. O. (2008). The Connections Project: A relational approach to engaging birth parents in visitation. *Child Welfare, 87*(6), 5–30.

Graham, G. (2015, September 28). DHS foster child deported within months of aging out of system. *Tulsa World*. Retrieved from www.tulsaworld.com/news/local/dhs-foster-child-deported-with . . . s-of-aging-out-of/article_ec4a67a9-2675-54ba-93c4-c55128113388.html

Grogan-Kaylor, A. (2000). Who goes into kinship care? The relationship of child and family characteristics to placement into kinship care. *Social Work Research, 24*(3), 132–141.

Haight, W. L., Kagle, J. D., & Black, J. E. (2003). Understanding and supporting parent-child relationships during foster care visits: Attachment theory and research. *Social Work, 47*(2), 195–207.

Havlicek, J. (2010). Patterns of movement in foster care: An optimal matching analysis. *Social Service Review, 84*(3), 403–435.

Levenson, M. (2016, January 23). As caseload soars, capacity raised at many foster homes. *The Boston Globe*, pp. 1, 12.

Mariscal, E. S., Akin, B. A., Lieberman, A. A., & Washington, D. (2015). Exploring the path from foster care to stable and lasting adoption: Perceptions of foster care alumni. *Children and Youth Services Review, 55*, 111–120.

Martinez, A. (2015, June 19). Foster parents accused of sexual abuse may have earned $1.6 million from state. *El Paso Times*. Retrieved from www.elpasotimes.com/news/ci_28348278/foster-parents-accused-sexual-abuse-may-have-earned?source=rss

McKim, J. (2014, December 16). Mass appeals court upholds ruling dismissing DCF lawsuit. *New England Center for Investigative Reporting*. Retrieved from http://necir.org/2014/12/16/ma-appeals-court-upholds-ruling-dismissing-dcf-lawsuit

Meiksans, J., Iannos, M., & Arney, F. (2015). Factors influencing decision making about the placement of children in care: Development of the Child Placement Questionnaire. *Children and Youth Services Review, 55*, 71–83.

Messing, J. T. (2005, March). *From the child's perspective: A qualitative analysis of kinship care placements*. Berkeley, CA: University of California at Berkeley, National Abandoned Infants Resource Center.

Mignon, S. I., & Holmes, W. H. (2013). Substance abuse and mental health issues within Native American grandparenting families. *Journal of Ethnicity in Substance Abuse, 12*(3), 210–227. doi:10.1080/15332640.2013.798751

North Carolina Department of Health and Human Services. (2012). *Helping teens make a successful transition from foster care to self-sufficiency*. Retrieved from www2.ncdhhs.gov/dss/links

O'Donnell, J. M. (1999). Involvement of African American fathers in kinship foster care services. *Social Work, 44*(5), 428–441.

Palmer, E., & Robertson, C. (2016, January 17). Mississippi fights to keep control of its beleaguered child welfare system. *The New York Times*. Retrieved from www.nytimes .com/2016/01/18/us/mississippi-fights-to-keep-control-of-itsbeleaguered -child-welfare-system.html?_r=0

Perlman, S., & Fantuzzo, J. W. (2013). Predicting risk of placement: A population-based study of out-of-home placement, child maltreatment, and emergency housing. *Journal of the Society for Social Work and Research, 4*(2), 99–113. doi:10.5243/jsswr.2013.7

Ryan, J. P., Hernandez, P. M., & Herz, D. (2007). Developmental trajectories of offending male adolescents leaving foster care. *Social Work Research, 31*(2), 83–93.

Rzepnicki, T. L. (1987). Recidivism of foster children to their own homes: A review and new directions for research. *Social Service Review, 61*(1), 56–70.

Stone, S., D'Andrade, A., & Austin, M. (2006). Educational services for children in foster care. *Journal of Public Child Welfare, 1*(2), 53–70.

Strijker, J., Knorth, E. J., & Knot-Dickscheit, J. (2008). Placement history of foster children: A study of placement history and outcomes in long-term family foster care. *Child Welfare, 87*(5), 107–124.

Swann, C. A., & Sylvester, M. S. (2006). The foster care crisis: What caused caseloads to grow? *Demography, 43*(2), 309–335.

U.S. Department of Health and Human Services. (2013, September). *Recent demographic trends in foster care* (Office of Data, Analysis, Research and Evaluation, Data Brief 2013-1). Retrieved from www.acf.hhs.gov/sites/default/files/cb/data_brief_ foster_care_trends1.pdf

Usher, C. L., Randolph, K. A., & Gogan, H. C. (1999). Placement patterns in foster care. *Social Service Review, 73*(1), 22–29.

Vaughn, M. G., Shook, J. J., & McMillen, J. C. (2008). Aging out of foster care and legal involvement: Toward a typology of risk. *Social Service Review, 82*(3), 419–446.

Wade, M. (2015, June 17). State ordered back to court over foster care. *MSNewsNow*. Retrieved from www.msnewsnow.com/story/29338028/state-ordered-back-to-court -over-foster-care

WakeGOV Human Services. (2014). *LINKS program*. Retrieved from www.wakegov .com/humanservices/children/links/Pages/default.aspx

Walters, E., & Ramshaw, E. (2015, December 17). Judge: Foster care system violates children's rights. *The Texas Tribune*. Retrieved from https://www.texastribune .org/2015/12/17/judge-foster-care-system-violates-childrens-rights

Yee, V. (2015, July 7). Suit to accuse New York City and State of keeping children in foster care too long. *The New York Times*. Retrieved from www.nytimes.com/2015/07/08/ nyregion/suit-accuses-new-york-city-and-state-of-keeping-children-in-foster-care -too-long.html?_r=1

ADOPTION

*A*doption is a very important way to create a family; however, it is sometimes misunderstood by people outside of the adoption world. Early in the 1900s, there was much secrecy about adoption, and children's birth records were typically sealed. "Matching" of children and families often focused around physical traits, especially race and religion (Nickman et al., 2005). Much has changed in the world of adoption, including greater acceptance of diversity in adoption practices. Chapter 8 examines the challenges and opportunities of adoption as well as the lifelong issues of the adopted child. This chapter examines the barriers to adoption. Because there is so much bureaucracy and considerable expense, it is true that only the deeply committed can become an adoptive parent. The financial expense almost ensures that those of low socioeconomic status are not offered the full range of opportunities to adopt available children.

We have known for many years that adopted children typically fare better than children raised in foster care or in institutions (Brodzinsky, 1993). In the best of circumstances, children can feel a sense of belonging and comfort in adoption that was not available to them in their biological or foster families. In the worst of circumstances, severe mental health and behavioral problems and ill-equipped adoptive parents can lead to disruption or dissolution of adoption.

In the 1970s, more parents from the middle class sought to adopt children, with fewer children available with "matched" physical characteristics. It was then that we saw the rise of attorney-arranged adoptions and private adoption agencies along with an accompanying rise in the costs of adoption (Nickman et al., 2005). We also began to see an increase in the number of children in foster care and therefore more children who became available for adoption.

There has been a dramatic decline in the number of infants available for adoption, from 9% before 1973 to 1% of infants born between 1996 and 2002 (Jones, 2009). Legalization and availability of abortion have been major contributors. This has brought with it a decrease in the number of women adopting children. The most recent National Survey of Family Growth found that 1.1% (0.6 million) of women aged 18 to 44 adopted children in 2002; 0.9% (0.5 million) adopted children between 2006 and 2010; and .61% (0.3 million) adopted children between 2011 and 2013 (Centers for Disease Control and Prevention, 2015). Changes over the last 25 years in adoption include less traditional adoptive arrangements such as kinship adoption; transracial adoption; single-parent adoption; and lesbian, gay, bisexual, transgender (LGBT) adoption as well as open adoption where birth parents may continue involvement with their children.

Women who adopt are typically older than birth mothers and typically have difficulty becoming pregnant (Jones, 2009). Women who have sought fertility treatments are far more likely to adopt than women who have not received fertility services. This speaks to a high degree of motivation to be a mother considering the expense and stress associated with fertility services (Jones, 2009). Importantly, willingness to adopt can also be associated with greater involvement with adoptive families (Bausch, 2006).

Typically in the United States, attitudes toward adoption are positive. Infertility in married couples is the reason most frequently cited for adopting a child (Bausch, 2006; Cudmore, 2005; Jones, 2009; Nickman et al., 2005). Adoption is not to be taken lightly, and research shows that more adults consider adoption than actually pursue it (Van Laningham, Scheuble, & Johnson, 2012). For example, in a sample of 579 Midwestern women aged 25 to 50, telephone interviews revealed 36% considered adoption, yet only 19.8% took any steps to actually apply for adoption (Van Laningham et al., 2012). Factors that affect the pursuit of adoption include infertility, race/ethnicity, formal or informal experience as a foster parent, and attitudes toward parenting.

Approximately 2% of American children are adopted (Child Trends Databank, 2012; Nickman et al., 2005). There are three ways by which children are adopted: private adoption, adoption from foster care, and international adoption. In 2007, private adoption without a public child welfare agency accounted for 38% of all adoptions; 37% of children were adopted from foster care; and 25% of children were internationally adopted through a private adoption agency (Child Trends Databank, 2012).

In a review of 10 years of published research on adoption, there were some important general findings (Nickman et al., 2005). Overall, the majority of adoptees have very good outcomes. Of course, a child's preadoption experiences and age at adoption influence the outcomes for adopted children. Better outcomes for children are often related to earlier age of adoption; however, that is not necessarily the case (Nickman et al., 2005). Identity formation difficulties can present in early adoption for both transracial and international adoption. Children placed after 1 year of age may be more likely to have developmental delays, attachment disorder, and posttraumatic stress disorder.

CHARACTERISTICS OF ADOPTIVE FAMILIES

There are many characteristics of adoption that impact the adoptee in childhood, adolescence, adulthood, and throughout life. Children can be impacted in different ways by transracial adoption, international adoption, open adoption, and placement in adoption because birth parents have had their rights terminated, adoption by LGBT parents, and learning about one's adoption as an adult (Child Welfare Information Gateway, 2013a).

Zill (2015) described the paradox of adoption. Adoptive parents are more likely to be better educated and have more financial resources than biological parents, and give more time and attention to parenting. Yet adopted children are more likely to have difficulty adjusting to school and more likely to have difficulty achieving academically. In a review of data on 19,000 children in kindergarten and first grade, adopted children had more behavioral problems, less positive attitudes toward learning, and lower reading and math achievement scores. These difficulties may be related to attachment issues, traumatic stress, and genetics (Zill, 2015).

Attachment difficulties focus on a child's need for a warm and loving relationship with an adult, typically the mother. When that relationship is interrupted or terminated, the effects can impair other relationships. One review of adoption studies found that children adopted before the age of 1 had comparable levels of emotional attachment as biological children (van den Dries, Juffer, van IJzendoorn & Bakermans-Kranenburg, 2009). Stress can lead to emotional issues over the long term, and an adoptive family may have great difficulty coping (Zill, 2015). In fact, even significant financial and educational accomplishments of adoptive parents may not be able to overcome genetic problems of adoptees.

Studies show that adoptees can score lower on measures of self-esteem and self-confidence (Child Welfare Information Gateway, 2013a). Some adoptees feel that secrecy surrounding their adoption contributed to low self-esteem. Further, they may feel different from others who have biological connections to their families. Two or more adopted children within a family can provide mutual support as well as strengthen positive feelings about adoption. Importantly, adoption remains a significant part of a person's identity throughout adulthood.

There is agreement in the literature about the challenges of adoption and what creates a positive adoptive experience. Some of the specific issues that adopted children deal with include difficulty accepting family rules for behavior, arguments with adoptive family members, disagreements about contacts with the birth family, and unequal treatment of biological and adoptive siblings (Hanna, Tokarski, Matera & Fong, 2011; Mariscal, Akin, Lieberman, & Washington, 2015). Sometimes adopted children can feel that the biological children in the home have greater status within the family (Mariscal et al., 2015). This can create a lot of tension and stress in a family.

Adopted children, especially adolescents, are more likely to receive mental health services (Brodzinsky, 1993). This can be related to preadoption experiences, especially for children in neglectful and abusive institutional care settings. An overview of research consistently found that even though levels of behavioral problems are comparable between adoptees and biological children, adoptees are more likely to receive psychiatric care (Nickman et al., 2005). This may be related to greater financial resources of adoptive parents and a stronger commitment from parents to ensure their adopted children get the needed services.

Some of the factors that create successful adoption include good parenting skills, strong commitment to the family, and open communication among family members (Brodzinsky, 2006; Hanna et al., 2011). One study that featured the voices of adopted youth found agreement that the things that contribute to successful adoption are the parents' motivation to help, honesty, genuineness, and trustworthiness (Mariscal et al., 2015). Of course, having adequate financial resources in a family can reduce stress.

Identity issues become more of a concern as a child reaches adolescence and questions about birth parents and siblings can become more probing. Although these questions can be challenges to adoptees, over time the issues can be resolved in positive ways. In a sample of 100 adoptees aged 35 to 55, five phases of identity development for adult adoptees were identified: (1) The lack of awareness or denial of adoption issues; (2) Emerging awareness where the adoptee can acknowledge the positive influence of adoption, but does not want an in-depth examination; (3) Drowning in awareness refers to feeling overwhelmed by anger and loss; (4) Reemerging from awareness refers to acknowledging the feelings and accepting reality; and (5) Finding peace is the state of having worked through the issues of adoption (Penny, Borders, & Portnoy, 2007).

It is critical for children and adoptive parents to receive support to adjust to the adoption experience (Mariscal et al., 2015). Some themes of adoption that children must cope with include grief and loss, identity development, and self-esteem issues (Child Welfare Information Gateway, 2013a). It is understandable that children think about their birth parents and why they were adopted (Neil, 2012). These are inevitable questions about birth parents that at times cannot be answered, especially in international adoption. For those adopted from other countries, there can be the loss of the cultural connections and language.

For those adopted at older ages, there is the stress associated with the loss of their home, their foster family, their communities, and their schools. Not surprisingly, children who feel secure and loved in their adoptive homes are better equipped to handle issues of loss (Child Welfare Information Gateway, 2013a).

ADOPTION FROM FOSTER CARE

Adoption from child welfare agencies typically occurs after foster care placement when it becomes apparent that birth parents will be unable to reunite with their children. Each year in the United States, approximately 51,000 children are adopted from foster care (U.S. Department of Health and Human Services, 2014).

Attitudes of children toward adoption are very much related to their experiences in foster care, both positive as well as negative (Chambers, Zielewski, & Malm, 2008). In a study of adolescents in Illinois, those with a strong relationship with their birth mothers were more likely to return to live with them. In contrast, a sense of belonging within a foster home predicted adoption by the foster family (Leathers, Falconnier, & Spielfogel, 2010). We will hear the voices of children regarding their adoption experiences in Chapter 9.

In the 2007 National Survey of Adoptive Parents, the first and only nationally representative survey, the motivation for parents to adopt fell into several categories. Eighty-six percent said they wanted to be able to provide a permanent home for a child or for children, 61% wanted to expand their family, 39% had fertility problems, 24% were seeking a sibling for their biological child, and 11% had adopted siblings of the available child (Malm, Vandivere, & McKlindon, 2011). Sixty percent of adoptive parents chose to adopt a child from foster care because of the lower costs, and 28% said it was faster than other forms of adoption.

The 2007 National Survey of Adoptive Parents found that overall, children adopted from foster care adjusted very well and adoptive parents were satisfied with the adoption experience (Malm et al., 2011). In hindsight, 92% of parents said they probably or definitely would make the same decision to adopt. In 2007, 22% of adoptions from foster care were completed by foster parents. Twenty-three percent were relatives, counting as kinship care, although 6% of kinship adoptive parents did not know the children before the adoption. The highest percentage of adoptive parents, 55%, did not know the child before adoption (Malm et al., 2011).

Child welfare agencies can seek adoptive families in a variety of ways. As already described, children in long-term foster care can be available for adoption and may be adopted by the foster family. For others, a new family must be found. A commonly used forum is the "adoption party," where interested adults can "shop" for children available for adoption through their state child protection agency. This is reminiscent of the orphan trains of the late 1800s, as described in Chapter 2, where children stood on the train platform in groups, had the opportunity to eat a meal with a family, and then were picked by the adults to join their families. Certainly, it is very stressful to be put in the situation of having a "fun" party where your future can be determined.

Media attention can be given to children who are free for adoption. November is known as "National Adoption Month," and organizations develop special media campaigns to support finding adoptive homes for children in need. In Boston, long-time television news anchor Jack Williams started Wednesday's Child that features children available for adoption through a special segment on the news. See Box 8.1 for a description of this important effort to expand adoption.

Not all adoption agencies are dedicated to finding homes for children in need. Some adoption agencies are actually scams that rip off potential adoptive parents for many thousands of dollars. Potential adoptive parents can be especially vulnerable to scams because they have such a high emotional investment in the adoption experience. For example, an Iowa couple was scammed several times by people claiming to be pregnant women looking to choose adoptive parents (Moore, 2015). In one instance, the couple paid $10,000 to an adoption agency and gave the woman money for rent, only to find this was all a lie. They

---

BOX 8.1 *Jack Williams and* **Wednesday's Child**

In 1981, television news anchor Jack Williams created the Wednesday's Child segment on the evening news. Williams collaborated with the Massachusetts Adoption Resource Exchange to find adoptive families for children with special needs in the care of the Massachusetts Department of Children and Families. Each week, Wednesday's Child featured one child available for adoption. When Williams retired in 2015, he had helped over 700 children with special needs find adoptive homes.

One young woman's letter to Jack Williams thanked him for all he did for her to find a home. She said she had lived without a home and without love. At age 10 she appeared on Wednesday's Child. She was grateful for the help she received and acknowledged the many children who were waiting for his help in finding adoptive homes.

——————
Adapted from Jack Williams Wednesday's Child (2015).

were not able to get their money back. The wife commented: "These women prey on families that just want to be families, they're desperate to have a child and you're vulnerable and you believe what you want to believe." Eventually, this couple was able to adopt two girls (Moore, 2015).

There are also the stories of adopted children who are abused within their adoptive homes. One example of a horrific adoption story received national attention. Eight adoptees won their lawsuit in the amount of $17.5 million against three adoption agencies in New York for the severe abuse and neglect they suffered at the hands of their adoptive mother (Associated Press, 2014).

RACIAL AND ETHNIC ISSUES IN ADOPTION

Race and ethnicity are among the most controversial issues in adoption practices and typically focus on whether it is preferable to place a child with a family of a different race/ethnicity if a family of the same race/ethnicity is unavailable. Two laws were passed to increase the number of children of color who could be adopted and to reduce their waiting time for adoption. The Multiethnic Placement Act of 1994 specifically prohibited using race to delay or deny adoption even though race could continue to be a factor in placement decisions (Brooks, Barth, Bussiere, & Patterson, 1999). This was further refined in 1996 with the Interethnic Adoption Provisions that foster care or adoption arrangements cannot "deny to any person the opportunity to become an adoptive or foster parent, on the basis of the race, color, or national origin of the person, or the child involved" (Brooks et al., 1999, p. 171).

Some have argued that transracial adoption can harm the development of adopted children and keep them from developing a positive racial identity. It has been of concern that transracial adoption can reduce efforts to seek adoptive same-race parents. In a position statement of the National Association of Black Social Workers in 1994, the Association supported as their top priority family preservation and reunification, and kinship care (Hollingsworth, 1998). A second priority was to place children with families of their own race, with transracial adoption considered only after same-race placements were unsuccessful. This included the proviso that African American community representatives had to be supportive of transracial placement.

As discussed, a disproportionate number of racial and ethnic minority children are found within the entire range of services provided by the child welfare system. Thus, it is not surprising that this is also the case in adoptions from foster care. Using data from the National Survey of Adopted Children from 2007, African American children were 14% of the American population, yet accounted for 35% of children adopted from foster care. White children were

56% of the American population, but accounted for 37% of children adopted from foster care (Malm et al., 2011).

One study focused on 1,550 children who were removed from their homes in Kansas by the child welfare system and placed in foster care for adoption (Kapp, McDonald, & Diamond, 2001). African American children were removed more quickly from birth families than White children. It took 1 to 2 months longer to match African American children with an adoptive family than White children or other children of color (Kapp et al., 2001). More efforts need to be made to understand the reasons for differential treatment of African American children, and to recruit African American families for adoption.

Similar issues have been raised for Native American children in the United States. The Indian Child Welfare Act (ICWA) of 1978 was designed to promote the best interests of Native American children yet simultaneously promote the stability of Native families and communities. This gave greater opportunity for children to be placed in Native American foster and adoptive homes, reducing the number of Native children placed with White families. This Act has been controversial, as demonstrated in the case of Baby Veronica, discussed in Chapter 2, where the debate is over whether the biological father who had Cherokee lineage was entitled to take his daughter from her adoptive home under the ICWA.

In 2015, the federal Bureau of Indian Affairs released updated ICWA guidelines to respond to continuing concerns about taking Native children away from families and placing them with non-Native families (Lakota Law Project 2015). It was noted that in South Dakota, Native children represent 15% of residents, yet they are 54% of the foster care population. Updated guidelines state that if a child is removed from a home, the child must be considered Native American until an investigation shows the child is not. Emergency removals of children from homes must meet a higher standard involving imminent danger or harm. Additionally, any professional called to testify in ICWA cases must have expertise in Native culture and customs (Lakota Law Project, 2015).

Religious beliefs and faith also play a role in adoption. In a study of 113 families, faith and church attendance were related to the decision to adopt, and resulted in lower adoptive parent stress and improved adoption outcomes, especially for African American families (Belanger, Copeland & Cheung, 2008).

Almost 20 years ago, it was clear that more needs to be done to minimize the need for transracial adoption by bolstering efforts to recruit adoptive families of color (Hollingsworth, 1998). Many years later, these recommendations are still being made. At the same time, with the tremendous growth of minority groups in the United States in recent years, same-race and ethnic adoptive placement may be less important than it once was. One psychiatrist concluded that in his view, "African-American children in white families may play an important role in helping other children and their parents overcome racial stereotypes" (Schetky, 2006).

CLOSED AND OPEN ADOPTION

It is very difficult to find a middle ground among adoptees who need and want information about their preadoption life and birth parents, the rights of the birth parents themselves, and the rights of adoptive parents to choose how to best raise a child (Nickman et al., 2005). "Closed" adoption refers to sealing records and not providing adoption information to the child or birth parent, ensuring that there is no contact. This was the state of adoption in the 1950s. In the 1970s and 1980s, there was a move toward open adoption, allowing direct contact between birth and adoptive families (Child Welfare Information Gateway, 2013b). "Open" adoption refers to the opportunity to interact with the birth mother to varying degrees. Frequency of contact is typically determined by both the birth and the adoptive families. Clearly, adoptees in open adoption have more information about their histories, which can be nagging issues for those in closed adoption. See Box 8.2 for an example of a closed adoption.

There is agreement among mental health clinicians specializing in adoption that children should be told of their adoption, but there is no consensus on when and how the child should be told (Nickman et al., 2005). These issues are good reasons to seek counseling from mental health clinicians who specialize in adoption. Counseling can help to bolster self-esteem and counteract fears of abandonment. Older children coming from multiple foster care placements may need mental health services over a longer period of time (Nickman et al., 2005).

There is a growing literature on the positive effects of open adoption for children, birth mothers, and adoptive parents (Crea & Barth, 2009; Ge et al., 2008). Siegel interviewed 21 sets of parents every 7 years starting in 1988. All parents and children were White and middle class. Siegel (2003) found that adoptive parents were very positive about open adoption when their children were infants, believing it best for the child. Siegel (2008) reaffirmed the earlier findings when the children were 6 to 7 years old, as no parent respondents desired less contact with the biological family. In the most recent follow-up, adoptive parents were still as positive about knowing their children's birth parents and said open adoption had been helpful to their children in addressing issues of identity (Siegel, 2013).

Von Korff and Grotevant (2011) found that contact with birth families is associated with more conversation about adoption between children and adoptive parents, and provides the opportunity to work through issues and

BOX 8.2 Closed Adoption Example in California

A 17-year-old adolescent named Jordan Rodriguez had helped to raise her five nieces and nephews in San Jose, California, but had difficulty obtaining permission to visit them. Rodriguez herself went into kinship foster care with her grandmother at the age of 13 when child protective services removed her from her home. Her nieces and nephews entered the child welfare system not long after. Rodriguez described the children's fear when they had a last visit with her and other family members just before they were readied for adoption. "After the visit, I was very mad that I couldn't do anything to keep them with me and that I had no say so about what the parents decided. I started crying a lot. It just broke my heart to see them leave" (p. 2). The four older children went to the same adoptive home and the youngest, her 2-year-old nephew, was placed in a different home. The family with the older children was clear they were not interested in allowing Rodriguez to maintain a relationship with the children. The parents of the youngest child have allowed visits.

In closed adoption, the birth and adoptive parents do not typically have contact after the legal proceeding has been finalized. The adoption records remain sealed until the child turns age 18. In February 2016, Rodriguez and members of the group California Youth Connection made a presentation to state legislators to support a bill that gives rights to biological family members to maintain connections.

Source: Loudenback (2016). Reprinted with permission from *The Chronicle of Social Change*.

support positive adoptive identity formation. This can assist with the psychological adjustment of adolescents (Van Korff, Grotevant, & McRoy, 2006). The Minnesota/Texas Adoption Research Project found that family members in open adoption were more satisfied than those in closed adoptions (Grotevant, McRoy, Wrobel, & Ayers-Lopez, 2013). Satisfaction by families with the level of contact between children and birth parents was associated with better adjustment by adopted adolescents. Twelve to 20 years after placing their children, birth mothers suffered less unresolved grief in open adoptions (Grotevant et al., 2013). Other research has also shown that open adoption can have a positive association with the adjustment of the birth mother after the child was placed (Ge et al., 2008). See Box 8.3 for ways that adoption professionals can contribute to successful open adoptions.

BOX 8.3 Ways Adoption Professionals Can Support Successful Open Adoption

1. Ensure that the child's needs are the focus of the open adoption process.
2. Make sure that birth and adoptive parents are educated about open adoption in its varying forms.
3. Help adoptive and birth parents determine what form of open adoption is best for them.
4. Assist adoptive and birth parents in relationship building and defining parameters for the relationships.
5. Help families to prepare for changes in the relationship as the child matures.
6. Provide all family members with opportunities for counseling at any time there is a need, especially to assist with communication among family members.

Source: Child Welfare Information Gateway (2013b).

INTERNATIONAL ADOPTION

Many adoptive families tout the importance and success of international adoption. International adoption became available after World War II and began to expand in the 1970s. The purpose of international adoption has been to provide homes for children who could not be cared for within their home countries, although it is not always clear who has made the decision that adoption is in the best interests of the child (Cantwell, 2014). International adoption is an example of how only those with funds to pay high fees, and jump through many hoops, would be eligible for out-of-country adoptions. One need only examine the website of the U.S. Citizenship and Immigration Services (USCIS), a division of the Department of Homeland Security, to see the complexity in international adoption. The USCIS must determine eligibility to become an adoptive parent based on U.S. citizenship, and if married, it must be a joint adoption. An adoption applicant must meet certain requirements such as not having a criminal history and completing a successful home study by an authorized adoption agency. Costs can vary widely by country and adoption agency, and finalized international adoptions can typically cost between $20,000 and $30,000.

Overall, internationally adopted children fare well and do not seem to experience many deficits, especially if they have been adopted early and have had good care while awaiting adoption. A review of research on international adoption studies found that, if no abuse, neglect, or late adoption was present, children of single parents had the same strong level of social adjustment as those of two-parent families (Nickman et al., 2005). However, children adopted from other countries may feel a sense of rejection by birth parents and even by their home country.

The majority of children adopted internationally since 1994 have been from China, predominately girls under the age of 2 (Tan, Marfo, & Dedrick, 2007). More recently, changing policies in China have meant fewer children available for out-of-country adoption and more eligibility restrictions for potential adoptive parents. Although some research has shown lower academic performance among adoptees, a sample of 77 adopted children from China showed comparable academic performance when matched with 77 Norwegian children (Dalen & Rygvold, 2008).

The ability to adopt from other countries is often closely intertwined with politics. For example, President Vladimir Putin of Russia signed a ban against American adoption in December 2012, terminating 259 pending adoptions of Russian children (Chizhova, Voltskaya, & Bigg, 2014). Advocates of human rights and others such as adoptive families point to the willingness of the Russian government to sacrifice the lives of children for political reasons. It is hard to think of anything more atrocious.

There is also an underside to international adoption that includes fraud and corruption. The Schuster Institute for Investigative Journalism (2012) at Brandeis University compiles documented cases of fraud in international adoption and provides links to stories of international adoption gone wrong. Cases of bribery, fraud, and other corrupt practices have been identified in countries including Guatemala, Sierra Leone, Cambodia, and Vietnam.

LESBIAN, GAY, BISEXUAL, AND TRANSGENDER ADOPTION

Gays and lesbians who adopt children face stigma in American society (Nickman et al., 2005). Although gay marriage is now federal law, attitudes toward LGBT individuals have not necessarily softened, especially when it comes to adoption of children.

Although there is little research on sexual orientation of parents and adoption, for the research that does exist, outcomes are positive. In comparing 106 families with gay, lesbian, and heterosexual couples, one study found that young children in gay and lesbian families were as well adjusted as children headed by heterosexuals (Farr, Forssell, & Patterson, 2010). In addition, children were found to have typical gender development. Rather than the sexual orientation of parents, it was the qualities of lower parenting stress, effective tools for disciplining children, and strong couple relationships that were associated with children being well adjusted. Another study comparing gay-, lesbian-, and heterosexual-parented families found that young adopted children's adjustment was not associated with family type (Goldberg & Smith, 2013). It was the positive family context of parents who were prepared for parenting and had a strong couple relationship that predicted good adjustment of children.

Sexual orientation of adoptive children can be problematic and is a risk factor for adoption disruption (Mariscal et al., 2015). One youth in a focus group who had two disrupted adoptions remarked: ". . .[T]hey (prospective adoptive parents) found out I was a member of the gay community and. . .they're all, never mind. . ." (Mariscal et al., p. 115). Much more must be done so that LGBT youth have the same level of supportive adoptive homes as all other children.

ADOPTION DISRUPTION AND DISSOLUTION

"Adoption disruption" is a generic term for adoptions that do not work out. Disruption has been further defined to mean removal from the home before adoption has been legalized. This can mean the return to foster care or placement with another adoptive family (Child Welfare information Gateway, 2012). In contrast, "adoption dissolution" refers to leaving the adoptive home after the adoption has been legalized and the relationship is severed, voluntarily or involuntarily (Child Welfare Information Gateway, 2012; Mariscal et. al., 2015). Rates of adoption disruption are known to be between 10% and 25% for children in the U.S. foster care system who have moved into adoption (Child Welfare Information Gateway, 2012; Mariscal et al., 2015). Estimates of adoption dissolution are between 1% and 5% (Child Welfare Information Gateway, 2012). See Box 8.4 for an example of an extreme case of adoption dissolution.

The exact number of adoption disruptions and dissolutions that result in the child leaving the adoptive home is unknown (Selwyn, Wijedasa, & Meakings, 2014). A study of adoptions in the United Kingdom over 12 years found that 3.2% of children experienced adoption disruption (Selwyn et al., 2014; in their study, Selwyn et al. did not use the term "dissolution," but instead used the term "disruption.") Importantly, 66% of parents stated the adoption experience was positive over time.

Most disruptions occur during the teenaged years when, typically, the fewest professional support services are available to adoptees (Selwyn et al., 2014). Parents reported that problems stemmed from mental health problems as a result of a history of neglect, family violence, or sexual victimization. Of the 35 families that experienced disruption, 91% of children had witnessed family violence before adoption, and 34% were sexual abuse victims before adoption. In 80% of disrupted adoptions, violence on the part of the child

> ### BOX 8.4 7-Year-Old Boy Returned to Russia After Failed Adoption
>
> In a disturbing case of international adoption, a 7-year-old boy was returned to Russia by his American mother, a nurse, who lived in Tennessee. The child was adopted in 2009 and remained in the adoptive home for about 1 year. The woman gave him a letter to give to the Russian authorities after he was returned to the orphanage.
>
> The letter to the Russian authorities accused them of lying to her about his behavior. She felt that his severe mental behavioral problems must have been evident prior to the adoption and that these were minimized in order to move him out of the orphanage into an adoptive home.
>
> This horrific case garnered considerable media attention. How can we know if the adoptive mother was lied to and the situation misrepresented to her? What constitutes a reasonable effort to care for a child with severe behavioral problems? What supports, if any, could have helped the mother parent this child?
>
> ⎯⎯⎯
> Adapted from Stewart (2010).

was involved. An astonishing 97% of children in disrupted adoptions had mental health problems. It was uncommon to receive referrals to support services that could have helped avoid disruption. The children leaving adoptive homes typically reentered some kind of foster care or group care, and their behavioral issues continued. These problems included self-harming behaviors, fire-setting, assaults on care workers, and committing serious crimes (Selwyn et al., 2014). Yet the numbers do not tell us the background and circumstances that led to the disruption.

A number of practices can be implemented to prevent adoption disruption. Stress levels of children moving from foster care to adoption can be reduced with professional assistance to better help children transition better (Selwyn et al., 2014). Early identification of a child's aggression, especially aggression toward an adoptive parent, can provide the opportunity for early intervention and treatment. Child and family members may need to be assessed for support services, and professionals must ensure that services are provided (Selwyn et al., 2014).

Seeking agreement on the definitions of disruption and dissolution will assist in comparing outcomes of research. Although there is greater research interest today, there is no national data on adoption disruption and dissolution (Child Welfare Information Gateway, 2012). Research that examines reasons for disruption/dissolution can aid in the design of preventive services.

RECOMMENDATIONS AND PROMISING PRACTICES

The well-being of children should be much more important than administrative policies, procedures, and any system of reimbursement (Mariscal et al., 2015). Unfortunately, this is not the case today, so much more work must be done to support adopted children and families.

Adoptive parents need better preparation to understand the trauma, grief, and loss issues of children (Mariscal et al., 2015). Counseling to address attachment issues, and the provision of support services, including support groups for both adoptees and parents, can be very helpful (Nickman et al., 2005). Adoptive parents must be realistic in their expectations of children and also mindful of children's early experiences, including trauma. All adoption participants need time to build the relationship before the adoption. Children, especially older children, need to receive more information about the prospective adoptive family.

Postadoption support services for children and parents can be very helpful. In a study of adoptive families receiving assessment and referrals for services including health care, mental health, and educational services, adopted youth had fewer behavioral problems, lower rates of disruption, and higher levels of parental commitment to maintaining the relationship (Liao & Testa, 2014). Recommendations from adoptees themselves include better matching according to cultural factors, child and family interests, and temperaments (Mariscal et al., 2015).

An important recommendation is to provide subsidies to adoptive families. Adoption is known to increase when financial supports are offered. This can be the case especially for foster parents adopting children (Buckles, 2013).

Many resources exist today to assist adoptees. The American Adoption Congress provides education and advocacy in support of adoptive families. The Adoptee's Liberty Movement Association advocates for adoptees to have access to their birth and adoption records, and offers a registry to help connect adoptees with their birth families. There are also a variety of adoption organizations at the international level. For example, Families with Children from China is an important supportive resource for families that have completed their adoptions as well as for those considering adoption from China.

SUMMARY AND CONCLUSION

It is critical to have a much better understanding of how to make timely and lasting adoption experiences for children and families. Children deserve to be raised in loving homes where their needs can be met by capable supportive adults. Adoption from foster care and international adoption can be very positive experiences for children and families. We need increased adoption support services for children as well as for adoptive and birth parents. Services to support adoptive families should be based on family-specific needs rather than simply providing services that are available. Very little research attention has focused on adopted children's perspectives on how to improve adoption outcomes. If at all possible, children must be given a voice in their adoptions.

Considerably more effort needs to be made to find adoptive homes for children, especially children in foster care who have no hope for reunification with birth family members. Media strategies and financial incentives can be successful in increasing the numbers of children adopted. Engaging with churches and other religious organizations can also be helpful in increasing adoptions. Greater opportunities to see successful adoptive families can be a powerful motivator for those considering adoption. Although adoption disruption and dissolution occur infrequently, it is a traumatic experience when it does occur. Greater efforts are essential to determine ways to prevent adoption disruption and dissolution.

DISCUSSION QUESTIONS

1. What challenges are associated with being an adopted child?
2. What kinds of services should be offered to children in the adoption process?
3. What are the issues of adult adoptees?
4. What can be done to reduce adoption disruption and dissolution?
5. What role can religious organizations play in adoption?
6. What can be done to prevent those looking to adopt children from being scammed?
7. Do age, gender, race/ethnicity, and sexual orientation impact the success of adoption?
8. What can the child welfare system do to facilitate adoptions?

9. What are the challenges for children adopted internationally, and for their parents?

10. Discuss your own ideas for improving and expanding opportunities for children to be adopted.

REFERENCES

Associated Press. (2014, August 30). 8 adoptees win $17.5m abuse suit. *The Boston Globe*, p. A2.

Bausch, R. S. (2006). Predicting willingness to adopt a child: A consideration of demographic and attitudinal factors. *Sociological Perspectives, 49*(1), 47–65.

Belanger, K., Copeland, S., & Cheung, M. (2008). The role of faith in adoption: Achieving positive adoption outcomes for African American children. *Child Welfare, 87*(2), 99–123.

Brodzinsky, D. M. (1993, Spring). Long-term outcomes in adoption. *The Future of Children, 3*(1), 153–166.

Brodzinsky, D. M. (2006). Family structural openness and communication openness as predictors in adjustment of adopted children. *Adoption Quarterly, 9*(4), 1–18. doi:10.1300/J145v9n04_01

Brooks, D., Barth, R. P., Bussiere, A., & Patterson, G. (1999). Adoption and race: Implementing the Multiethnic Placement Act and the Interethnic Adoption Provisions. *Social Work, 44*(2), 167–178.

Buckles, K. S. (2013). Adoption subsidies and placement outcomes for children in foster care. *Journal of Human Resources, 48*(3), 596–627.

Cantwell, N. (2014, March). *Innocenti Insight: The best interest of the child in intercountry adoption*. Florence, Italy: UNICEF Office of Research.

Centers for Disease Control and Prevention. (2015). *National Survey of Family Growth*. Retrieved from www.cdc.gov/nchs/nsfg/key_statistics.htm

Chambers, K., Zielewski, E. H., & Malm, K. (2008). *Foster youths' views of adoption and permanency*. Washington, DC: The Urban Institute Child Welfare Research Program.

Child Welfare Information Gateway. (2012). *Adoption disruption and dissolution*. Washington, DC: U.S. Department of Health and Human Services, Children's Bureau.

Child Welfare Information Gateway. (2013a). *Impact of adoption on adopted persons*. Washington, DC: U.S. Department of Health and Human Services, Children's Bureau.

Child Welfare Information Gateway. (2013b). *Working with birth and adoptive families to support open adoption*. Washington, DC: U.S. Department of Health and Human Services, Children's Bureau.

Child Trends Databank. (2012, August). *Adopted children. Indicators on children and youth.* Bethesda, MD: Author. Retrieved from www.childtrends.org/?indicators=adopted-children

Chizhova, L., Voltskaya, T., & Bigg, C. (2014, December 31). *Two years after Russian ban, 'taboo' hangs over Russian children denied U.S. adoption.* Radio Free Europe/Radio Liberty. Retrieved from http://rferl.org/content/russia-united-states-adoptions-orphans-taboo-ban/26771310.html

Crea, T. M., & Barth, R. P. (2009). Patterns and predictors of adoption openness and contact: 14 years postadoption. *Family Relations: Interdisciplinary Journal of Applied Family Studies, 58*(5), 607–620.

Cudmore, L. (2005). Becoming parents in the context of loss. *Sexual and Relationship Therapy, 20*(3), 299–308. doi:10.1080/14681990500141204

Dalen, M., & Rygvold, A.-L. (2008). Educational achievement in adopted children from China. *Adoption Quarterly, 9*(4), 45–58.

Farr, R. H., Forssell, S. L., & Patterson, C. J. (2010). Parenting and child development in adoptive families: Does parental sexual orientation matter? *Applied Developmental Science, 14*(3), 164–178.

Ge, X., Natsuaki, M. N., Martin, D., Leve, L., Neiderhiser, J., Shaw, D. S., . . . Reiss, D. (2008). Bridging the divide: Openness in adoption and post-adoption psychosocial adjustment among birth and adoptive parents. *Journal of Family Psychology, 22*(4), 529–540.

Goldberg, A. E., & Smith, J. Z. (2013). Predictors of psychological adjustment in early placed adopted children with lesbian, gay, and heterosexual parents. *Journal of Family Psychology, 27*(3), 431–442.

Grotevant, H. D., McRoy, R. G., Wrobel, G. M., & Ayers-Lopez, S. (2013). Contact between adoptive and birth families: Perspectives from the Minnesota/Texas adoption research project. *Child Development Perspectives, 7*(3), 193–198. doi:10.1111/cdep.12039

Hanna, M., Tokarski, K., Matera, D., & Fong, R. (2011). Happily ever after? The journey from foster care to adoption. *Adoption Quarterly, 14*(2), 107–131.

Hollingsworth, L. D. (1998). Promoting same-race adoption for children of color. *Social Work, 43*(2), 104–116.

Jack Williams Wednesday's Child. (2015). Retrieved from www.jackwilliamswednesdays child.com

Jones, J. (2009). *Who adopts? Characteristics of women and men who have adopted children* (NCHS Data Brief No. 12). Hyattsville, MD: National Center for Health Statistics. Retrieved from www.cdc.gov/nchs/data/databriefs/db12.pdf

Kapp, S. A., McDonald, T. P., & Diamond, K. L. (2001). The path to adoption for children of color. *Child Abuse & Neglect, 25*, 215–229.

Lakota Law Project Report. (2015, February 26). *Feds strengthen ICWA guidelines*. Retrieved from https://lakotalawproject.wordpress.com/2015/02/26/feds-strengthen-icwa-guidelines

Leathers, S. J., Falconnier, L., & Spielfogel, J. E. (2010). Predicting family reunification, adoption, and subsidized guardianship among adolescents in foster care. *American Journal of Orthopsychiatry, 80*(3), 422–431.

Liao, M., & Testa, M. (2014). Postadoption and guardianship: An evaluation of the Adoption Preservation, Assessment and Linkage Program. *Research on Social Work Practice*. doi:10.1177//1049731514564600

Loudenback, J. (2016, January 20). Closed adoption law separates California teen from her family. *The Chronicle of Social Change*. Retrieved from https://chronicleof socialchange.org

Malm, K., Vandivere, S., & McKlindon, A. (2011, May). Children adopted from foster care: Child and family characteristics, adoption, and well-being. *ASPE Research Brief*. Washington, DC: U.S. Department of Health and Human Services.

Mariscal, E. S., Akin, B. A., Lieberman, A. A., & Washington, D. (2015). Exploring the path from foster care to stable and lasting adoption: Perceptions of foster care alumni. *Children and Youth Services Review, 55*, 111–120.

Moore, S. (2015, March 5). Iowa family falls victim to adoption scam. *WHO Channel 13 TV*. Retrieved from http://whotv.com/2015/03/04/iowa-family-falls-victim-to-adoption-scam

Neil, E. (2012). Making sense of adoption: Integration and differentiation from the perspective of adopted children in middle childhood. *Children and Youth Services Review, 34*(2), 409–416.

Nickman, S. L., Rosenfeld, A. A., Fine, P., MacIntyre, J. C., Pilowsky, D. J., Howe, R.-H., . . . Sveda, S. A. (2005). Children in adoptive families: Overview and update. *Journal of the American Academy of Child and Adolescent Psychiatry, 44*(10), 987–421.

Penny, J., Borders, L. D., & Portnoy, F. (2007). Reconstruction of adoption issues: Delineation of five phases among adult adoptees. *Journal of Counseling & Development, 85*(1), 30–41.

Schetky, D. H. (2006). Commentary: Transracial adoption—Changing trends and attitudes. *Journal of the American Academy of Psychiatry and the Law, 34*(3), 321–323.

Schuster Institute for Investigative Journalism. (2012). *Fraud & corruption in international adoptions*. Waltham, MA: Brandeis University. Retrieved from http://brandeis.edu/ investigate/adoption

Selwyn, J., Wijedasa, D., & Meakings, S. (2014, April). Beyond the adoption order: Challenges, interventions and adoption disruption. Retrieved from https://www.gov.uk/government/ publications/beyond-the-adoption-order-challenges-intervention-disruption

Siegel, D. H. (2003). Open adoption of infants: Adoptive parents' feelings seven years later. *Social Work, 48*(3), 409–419. doi:0037-8046/03

Siegel, D. H. (2008). Open adoption and adolescence. *Families in Society: The Journal of Contemporary Social Services, 89*(3). doi:10.1606/1044-3894.3762

Siegel, D. H. (2013). Open adoption: Adoptive parents' reactions two decades later. *Social Work, 58*(1), 43–52. doi:10.1093/sw/sws053

Stewart, W. (2010, April 9). Fury as U.S. woman adopts Russian boy, 7, then sends him back alone with note saying: 'I don't want him anymore.' *Daily Mail.com.* Retrieved from http://www.dailymail.co.uk/news/article-1264744/American-sends-adopted -Russian-boy-behavioural-problems.html

Tan, T. X., Marfo, K., & Dedrick, R. F. (2007). Special needs adoption from China: Exploring child-level indicators, adoptive family characteristics, and correlates of behavioral adjustment. *Children and Youth Services Review, 29,* 1269–1285.

U.S. Department of Health and Human Services. (2014). *Trends in foster care and adoption FFY 2002–2013.* Retrieved from www.acf.hhs.gov/sites/default/files/cb/ trends_fostercare_adoption2013.pdf

Van den Dries, L. Juffer, F., van IJzendoorn, M. H., & Bakermans-Kranenberg, M. J. (2009). Fostering security? A meta-analysis of attachment in adopted children. *Children and Youth Services Review, 31*(3), 410–421.

Van Laningham, J. L., Scheuble, L. K., & Johnson, D. R. (2012). Social factors predicting women's consideration of adoption. *Michigan Family Review, 16*(1), 1–21.

Von Korff, L., & Grotevant, H. D. (2011). Contact in adoption and adoptive identify formation: The mediating role of family conversation. *Journal of Family Psychology, 25*(3), 393–401. doi:10.1037/a0023388

Von Korff, L., Grotevant, H. D., & McRoy, R. G. (2006). Openness arrangements and psychological adjustment in adolescent adoptees. *Journal of Family Psychology, 20*(3), 531–534. doi:10.1037/0893-3200.20.3.531

Zill, N. (2015, October 7). *The paradox of adoption.* Charlottesville, VA: Institute for Family Studies. Retrieved from family-studies.org/the-paradox-of-adoption

PARENT AND CHILD PERSPECTIVES ON CHILD WELFARE SERVICES

Surprisingly little research exists on parent and child experiences within the child welfare system. Chapter 9 examines the experiences of children and parents receiving interventions and services from child protection agencies. It describes positive experiences of parents and children, and discusses the challenges parents and children face regarding allegations of abuse and neglect. The chapter also examines experiences of children and youth in foster care placement and adoptive homes, and the importance of children having a say in their own futures.

Parents and children can have remarkably different perceptions of services they receive and the reasons for intervention, especially if children are removed from the home. Children tend to focus on their personal experiences and treatment by parents and child welfare agencies. Parents are more likely to offer insights into the process and their own treatment by child welfare systems. In cases where the child is removed from a birth parent by child protection services, it can result in a feeling of horror and confusion for the child. Alternatively, being removed from a severely abusive home can bring substantial relief to the child or children. The stories told by parents and children are an important part of their identity, reveal their understanding of the situations they are in, and importantly guide their future decisions and actions (Latty & Burns-Jager, 2001).

An underlying commitment within child protection services is that professionals will respond to families in ways that can support them in caring for their children or help them in the future to reunify with their children

(Hurlburt, Barth, Leslie, Landsverk, & McCrae, 2007). Participation of family members in determining care plans, child welfare practices, and case reviews can be invaluable as well as challenging (Morris, Brandon, & Tudor, 2015). It is critical that child protection workers have an understanding of how parents experience their intervention if workers are to be accepted as helpful (Dumbrill, 2006; Latty & Burns-Jager, 2001). Parents can feel apprehension about contact with child protection workers; however, successful relationships can be formed (Spratt & Callan, 2004). It is especially important yet difficult to cultivate effective relationships between parents and child protection workers because of the emotionally laden context of abuse and neglect, and the fact that families are involuntary clients of the child protection agency (Altman, 2008; Drake, 1994; Kemp, Marcenko, Hoagwood, & Vesneski, 2009). There is a delicate balance between working "with" clients yet also having the authority to remove children from the home (Healy & Darlington, 2009). Although communication and a positive relationship are essential, there must be motivation on the part of parents to improve the health of the family (Altman, 2008). Cultural differences can have a negative impact on the willingness to engage on the part of parents (Larsen-Rife, & Brooks, 2009). The ability to work successfully with difficult family situations can be a testament to the skills of the child protection worker. We will hear the voices of child welfare professionals in Chapter 10.

In one study of both child welfare clients and child welfare workers, there was remarkable agreement between both groups regarding the attitudes and competencies needed to work successfully together (Drake, 1994). There was agreement that child welfare workers must be respectful, have an appropriate nonjudgmental attitude, have the ability to stay calm, and be able to communicate effectively by speaking at the client's level of understanding.

In a qualitative study of parents and child protection workers, there was agreement that to cultivate a productive relationship, workers must have a positive disposition, be authentic in the relationship, and show compassion (Bundy-Fazioli, Briar-Lawson, & Hardiman, 2009). Workers and parents also agreed that a positive relationship is built when workers are knowledgeable, look for ways to empower parents, and serve as an intermediary between powerful bureaucratic systems such as the child protection agency and family courts.

FAMILY PRESERVATION

Parents can have different perceptions of the power of child welfare workers and their agencies. Parents who perceive that the agency has power and control over them are less satisfied than parents who feel that power can be used to support them in their parenting. The reality is that child welfare workers and their agencies do have substantial power and authority over parents in child maltreatment cases (Marcenko, Brown, DeVoy, & Conway, 2010). In general, parents who are receiving child welfare services while their children remain in the home tend to be more satisfied with services than those whose children are removed (Chapman, Gibbons, Barth, & McCrae, 2003; Kemp, Marcenko, Lyons, & Kruzich, 2014). The most satisfied parents were those assigned fewer than two caseworkers with whom they had recent contact, and also felt that they quickly received helpful services (Chapman et al., 2003).

In a qualitative study of 18 parents, these parents perceived the use of power by child welfare professionals as a way to support them or, in contrast, as a mechanism of control over parents (Dumbrill, 2006). All parents in the study thought of child protective workers as more powerful than themselves, and 16 of 18 parent respondents felt that power was used in negative ways. Several recounted experiences where decisions had already been made to place the children in care, and the parents felt their input was discounted. However, nine parent respondents felt that the worker used power in ways that were helpful by offering concrete services. For example: "The worker was very very helpful. . . . She took us everywhere we needed to go and she was there for us, different ideas about different things and so we had a really good rapport with child protection services" (Dumbrill, 2006, p. 32).

Parent responses to child protection workers depended on their percep-tions of the use of power. Typically, parents responded in one of three ways: (1) by fighting with and challenging workers, even taking them to court; (2) by "playing the game," and appearing to be cooperative; or (3) by working collab-oratively with child protection workers (Dumbrill, 2006). Parents who thought child protection workers used power in collaborative ways responded by being cooperative themselves. Parents who perceived that power was used over them responded by challenging or "playing the game" with workers (Dumbrill, 2006).

There must be give-and-take and a real effort for parents to work with child protection workers. Here is what one mother, Nancy, had to say:

> I am the parent. I want the agency worker to know that this means I have certain rights. I know that it means I have certain responsibilities also. My major piece of advice—hard as it is sometimes—is to try to make the agency worker's job easier, not harder, whenever you can. I make a point of thanking her for special acts like buying my son his favorite candy bar. I do this even if I'm also frustrated by other decisions she is making. I try not to complain about little things—like an appointment having to be changed—as long as it is obvious that she is working as hard as she can. I give her information (insurance information, for example). I make calls to school personnel and others. Then I tell her what I find out.

This can help her out. It also helps my child and is a constant reminder that I am the parent. (McCarthy et al., 2003, p. 86)

It is no surprise that parents who receive in-home services tend to be happier with child protection services than those whose children are removed from the home. In-home services can lead to a more collaborative experience for families than when child protection workers determine that a child must be removed from the home. Lisette tells the story of how child protective services helped by arranging for services that could keep her family together. See Box 9.1 for Lisette's story.

Parents of children receiving child protective services stated in interviews that their most positive experiences occurred when they were treated with respect and felt supported by the child protection worker (Palmer, Maiter, & Manji, 2006). Referrals for helpful resources were appreciated, including referrals for daycare, educational programs, mental health services for the child and/

BOX 9.1 *Lisette's Story*

Lisette describes keeping her family together in her own words:

> I am a single mother of four boys. I was living with my boy-friend and there were lots of fights in my home. . . . Most of the times the protective services worker found that I did not hurt the children. But when my 6-year-old set his bed on fire, the protective services worker said that my family needed help. We agreed to accept in-home services. . . . Once the worker and I began to work together, we found out that all four of my sons needed help with their mental health. . . . The in-home services worker helped us get Section 8 housing. She helped us get food and clothes so we could all live together again. She took us to a community mental health program. I found out my sons . . . had ADD, ADHD, learning disabilities, and one had epilepsy. . . .

Lisette was appreciative of the services that were provided, and her family was still together and receiving mental health services. In addition, the family received ongoing services from a case manager and a family advocate.

Source: McCarthy et al. (2003).

or the parents, and even temporary placement of the child. Thirty-one percent talked about the emotional support they received. For example, ". . .they were so understanding and they weren't looking down on you for faults that you might think you have. And they try and explain that [although she placed her son temporarily in care] you're not a bad parent . . . they're always reassuring you on that" (Palmer et al., 2006, p. 817). See Box 9.2 for an example of intensive services to keep a family together provided by HOMEBUILDERS.

BOX 9.2 HOMEBUILDERS

HOMEBUILDERS was established in 1974 and is the oldest intensive family preservation service, having assisted over 15,000 families. To receive services, children and families must be referred by state child welfare agencies and be at significant risk of foster care or institutional placement. A variety of services are provided to reduce the risk of harm to children and to enable parents to learn new skills. The staff manages small caseloads of two to three families and offers round-the-clock availability. Additional key program features include crisis intervention, treatment within the home and community setting, responsiveness of staff, and flexible services based on evidence-based practices. Families typically receive 40 to 50 hours of direct service within a 4-week period.

Several program evaluations have attested to the success of HOMEBUILDERS. The website touts positive outcomes for families: 6 months after participation in HOMEBUILDERS, 86% of children in the program were able to remain in their homes, avoiding foster care or institutional placement.

One single mother who was physically abusive to her three children aged 3, 5, and 10 had this to say about the value of the HOMEBUILDERS program:

> Without HOMEBUILDERS we would not be together. Our therapist had a hands-on approach. He walked us through everyday stuff. I broke the cycle of violence in my family. If it worked in my family it could work with others, because we were the worst of the worst.

Source: Institute for Family Development (2013).

Overall, a family assessment must include the strengths of the family and a determination of their needs rather than a punitive, adversarial approach (Larsen-Rife & Brooks, 2009). An individualized approach to each family is needed with services based on the risk to the child (or children), vulnerability of the children based on age and other factors, and the protective factors present in the home. Effective engagement between child welfare workers and parents can be made more difficult when parental substance abuse, mental illness, and/or violence are present in the family (Bundy-Fazioli et al., 2009; Larsen-Rife & Brooks, 2009).

Parents can also have negative experiences with child protection workers and can struggle to maintain the relationship. As discussed, this is especially so if children are removed from the home. Palmer et al. (2006) found that 21% of the parents felt a child protection worker had betrayed them when they had withheld information or used confidential information against them in court. The following example is from a parent whose child was removed from the home: "they had promised me that [daughter] would be coming home that night. . .[then placed her in care]. They said, 'I'm sorry, we have to protect the children first and we were trying to calm you down at your house.' Which I didn't think was fair—they lied to me" (Palmer et al., 2006, p. 818).

There are extreme cases where children are abruptly removed from their homes in ways that are traumatic for them and their parents. A single 38-year-old mother with three children stated: "They came into the mall, in public, and snatched my kids right out of my hands. . .having people see this and having them ripped out of my arms and being treated as if I was a bad person. . .I ended up in hospital for a long time" (Palmer et al., 2006, p. 819).

BIRTH PARENT PERSPECTIVES

It can be extremely traumatic for birth parents to lose their children to the foster care system, and then to adoption. However, there are ways to reduce the trauma to the children and the birth parents. As discussed in Chapter 8, open adoption is more likely to be available to children and families today, so there can be continued contact. For example, a mother named Elena found that an open adoption worked well for her children and for her. Elena had been using drugs, and her child was abused in the homes of her sisters. Elena talked about how her children were placed in foster care, and the foster family sought adoption:

I was told that I had used up all my chances and that my time was up. This family adopted my girls, but they also write me letters and send me pictures, so I don't have to worry. I have had a couple of visits with my children—at Christmas one year, so I know they are OK. The letters and pictures they send me help a lot, too. Sometimes, they even send me some examples of their school projects or videos of them as a family. The letter and videos can be sad, but it's great to know that my children have a good life with their new family. (McCarthy et al., 2003, p. 67)

FOSTER PARENT PERSPECTIVES

Some families are interested in serving as foster families for short or long periods of time. When children in foster care fit in well, foster parents may seek to adopt them. However, there are a number of barriers to adoption faced by families seeking to adopt from foster care. In a sample of families seeking to adopt foster children, major obstacles included the logistics of the adoption process, communication issues, lack of responsiveness and emotional support from the agency, and lack of services (Chanmugam et al., 2016). These challenges were so arduous that only 98 families in the study completed the adoption process, whereas 102 families decided to discontinue the process. It is a strong indictment of the adoption process that more than half of the applicant families chose not to complete the process. Clearly, much more must be done to streamline the foster care to adoption policies and procedures.

CHILDREN'S PERSPECTIVES

Children's voices must be heard when it comes to placement in foster care or when efforts are made by birth parents, foster parents, or child welfare professionals to pursue adoption. Children must be heard from directly. They may need guardians ad litem, professionals appointed by the court, to protect them in abuse and neglect court proceedings, and they may need their own lawyers. As stated by Robinson (1993): "Children should not be silenced by what adults have deemed to be in their best interests in situations in which both the state and their parents have repeatedly acted to the detriment of those interests. Children need to be involved in the fundamental decisions that shape their own future" (p. 415).

Not surprisingly, children's views of their placement, whether in foster care or adoption, depend a great deal upon age and previous experiences. A 7-year-old boy experienced confusion and difficulty in understanding his experience: "Do I have one family or two? My mom and dad didn't make me . . . I was born to another lady somewhere . . . so is she my mother too? . . . It gets kind of confusing sometimes" (Brodzinsky, 2011, p. 201).

Adoption Views

The experiences children have in foster care greatly influence their attitudes toward adoption, and therefore it is understandable that they have questions and concerns (Chambers, Zielewski, & Malm, 2008). A sample of 43 English children, adopted while under age 4, were interviewed about their adoption experiences when they were between the ages of 5 and 13 (Neil, 2012). At an average of 8.6 years old, almost all children felt integrated into their adoptive families. Positive comments included: "it's just they care for me in every way" and "they think I am nice, and they just love me" (Neil, 2012, p. 411). About one quarter of the children said life with their adoptive parents was better than their previous lives. For example, one child said: "it's better than what it could have been" (Neil, 2012, pp. 411–412). Most of the adoptive families had some contact with birth families; however, it was surprising that almost three quarters of children lacked basic information about their birth families. This could be because adoptive parents were not given information by birth families or that adoptive parents did not know the children wanted more information (Neil, 2012). It could also be that children did not ask questions because they were not emotionally prepared to learn about their birth families.

In trying to make sense of their adoption, over two thirds of the children said that their birth parents were unable to take care of them, typically for health reasons (Neil, 2012). For example, one child said: "My mummy was too poorly," and another child said: "She had this really bad headache" (p. 414). Only a few children addressed issues of mental health rather than physical health: "Well adoption means that. . .your real family is not right in the head. . .Like they've, like this really weird virus and, and they can't really look after the child very good" (p. 414).

Older children find it much more difficult to be adopted. Few families have an interest in adopting an older child, and child protection workers may not actively seek adoptive homes (Chambers et al., 2008). In focus groups with foster children aged 11 to 19, most said that they had an initial goal of family reunification that did not work out. Children and youth seemed to be well aware that their chances were reduced because of their older age. They objected to adoption, feeling that they were too old and preferred to find an independent living program (Chambers et al., 2008). Some youth felt there was something wrong with them because they had been in foster care for so long. The older youth felt they would be "picky" about finding an adoptive home: "They stereotype us [youth] and we stereotype them [adoptive parents]" (Chambers et al., 2008, p. 2).

Some youth interested in adoption thought they might have more freedom in an adoptive home, whereas others thought they might have less freedom and are "stuck" (Chambers et al., 2008, p. 3). Some youth questioned the motives of potential adoptive families: "Some people think if they are like 'I adopted this child and it's not mine,' that they get put up for some sort of glory" (p. 3). Other youth said their birth parents did not want to give up parental rights. One child said his mother refused to discuss adoption, feeling "every time she heard the word [adoption], she didn't like it because she felt like I was being taken away from her" (Chambers et al., 2008, p. 1).

One very interesting qualitative study of adolescents and their adoptive parents found that there were indeed challenges but that overall, adoption was a positive experience (Wright & Flynn, 2006). This study of 37 adolescents and 58 adoptive parents found considerable agreement that being a family was especially important and meaningful. Fifty-seven percent of parents said the adoption was successful because they really felt like a family. Nine-five percent of adolescents said they would choose adoption again. Yet neither parents nor adolescents painted an overly rosy picture of adoption. Indeed, 26% of parents had considered disruption (termination) of the adoption because of challenging behaviors and arguments. Forty-four percent of parents said the stress and emotional challenges associated with the child's behavioral problems were most difficult. One mother considered not going through with the adoption until she realized that they were being put to the test: "The closer we got to the day to sign those papers the worse he got. He was just testing us to see if we really wanted him" (Wright & Flynn, 2006, p. 499). Overall, there was a strong mutual relationship—parents chose the adolescent, and the adolescent chose the parents. Beyond the initial choice, both parents and adolescents had to commit to making the adoption work.

Adolescence is the time when adoption disruption or dissolution is most likely to occur, and success of adolescent adoption is typically seen in terms of no adoption disruption (Wright & Flynn, 2006). There is much more to learn about adoption of this group of adoptees and how to help them adjust to adoption and focus on building a successful future. See Box 9.3 for advice for adoptive parents of adolescents.

Children's Perceptions of Adoption Recruitment Activities

The process of matching children and adoptive parents is not an easy one, especially if children are repeatedly subjected to foster and adoptive parent recruitment activities. Youth who were asked about their experiences said they were more likely to see advertisements to help children in Africa and other countries than to help children in the United States (Chambers et al., 2008). They were not aware of events such as local media efforts that featured individual children available for adoption. There was a clear preference not to participate

---

BOX 9.3 *Professional Advice for Adoptive Parents*

1. It is normal for children to want to learn about their adoption, and it is helpful to their developing identity.
2. Adolescents may show intense interest in their adoptions and birth families or may have no interest in this information at this time in their lives.
3. Understand that adoption plays an important role in the developing identity of children and is influenced by the children's personality characteristics, their family members, as well as their experiences in the community, in school and with peers.
4. Parents need to be open and supportive themselves about adoption and can help the child develop a positive self-identity as an adoptee.
5. Information about birth parents and the reason for adoption, as well as contact with birth family members, can help adoptees develop positive self-esteem.
6. Transracial adoption adds to the complexity of identity development for adoptees, and positive role models can help ensure success in identity development.

Source: Brodzinsky (2011).

---

in adoption "parties." One said about media recruitment opportunities: "You don't want no one to feel sorry for you, because it's hard enough that we have to be in the system, hard enough that we have to be a statistic" (Chambers et al., 2008, p. 4). Several youth were asked to participate in recruitment of adoptive parents by filming an adoption segment for television. Most said they did not want to participate in any media recruitment events because of embarrassment: "all your friends would look at you and know you had no place to go" (p. 4).

Typically, the children participating in recruitment events were aged 13 to 15 and reported negative experiences (Chambers et al., 2008). One girl described how she was at a "matching" party but did not immediately understand the purpose of the event. It was only after she was questioned by adults and asked to fill out forms that she realized what was going on. She asked to withdraw from adoption consideration because she said she was not interested in adoption. Of course, it is entirely possible that by choosing to reject adoption, she was trying to avoid another disappointment and rejection by a family.

In recent years, more attention has been paid to participation of children and birth parents in developing a care plan. One reason is that the United Nations

Convention on the Rights of the Child of 1989 specifically addresses the right of children's views to be known and considered in care planning, based on their age and level of maturity (Healy & Darlington, 2009). The participation of human services clients in decisions about themselves has been recognized as essential. This is often referred to as the "right to self-determination." Greater openness to child and parental involvement in care planning represents a departure from paternalistic ideas, and has been supported as a "best practice." Of course, ethical concerns still exist about very young children participating in their care planning, and it is difficult to determine at what age and maturity level children can most appropriately participate (Healy & Darlington, 2009).

Transracial Adoption

In Chapter 8, we discussed both transracial adoption within the United States and international adoption. We learned that social and political factors can intersect to make intercountry adoption available or, as in Russia, no longer possible. In addition, social factors such as poverty and war can affect adoption efforts and outcomes. For example, Korean adoptions, at one time the largest adoption program available to Americans, began after the end of the Korean War in the 1950s (Lee, 2003).

One study of African American children adopted by Whites found that in the early years, parents encouraged positive identification with their race and culture (DeBerry, Scarr, & Weinberg, 1996). In the initial study, 42% of families had supported bicultural socialization. However, 10 years later as the children became adolescents, only 20.4% of families were considered bicultural. Thus over time, parents were less likely to emphasize racial identity, and children became less likely to identify with African American culture.

> Regarding a very positive transracial adoption, one seventeen year-old boy said: I grew up in a very integrated community and went to very integrated schools . . . I've always had both African American and White friends . . . and some Asian friends too . . .being Black has never been an issue for me . . . I'm very comfortable with who I am . . . my parents are very open and supportive . . . I feel good about being adopted by them . . . the fact that they aren't African American hasn't prevented me from feeling proud that I'm Black . . . they've helped me with that. (Brodzinsky, 2011, p. 203)

In a very small study of two adoptive families with a total of four children who were adopted internationally, parents faced challenges when children displayed emotional and behavioral problems (Deveny-Leggitt, 2012). Parents felt a full range of emotions from joy to fear. One mother expressed it in the following words:

. . . My thinking is that when you make a decision to adopt that. . .there isn't ever a question that this isn't your child. . .very quickly it doesn't have too much to do with how you got them. It's just now you got them, how do you take care of them? (p. 62)

Transracial adoptees are not simply passive recipients of their racial and ethnic perceptions of themselves and their perceptions of racism (Lee, 2003). Transracial adoptees are active participants in defining their own racial and ethnic identities as well as how they negotiate challenges or racism.

Overall, there are many positive stories about adoption told by adoptees themselves. See Box 9.4 for the views of a 27-year-old reflecting on the adoption experience.

It is by focusing their attention on the children themselves that child welfare professionals and researchers can better understand their situations and experiences, and then develop ways to help: "Researchers must listen closely to adoptees to hear their hopes and desires, their gratitude and their resentment, their joys, and sorrows" (Brodzinsky, 1993, p. 162). This important advice from almost 25 years ago has yet to yield significant improvements in the adoption process.

BOX 9.4 Adoption Experience

Here are the words of a 27-year-old looking back on the adoptive experience:

> I talk [with my adoptive parents] about how drama filled the [birth] family and I'm glad I'm on the inside. That I can be there for everyone, but then leave, and go to my respective [adoptive] family . . . who isn't perfect either. I feel it's [adoption] given me a lot. A complete sense of perspective that not a lot of children and young adults, or adults have for that matter. It has allowed me to be completely accepting of others' families, and be able to see issues with families that I wouldn't have normally been aware of or really even cared about. People who have known me for a while have asked the question, nature or nurture . . . I'm a prime example . . . a product of both. I like the view point it gives me.

Source: Von Korff and Grotevant (2011).

RECOMMENDATIONS AND BEST PRACTICES

When possible, it is imperative that child welfare systems engage openly and honestly with parents and children regarding case planning. In protective services, three core principles are recommended for working with families: (1) respect, (2) appropriateness, and (3) transparency (Healy & Darlington, 2009; Morris et al., 2015). *Respect* refers to child protection workers acknowledging the value of opinions of family members and recognizing that each has a right to his or her own opinion. This can also lead to greater respect among family members for each other's opinions, and contributes to the development of a "shared understanding" of the family's issues (Healy & Darlington, 2009, p. 425). *Appropriateness* refers to exploring options that are both reasonable and realistic for the child and the family. This includes determining the extent of participation of children in the process. In one study, child protection workers were not comfortable with the participation of children under age 5 (Healy & Darlington, 2009). Workers also expressed concern that they did not have adequate time with families, an important issue that will be discussed in the next chapter. *Transparency* refers to having a clear purpose for the child protection intervention as well as a clear process for determining the care plan. An important element of transparency is that child protection workers must be clear about their professional boundaries by informing parents of the restrictions in their participation. Parents need clear messages on how child protection workers perceive the family problems and what changes should be made to provide a healthy home for children (Healy & Darlington, 2009).

An initial meeting in a supportive environment can go a long way to engage patients in treatment. For example, in a study of depressed low-income clients, the 1-hour intake session helped to increase future patient participation in treatment (Swartz et al., 2007). An adage among psychotherapists is that the job of therapists in an initial session is to do their best to ensure that clients come back for a second session. The same can apply to child welfare interventions as well.

Parent trainings for families in the child welfare system can also be helpful. Historically, parent-training programs focused on ways for parents to manage the problem behaviors of their children. More recent efforts have focused on bringing parent-training programs within the realm of child protection services (Hurlburt et al., 2007). These programs focus on expanding the child development knowledge of parents as well as changing parental behavior and improving parenting skills. Improvements can be seen in boundary setting and using consistent disciplinary measures. At this time, it is not clear which types of child maltreatment are most likely to be reduced through parenting classes. Parenting classes are frequently offered by local family service and other kinds of human service agencies. Greater use of parenting programs by those in the child welfare system can provide additional data on what approaches work best and for whom.

Another innovation is a parent-mentoring program where foster parents who have deep knowledge of the child welfare system offer individualized support to parents who are working on family preservation (Marcenko et al., 2010). Mentors work with parents on a wide variety of issues such as discipline, budgeting, developing a support network, and referrals to community human service agencies.

Finally, the need for continued innovations on behalf of children receiving child welfare services is critical. See Box 9.5 for a description of the Treehouse at Easthampton Meadow program in Massachusetts.

SUMMARY AND CONCLUSION

Planning for children within the child welfare system must include the perspectives of the children. It must also include, to the fullest extent possible, the needs and desires of the birth parents. Ideally, parents, child welfare workers, and

BOX 9.5 The Treehouse at Easthampton Meadow in Massachusetts

Opening in 2006, the Treehouse at Easthampton Meadow is a mixed-income rental community for children to move out of foster care placement and into permanent adoptive homes with postplacement support services. The mission is to "inspire a re-envisioning of foster care in America," with a vision of "every child rooted in family and community." The multigenerational planned community has apartments and homes around a central Community Center. Seniors who move to Treehouse choose to be active participants in the lives of children. Over 100 people from ages 3 to 90 live in the community.

The Treehouse program is widely considered an innovative program that can meet the needs of children and elders alike. It serves as an important model for moving children from foster care into adoptive homes and could be expanded to all regions of the United States.

Adapted from Massachusetts Housing Finance Agency (2015); Treehouse Foundation (2016).

children should work collaboratively to preserve the family. Parental satisfaction with child protection services tends to be highest when the child remains in the home and services are provided. If family preservation is not possible, the least restrictive measures to ensure the safety of children are essential. Youth receiving child protective services must feel empowered to have a say in their own futures.

Child welfare agency requirements can be obstacles to successful family engagement, especially when they involve removal of children against the wishes of family members. Child protection workers must adhere to the principles of respect, appropriateness, and transparency when working with families. A variety of services can meet the needs of children and their families including parent trainings, intensive home services through programs such as HOMEBUILDERS, and innovative housing such as the Treehouse program.

DISCUSSION QUESTIONS

1. In what ways can child protection workers be helpful to families?

2. What are potential reactions of birth parents to child protection workers?

3. Discuss the importance of family preservation services.

4. How are power and authority used by child protection workers?

5. Why might children in foster care shy away from media attention designed to find an adoptive home for them?

6. What are the special issues regarding adoption of adolescents?

7. In what ways can parent-training programs be useful?

8. How does transparency help child protection workers deal with foster care placement and adoption situations?

9. Why is it important to have children in the child welfare system participate in decisions about their future?

10. What are your own suggestions for helping children in the child protection system to get their needs met and to plan for a successful future?

REFERENCES

Altman, J. C. (2008). Engaging families in child welfare services: Worker versus client perspectives. *Child Welfare, 87*(3), 41–61.

Brodzinsky, D. M. (1993, Spring). Long-term outcomes in adoption. *The Future of Children, 3*(1), 153–166.

Brodzinsky, D. M. (2011). Children's understanding of adoption: Developmental and clinical implications. *Professional Psychology: Research and Practice, 42*(2), 200–207. doi:10.1037/a0022415

Bundy-Fazioli, K., Briar-Lawson, K., & Hardiman, E. R. (2009). A qualitative examination of power between child welfare workers and parents. *The British Journal of Social Work, 39*(8), 1447–1464. doi:10.1093/bjsw/bcn038

Chambers, K., Zielewski, E. H., & Malm, K. (2008, January). *Foster youths' views of adoption and permanency* (Child Welfare Research Program Brief). Washington, DC: The Urban Institute.

Chanmugam, A., Madden, E. E., Hanna, M. D., Cody, P. A., Ayers-Lopez, S. J., McRoy, R. G., & Ledesma, K. (2016). Agency-related barriers experienced by families seeking to adopt from foster care. *Adoption Quarterly*, 1–19. doi:10.1080/1092675 5.2015.1121187

Chapman, M. V., Gibbons, C. B., Barth, R. P., & McCrae, J. S. (2003). Parental views of in-home services: What predicts satisfaction with child welfare workers? *Child Welfare, 82*(5), 571–596.

DeBerry, K. M., Scarr, S., & Weinberg, R. (1996). Family racial socialization and ecological competence: Longitudinal assessments of African-American transracial adoptees. *Child Development, 67*(5), 2375–2399.

Deveny-Leggitt, H. (2012). *Adoptive parents' experience with international adoption: Children with attachment or behavioral challenges* (Master of Social Work Clinical Research Papers, Paper No. 18). Retrieved from http://sophia.stkate.edu/msw_papers/18

Drake, B. (1994). Relationship competencies in child welfare services. *Social Work, 39*(5), 595–602.

Dumbrill, G. C. (2006). Parental experience of child protection intervention: A qualitative study. *Child Abuse & Neglect, 30*, 27–37.

Healy, K., & Darlington, Y. (2009). Service use participation in diverse child protection contexts: Principles for practice. *Child & Family Social Work, 14*, 420–430. doi:10.1111/j.1365-2206.2009.00613.x

Hurlburt, M. S., Barth, R. P., Leslie, L. K., Landsverk, J. A., & McCrae, J. S. (2007). Building on strengths: Current status and opportunities for improvement of parent training for families in child welfare. In R. Haskins, F. Wulczyn, & M. B. Webb (Eds.), *Child protection: Using research to improve policy and practice* (pp. 81–106). Washington, DC: Brookings Institution Press.

Institute for Family Development. (2013). *HOMEBUILDERS intensive family preservation services and intensive family reunification services*. Retrieved from www.institutefamily.org/aboutus_program.asp

Kemp, S. P., Marcenko, M. O., Hoagwood, K., & Vesneski, W. (2009). Engaging parents in child welfare services: Bridging family needs and child welfare mandates. *Child Welfare, 88*(1), 101–126.

Kemp, S. P., Marcenko, M. O., Lyons, S. J., & Kruzich, J. M. (2014). Strength-based practice and parental engagement in child welfare services: An empirical examination. *Children and Youth Services Review, 47*, 27–35.

Larsen-Rife, D., & Brooks, S. (2009, June). *The importance of family engagement in child welfare services*. Davis, CA: Northern Training Academy Supporting Children and Family Services.

Latty, C. R., & Burns-Jager, K. (2001). Narrating confluent experiences in a child welfare case. *International Review of Qualitative Research, 4*(1), 59–80.

Lee, R. M. (2003). The transracial adoption paradox: History, research, and counseling implications of cultural socialization. *Counseling Psychology, 31*(6), 711–744.

Marcenko, M., Brown, R., DeVoy, P. R., & Conway, D. (2010). Engaging parents: Innovative approaches in child welfare. *Protecting Children, 25*(3), 23–34.

Massachusetts Housing Finance Agency. (2015, March 9). *Innovative, multigenerational housing for seniors and families adopting children from foster care in Easthampton completed and occupied*. Retrieved from https://www.masshousing.com/portal/server .pt/search?in_hi_opt_comm_community=217&in_se_sel_1=everything&q=innov ative%2C+multigenerational

McCarthy, J., Marshall, A., Collins, J., Arganza, G., Deserly, K., & Milon, J. (2003, December). *A family's guide to the child welfare system*. Washington, DC: Georgetown University Center for Child and Human Development.

Morris, K., Brandon, M., & Tudor, P. (2015). Rights, responsibilities and pragmatic practice: Family participation in case reviews. *Child Abuse Review, 24*, 198–209. doi:10.1002/car.2272

Neil, E. (2012). Making sense of adoption: Integration and differentiation from the perspective of adopted children in middle childhood. *Children and Youth Services Review, 34*, 409–416.

Palmer, S., Maiter, S., & Manji, S. (2006). Effective intervention in child protective services: Learning from parents. *Children and Youth Services Review, 28*, 812–824.

Robinson, S. (1993). Remedying our foster care system: Recognizing children's voices. *Family Law Quarterly, 27*(3), 395–415.

Spratt, T., & Callan, J. (2004). Parents' views on social work intervention in child welfare cases. *British Journal of Social Work, 34*, 199–224.

Swartz, H. A., Zuckoff, A., Grote, N., Spielvogle, H. N., Bledsoe, S. E., Shear, M. K., & Frank, E. (2007). Engaging depressed patients in psychotherapy: Integrating techniques from motivational interviewing and ethnographic interviewing to improve treatment participation. *Professional Psychology: Research and Practice, 38*, 430–439.

Treehouse Foundation. (2016). *An inter-generational community: Vital living opportunities and community connections for all ages*. Retrieved from http://refca.net/community/ treehouse-easthampton/multi-generational-community

Von Korff, L., & Grotevant, H. D. (2011). Contact in adoption and adoptive identity formation: The mediating role of family conversation. *Journal of Family Psychology, 25*(3), 393–401.

Wright, L., & Flynn, C. C. (2006). Adolescent adoption: Success despite challenges. *Children and Youth Services Review, 28*, 487–510.

RE PROFESSIONALS

10

eld of child welfare is never easy. Each day there be made that affect the future of children and their families. Often, these decisions must be made within a nonsupportive organizational climate where child welfare workers have too few resources to offer. Chapter 10 examines the professional and personal realities of those who work within the system. There are different roles within child welfare systems, including intake workers who respond when initial telephone reports of abuse and/or neglect are made, workers who focus on investigations of child abuse and neglect, and ongoing workers who work for family preservation or foster care placement. Each position is stressful in its own way.

The pressures for child welfare workers come from a number of sources. These include how the agency is organized and the bureaucratic rules that must be closely followed, especially the overwhelming documentation requirements. Child welfare systems can be state-level or county-level agencies, or child protection professionals can work for private agencies. All agencies have their own specific requirements that must be met by staff.

Administrators, as well as parents and supervisors, can exert pressure on child welfare workers, and then of course, there are the needs of the children. Organizational pressures can include time limits for completing work and the availability of only very limited resources (adapted from Smith & Donovan, 2003). There can also be large differences between child welfare policies and actual child welfare practices. Work environments can bolster confidence and empower child welfare workers or, on the other hand, can disempower them (Wallach & Mueller, 2006).

Little research has been done on the context in which child welfare workers function and their own views on the roles in which they serve.

ETHICS AND CHILD WELFARE PRACTICE

Expected to adhere to agency policies, child protection workers can feel caught between the bureaucracy and doing what they think is best to address the issues of their clients and families. Child welfare workers are in the unique position of identifying agency problems with negative consequences for their clients and themselves, and yet they are unable to resolve those problems. Frustration can be associated with not being able to improve a dysfunctional organizational system.

Too often, child welfare workers are called upon to deal with situations that challenge their integrity and ethical standards. Yet a concern for ethics should permeate all child welfare decisions (Maluccio, Pine, & Tracy, 2002). Professional boundary issues occur relatively frequently in the practice of child welfare (Brenner, Kindler, & Freundlich, 2010). Workers are expected to be ethical, although the path to ethical decision making can pit the needs of children and their families against the needs of the agencies. In the child welfare system, much stress can stem from the bureaucratic rules and administrative pressures as well as from client and family problems. These competing concerns are a challenge to work priorities, analyzing situations and options, and making knowledgeable and reasonable decisions.

Time constraints and the need to cut costs can weigh heavily on child welfare workers. In a qualitative study of child welfare workers in Chicago, those working in foster care strongly felt pressure not to place children because of the expense of foster care. Efforts to reduce the financial expenditures for foster care can result in very high caseloads (adapted from Smith & Donovan, 2003). It is clear that the needs of children are not a top priority.

With so many factors competing for a caseworker's time, biological parents may not be considered a high priority. Biological parents can receive less attention from child welfare workers since the child has been removed and the workers' time is more likely to be spent with the child and foster parents (adapted from Smith & Donovan, 2003).

Caseworkers can assume that parents are responsible for a lack of contact and interpret it as disinterest in reunifying the child with the family. Thus workers will rely on parents to contact them for assistance rather than reaching out to parents (adapted from Smith & Donovan, 2003). Child welfare professionals often blame parents for the toll that large caseloads and time pressures take on them.

Adherence to rigid rules can take precedence over seeking genuine positive change in parents. Rather than focus on a parent's progress toward fitness to resume care for a child, the emphasis is often placed on whether the parent completed certain programs. The result is a "test" of whether parents can complete the obstacle course set for them. The ability of parents to complete programs required of them by child welfare professionals serves as a positive sign that the parents want the child to be returned home and are willing to work toward that plan (adapted from Smith & Donovan, 2003).

Workers can choose to overlook the needs of biological parents and concentrate on the families that are easier to help. These workers may not recognize their responsibility to help parents become better parents, and can be inclined to blame parents when the workers themselves experience organizational pressures (adapted from Smith & Donovan, 2003).

It is of critical importance to examine the organizational context in child welfare work and not assume that poor quality practices are attributable to individual workers. See Box 10.1 for an example of how adherence to bureaucratic rules can prevent workers from being helpful and can actually land them in trouble.

Child protection work is not without its dangers. Although taking the life of a child welfare worker is rare, it does occur and should be considered an important occupational hazard (Tham, 2007). See Box 10.2 for an example of how a child welfare worker lost her life at the hands of a child's mother.

BOX 10.1 Social Worker Faces Disciplinary Action for Helping a Child

Karey Cooper, a child welfare worker for the Kentucky Cabinet for Health and Family Services, apparently made a big mistake when she actually helped a 7-year-old girl in need. Cooper had been the child's caseworker and then was moved to "state investigations," where she investigated the most challenging and serious maltreatment cases. The child and her family were assigned to another ongoing caseworker who had officially closed the case. Relatives contacted Cooper about continued abuse and neglect and, in response, Cooper visited the girl at her school to find her unkempt and without adequate food. At the time Cooper was unaware the child protection case had been closed.

Cooper was informed she violated agency policy by visiting a child in a family that had a closed case. Cooper had earlier earned

(continued)

> ### BOX 10.1 Social Worker Faces Disciplinary Action for Helping a Child (continued)
>
> accolades for the quantity and quality of her work. Although 18 cases were recommended, Cooper had handled 102 cases. The agency had been under criticism for very high caseloads, caseworker turnover, and 92 families that were "lost" in the system and did not receive needed interventions. Cooper's fall from grace seemed to come after she wrote two letters to the child welfare commissioner in which she described her concerns about the handling of the case. Thereafter, her time sheets and travel vouchers came under scrutiny in ways they had not previously. Cooper said: "Here they've lost track of 92 cases and I'm in trouble because I went to see one kid" (Yetter, 2015, p. 1).
>
> This case seems to be about much more—one caseworker became the scapegoat for a deeply troubled child welfare agency. Perhaps it was Cooper's integrity and ethical standards that led her to become a whistle blower on behalf of a 7-year-old child.
>
> _____
> *Sources*: FoxNews.com (2015); Yetter (2015).

JOB SATISFACTION

There is agreement that the most satisfying part of child welfare work is to see the successes of the children and families (Whitaker, Reich, Reid, Williams & Woodside, 2004). Interest in the field of child welfare can begin with a positive internship experience in undergraduate and graduate programs (Alperin, 1998).

Typically, the child welfare workers who thrive on their work have strong coping strategies, strong social and emotional support, and an agency with positive organizational characteristics. The ability to provide empathic services to children and families supports a sense of professional and personal accomplishment. Many factors determine the professionalism of child welfare workers and the quality of their work. These factors include the personality of the worker, the level of job interest, the type and level of education, and the kinds of training offered by child welfare agencies.

In a study of staff turnover among new child welfare workers in California, job satisfaction was the best predictor of whether workers remained on the job (Weaver, Chang, Clark, & Rhee, 2007). Child welfare agencies can support job satisfaction by providing appropriate supervision, increasing

> ### BOX 10.2 *Murder of a Child Protection Worker in Berlin, Vermont*
>
> In August 2015, Jody Herring faced murder charges in the slaying of a Vermont Department for Children and Families caseworker, Lara Sobel. Herring was accused of also murdering two cousins and an aunt whom she felt had called the child welfare authorities. Sobel, age 48, was the caseworker as Herring lost custody of her 9-year-old daughter. Sobel had worked for over 14 years in child welfare and had two young daughters. She was shot twice as she was leaving her office.
>
> Mrs. Sobel was remembered at her funeral as an outstanding child protection worker who committed her life to helping children. The loss to her family and the community is immeasurable.
>
> ———
> Adapted from Crimesider Staff (2015); Ledbetter (2015); Rathke and Gram (2015).

caseloads slowly rather than overwhelming new workers with cases, and providing opportunities for continuing education. If job satisfaction can be increased, especially early after starting the job, the likelihood of turnover is reduced (Weaver et al., 2007).

CHALLENGES OF CHILD WELFARE WORK

There are many challenges to working within the child welfare system. As indicated, there are various needs to be met, including children's needs, family needs, and also the needs of staff in the organization. Some child welfare workers express frustration over the lack of resources for families in need: "It's difficult working with families who have extreme needs when resources are not available for them to meet basic needs no matter how hard they work" (Whitaker et al., 2004, p. 18). In their roles as case managers, child welfare workers must locate community resources to which they can refer children and families. This can be problematic, especially when the necessary resources are not available. Even if there are resources, families can wait months to receive services without any supports during that waiting period (adapted from Smith & Donovan, 2003).

There is a sensitivity to negative perceptions of child welfare workers, especially negative media attention. In the words of one worker: "The child welfare staff person is always the bad guy in the eyes of the press and other service providers" (Whitaker et al., 2004, p. 9). Negative perceptions of child welfare work can, over time, have a negative impact on workers. One supervisor commented, "Too often the agency fails to acknowledge, reward, and pay attention to good work" (Hess, Kanak, & Atkins, 2009, p. 27).

A staff survey by the Child Welfare League of America (2014) found that 70% of Massachusetts child welfare workers disagreed with the statement that the Department of Children and Families "values and rewards accountability, communication, responsiveness, and commitment to improvement" (p. 38). Certainly, this is a very revealing and damning statement, and serves as a critical reminder of how much work is required to improve the health of child welfare organizations. In focusing on how to achieve improvements, one child welfare worker stated: "I would like the work to be more respected, less bureaucratic, more focused on the people we serve" (Whitaker et al., 2004, p. 18).

Salaries

In 2016, the *U.S. News and World Report* listed the 2014 median annual salary of child welfare workers as $42,120. The top 10% earned $72,500, and the average of the lowest paid was approximately $27,500. Although these are certainly not top salaries, it is clear that no one enters the field of human services looking to make a lot of money. In addition to the personal rewards of helping children and families, child welfare jobs, especially those with state child protection agencies, are typically stable and secure, and often offer a pension in an era when pensions are rapidly disappearing from the workplace. Unfortunately, these generous benefits are a problem when earning benefits takes precedence over the needs of children and families. Staff not well suited to child protection work can continue to hold jobs long after they have stopped being effective in their roles.

Caseload and Workload

Very high caseloads have long been a problem in child welfare. Although there are recommended numbers of cases, all too often the maximum number is exceeded. As indicated, caseload refers to the number of cases assigned to each worker. Workload refers to the amount of time and effort that is required to provide services and to achieve a positive case resolution, and generally refers to the average amount of time required to handle specific kinds of cases (Child Welfare Information Gateway, 2010). According to the Boston Foundation in Massachusetts "... caseloads have increased extraordinarily and are the highest they have been in two decades" (Meltzer & Paletta, 2014). Reasonable caseloads contribute to worker satisfaction and have a positive impact on client families as well.

High caseloads not only affect workers and families, but create problems across the entire system:

> Simply hiring more workers will not be successful in reducing worker turnover and stabilizing the workforce if the hiring is done in isolation from other improvements such as improving training, supervision, supports for workers, relationships with private providers and the court, and the overall climate and culture of the work environment. (Meltzer & Paletta, 2014, p. 13)

Workload and caseload issues are not easy to address because they are a part of the larger problems of staff turnover and hiring and caseworker assignment practices (De Varon, Costello, & Edwards, 2008). Studies of workload and caseload issues can help justify requests for increasing child welfare budgets, and address work equity concerns (Edwards & Reynolds, 2008). Workloads should be reasonable and must be tied to the recommendations of licensing or accrediting bodies (Child Welfare League of America, 2013).

There are a number of strategies to effectively manage caseloads, and some agencies have developed specific workload measures and types of reports (Wagner, Johnson, & Healy, 2008). These can include computerized data management tools that help determine whether agency locations have too few staff or too many (Child Welfare League of America, 2013). Software has also been developed to allow supervisors and managers to assign case assessments and ongoing cases as part of an effort to distribute work more equitably among workers. Delaware has used a system that each month compares caseload numbers with a set of caseload standards (Child Welfare Information Gateway, 2010). Of course, measurement of workloads must be a part of a coherent methodology to determine the most appropriate staffing levels; they are very important in the development of strong management practices (Goodman & Hurwitz, 2008).

Staff Turnover

Staff turnover has long been a problem in human services, and it is very much the case in child welfare (Weaver et al., 2007). Staff turnover can be associated with high caseloads, low salary, poor staff morale, lack of autonomy, and few opportunities for promotion. Child welfare staff turnover can also be related to frustration with attorneys and courts that do not share the same goals and ethics in child welfare practice (Vandervort, Gonzalez, & Faller, 2008). It can be difficult to make comparisons regarding turnover because of the different ways of measuring turnover, and because of geographic differences (Weaver et al., 2007).

The U.S. Government Accounting Office (GAO, 2003) found the average time in a child welfare job is 2 years. This concurs with the findings of more recent research. In a study in Sweden of factors affecting decisions to leave child welfare, 54% of workers had been with their agency for 2 or fewer years (Tham, 2007). Significantly, 48% were planning to leave their jobs. Those intending to resign cited the demands of child welfare work, role conflicts, and concern about the potential for violence. Welfare workers who intended to remain in their jobs cited the positives in their work, had greater clarity in their roles, and had the ability to make independent decisions. The climate of the organization had a great impact on workers' job satisfaction. Those workers who felt management was concerned for them and their health and felt rewarded for doing their jobs well were more likely to want to continue in their jobs (Tham, 2007).

Staff turnover poses risks for maltreated children and their families if there is continual disruption in the continuity of care and services (Mor Barak, Levin, Nissly, & Lane, 2006). There is simply no substitute for the caseworker who can provide ongoing support and continuity for families where maltreatment has occurred. The absence from continuous service of a single worker can cause delays in receiving services and uncalled for changes in requirements for a family. Importantly, retention of child welfare workers can be correlated with foster care placement stability for children (Perry & Murphy, 2008).

Education and Training

Education provides a broad knowledge basis for handling the responsibilities of child welfare positions. However, there can be a huge disconnect between education, training, and the realities of the job. This is a significant reason why social work and human service undergraduate and graduate programs require field placements. There is no substitute for real-life experience in child welfare and other areas of human services practice.

Over time, there has been a gradual increase in the need for academic credentials as well as child welfare certifications and licenses. Typically, these requirements are determined by each state. Today, most child welfare workers have at least a bachelor's degree, and some have a master's degree (GAO, 2003). Child welfare workers typically earn a bachelor's degree in social work (BSW), human services, psychology, or sociology. A bachelor's degree should be considered the minimum educational level for child welfare practice. Some child welfare workers have a Master of Social Work (MSW) degree or a Master of Science in Human Services (MSHS) degree. Some social work and human services programs offer specific training and courses in child welfare that can lead to an advanced certificate in child welfare work. In the field of social work, students can earn a Doctor of Social Work (DSW) degree that focuses on clinical practice or a Doctor of Philosophy (PhD) degree in social work that concentrates on social work research.

One national study of child welfare workers found that those with any graduate degree had more job satisfaction than those without (Barth, Lloyd, Christ, Chapman, & Dickinson, 2008). Research has also shown that a BSW and/or MSW can be associated with better job performance and lower staff turnover (GAO, 2003).

It is very important for academic programs to teach the knowledge and skills that can improve child welfare practice. Indeed, it is the hallmark of an excellent undergraduate or graduate program when graduates find that they use their newly acquired knowledge and skills in the workplace. Education and training of workers tend to focus on providing strengths-based practices to support families, yet these practices may not be utilized within the child welfare agencies (adapted from Smith & Donovan, 2003). Academic programs focus more on recent relevant research findings on child welfare; however, new and innovative approaches can take years to find their way into child welfare practice.

Continuing education and training typically take place through workshops and course offerings within child welfare agencies themselves or other local agencies. The need for continuing education has been recognized for many years (Vinokur-Kaplan, 1987). Today, to maintain a license as a social worker, many states require a specific number of continuing education units ("ceus"). For example, in Massachusetts there are four levels of social work licensure. The highest level, the Licensed Independent Clinical Social Worker, requires 30 ceus over a 2-year period. Ongoing child welfare training and workforce development should focus on a wide variety of topics. See Box 10.3 for critical topics to be covered.

Supervision

Lack of excellent supervision within human service organizations is a chronic problem. However, few things in an organization are as important as quality clinical supervision. Supervisors impact how well policies are followed within an agency, set expectations for workers, and strongly influence staff turnover (Children's Services Practice Notes, 2008). It is imperative that supervisors in child welfare organizations hold a master's degree in social work, human services, or psychology. It is also imperative that they have experience in the field of child protection services before becoming supervisors.

The purposes of supervision are to deliver high-quality services to children and families, to support the work of the child welfare agency, to ensure the professional development of caseworkers, and to contribute to a positive culture within the

BOX 10.3 Workforce Development in Child Welfare Agencies

Workfare development with child welfare organizations must offer orientations, and educational and training programs to address the following for child welfare workers:

1. Children's rights
2. Child, youth, and adult development
3. Family rights and responsibilities
4. Cultural competency and cultural humility
5. Effects of trauma on children, youth, and families
6. Child welfare laws and regulations
7. Agency policies and procedures
8. Community partnerships
9. Agency communication and collaboration
10. Appropriate professional boundaries, including prevention of sexual exploitation
11. Stress management and self-care
12. Effects of secondary traumatic stress

Source: Child Welfare League of America (2013).

agency (Landsman & D'Aunno, 2012). More specifically, supervision must support a competent work environment, guide practice in the services offered, facilitate the acquisition of new knowledge and practices by caseworkers, respond to the needs of staff, and evaluate the quality of services and the staff that provides them (Center for Advanced Studies in Child Welfare, 2009; Landsman & D'Aunno, 2012). Supervision can be individual, with one supervisor and one worker, or it can be provided in a group. When clinical supervision is poor or nonexistent, workers can and should meet together to discuss cases in a peer supervision process.

There is ample evidence for the importance of quality supervision. A national study found that the quality of supervision of child welfare workers was the strongest predictor of job satisfaction (Barth et al., 2008). In a meta-analysis that examined the findings of 27 research studies, the importance of supervision was reaffirmed (Mor Barak, Travis, Pyun, & Xie, 2009). A positive supervisory relationship promotes job satisfaction and job retention (Hess et al., 2009). Strong supervisors who reflect their own knowledge and skill level offer valuable guidance to workers. Strong supervisors also provide social and emotional support to child welfare workers in their difficult jobs.

Every caseworker should have an experienced and knowledgeable supervisor (Child Welfare League of America, 2013). A strong relationship between worker and supervisor can cultivate and support feelings of empowerment, and bolster self-confidence in child welfare workers (Wallach & Mueller, 2006; Mor Barak et al., 2009). Strong supervision can help workers expand their own knowledge and encourage the development of new helping strategies for children and families (Wallach & Mueller, 2006). In praise of her supervisor, one child welfare worker said: "My supervisor's boundaries and ethics are so strong that I'm not even aware of what must be obstacles for her. This is powerful because I'm free to focus on my own work and not have additional concerns about her (Hess et al., 2009, p. 16).

Leadership

Few factors are as important as leadership and administrative practices in child welfare organizations. Leaders of child welfare organizations are responsible for establishing and maintaining the organizational climate for success for children and families as well as staff (Meltzer & Paletta, 2014). Academic credentials, a minimum of a master's degree and experience in child welfare settings, are the appropriate qualifications for leaders in child protection services. Politics should have no place in child welfare organizations, although often, leaders are political appointees.

Historically, there has been a lack of strong child welfare leadership in Massachusetts and other states (Meltzer & Paletta, 2014). The reader may recall from the Preface of this book that Massachusetts sought child welfare leadership from an individual who worked for the Massachusetts Registry of Motor Vehicles and had no child welfare experience. Leaders of organizations must have the experience, knowledge, and skills to plan and develop systems that are successful in helping children and families (Child Welfare League of America, 2013).

It is the responsibility of leaders of child welfare organizations to ensure that standards are set for the provision of services and that these standards are met by the agency. In 2013, the National Association of Social Workers (NASW) developed standards to guide practice within child welfare organizations. The NASW Standards serve a number of important purposes and can be utilized as standards by workers in other professions such as human services and psychology. The Standards remind us that no child welfare organization can meet all the needs of children, and that collaborations with children and families, as well as state and community-based organizations, are essential. The Standards define the scope of work for social workers in child welfare, help workers meet the expectations of children and families, and require the support of child welfare leadership. The Standards serve as an important reference guide and checklist to ensure the appropriate quality and quantity of child welfare services are provided. See Box 10.4 for the NASW Standards.

Burnout and Self-Care of Workers

Stress and "burnout" among child welfare workers create huge issues. The term "burnout" has been replaced in recent years with "compassion fatigue," "vicarious trauma," and most recently by "secondary traumatic stress." It is no secret that child welfare is among the most difficult and stressful work within human services (Drake & Yadama, 1996; Lizano & Mor Barak, 2015). Burnout is a response over time to the difficult work, and is associated with depression, anxiety, and irritability (Jayaratne, Chess, & Kunkel, 1986; Siegfried, 2008). These stress responses are likely to develop when the nature of the work is rooted

---

BOX 10.4 National Association of Social Workers Standards for Social Workers in Child Welfare Practice

Standard 1: Ethics and Values. Social workers in child welfare shall demonstrate a commitment to the values and ethics of the social work profession and shall use NASW's *Code of Ethics* as a guide to ethical decision making while understanding the unique aspects of child welfare practice.

Standard 2: Qualifications, Knowledge, and Practice Requirements. Social workers practicing in child welfare shall hold a BSW or MSW degree from an accredited school of social work. All social workers in child welfare shall demonstrate a working knowledge of current theory and practice in child welfare and general knowledge of state and federal child welfare laws.

Standard 3: Professional Development. Social workers in child welfare shall continuously build their knowledge and skills to provide the most current, beneficial, and culturally appropriate services to children, youth, and families involved in child welfare.

Standard 4: Advocacy. Social workers in child welfare shall seek to advocate for resources and system reforms that will improve services for children, youth, and families.

Standard 5: Collaboration. Social workers in child welfare shall promote interdisciplinary and interorganizational collaboration to support, enhance, and deliver effective services to children, youth, and families.

Standard 6: Record Keeping and Confidentiality of Client Information. Social workers in child welfare shall maintain the appropriate safeguards for the privacy and confidentiality of client information.

(continued)

BOX 10.4 *National Association of Social Workers Standards for Social Workers in Child Welfare Practice (continued)*

Standard 7: Cultural Competence. Social workers shall ensure that families are provided services within the context of cultural understanding and competence.

Standard 8: Assessment. Social workers in child welfare shall conduct an initial, comprehensive assessment of the child, youth, and family system in an effort to gather important information. The social worker shall also conduct ongoing assessments to develop and amend plans for child welfare services.

Standard 9: Intervention. Social workers in child welfare shall strive to ensure the safety and well-being of children through evidence-based practices.

Standard 10: Family Engagement. Social workers in child welfare shall engage families, immediate or extended, as partners in the process of assessment, intervention, and reunification efforts.

Standard 11: Youth Engagement. Social workers in child welfare shall actively engage older youth in addressing their needs while in out-of-home care and as they prepare to transition out of foster care.

Standard 12: Permanency Planning. Social workers in child welfare shall place children and youth in out-of-home care when children and youth are unable to safely remain in their homes. Social workers shall focus permanency planning efforts on returning children home as soon as possible or placing them with another permanent family.

Standard 13: Supervision. Social workers who act as supervisors in child welfare shall encourage the development and maintenance of a positive work environment that facilitates the advancement of social workers' skills, creates a safe and positive work environment, provides quality supervision to social workers, and ensures quality service delivery to clients.

Standard 14: Administration. Social workers who act as administrators shall promote an organizational culture that supports reasonable caseloads and workloads, adequate supervision, appropriate use of emerging technologies, and legal protection for employees' actions in the course of carrying out their professional responsibilities.

Source: National Association of Social Workers (2013). Copyrighted material reprinted with permission from the National Association of Social Workers, Inc.

in traumatic experiences for clients with the added burden of feeling a lack of support from agency supervisors and administrators.

It is certainly understandable that workers can be stressed by the nature of the work itself. Sources of the most extreme stress can be the death of a child or parent in the workers' caseload, chronic exposure to the accounts of child mal-treatment from the children and others, examining photographs of horrendous injury to children, and offering support to family members when a child has died (Siegfried, 2008). Work with children who have been sexually abused can be especially challenging and emotionally difficult for child protection workers.

The work of child welfare can also impact the personal lives of workers. Stress in workers can increase physical illness, cynicism about the work they do and their future accomplishments, and also create a sense of disconnection from others in the agency as well as in their personal lives (Siegfried, 2008). Child welfare workers can report lower marital satisfaction. In a study of 75 women working in child welfare and their husbands, there was a reciprocal relationship—stress at work increased marital stress, and conflictual marital relationships had a negative impact on job performance (Jayaratne et al., 1986).

Child welfare employers must share the responsibility for encouraging staff self-care (Child Welfare League of America, 2013). Self-care also extends to su-pervisors and administrators (Hess et al., 2009). This includes positive working conditions and a commitment to fair treatment for all.

RECOMMENDATIONS AND PROMISING PRACTICES

In general, poor child welfare management and administration can and should be improved, especially in light of the demanding work of child welfare (Tham, 2007). To improve child welfare clinical supervision, agencies should more clearly define job responsibilities and involvement of supervisors in improv-ing workflow (National Child Welfare Resource Center for Organizational Improvement, 2007). Training must be provided for supervisors, who must be active participants in training of caseworkers. It is imperative that continuing professional development be a priority for both new and experienced supervi-sors (Hess et al., 2009). In addition, supervisors need to have regular contacts with other supervisors in the agency and in other programs (National Child Welfare Resource Center for Organizational Improvement, 2007). One caseworker shared the following reflection:

> At the weekly staff meeting, supervisors are able to share issues and problems in cases and brainstorm. They can then report back to case-workers with ideas or solutions. This process helps them become better supervisors and collaborate more with each other. (Hess et al., 2009, p. 37)

Feedback and reflection should be ongoing reciprocal processes in the field of child welfare. This means that workers should continually question their ways of thinking about cases as well as the decisions they make. No one is immune from bias, especially in the complex world of child welfare. In a study of child welfare workers' perceptions of cultural awareness and racial biases toward African Americans in one county in California, the majority of workers rated themselves high in cultural competency and low in racial biases, yet many biases were present (Thompson, 2015). This study serves as an important reminder that a process of self-reflection and evaluation is critical for child welfare workers (National Conference of State Legislators, 2006). Although supervisors and administrators are charged with evaluating the quality of the work, child welfare workers must engage in a continuous process of self-examination to learn from their mistakes.

Child welfare managers and administrators can improve the work climate by taking a greater interest in reducing conflicts between the work and family responsibilities of caseworkers (Lizano & Mor Barak, 2015). It can be very useful to examine options outside of the traditional workweek such as flexible hours, compressing the same number of hours into fewer days, and working from home.

Child welfare agencies must seek new strategies to emotionally support their workers. Agencies have a duty to develop individual and group supports for prevention as well as coping with traumatic stress (Siegfried, 2008). They should also provide the services of an employee assistance program where workers can receive confidential and supportive counseling, if needed (Siegfried, 2008). An important component of counseling can be learning specific relaxation techniques (Dane, 2000).

Agencies, outside evaluators, administrators, supervisors, and child welfare workers need to engage in an ongoing process to determine whether redesign or restructuring of the workplace is necessary to better meet the needs of clients and staff (Cohen, 1992).

Improved child welfare outcomes depend largely on the attention given to the needs of child welfare professionals. Agencies must hire and work to retain qualified child welfare workers (Pace, 2015). Policies and practices must build a healthy work climate by providing quality supervision and professional development opportunities to all staff. Evidence-based research findings must be utilized in work with children and their families as well as in strategies for good hiring and retention practices (Pace, 2015). Child welfare practice must focus more closely on whether desired client outcomes are actually achieved rather than simply whether services were provided (Lohrbach et al., 2005). One child welfare worker offered the following advice to new workers: "I would tell them to approach work from a strengths perspective, and to become an advocate for social justice, to practice self-care, and to keep their practice based on research" (Whitaker et al., 2004, p. 19). Simple to say, hard to do.

SUMMARY AND CONCLUSION

The role of the child welfare worker is extremely difficult. High caseloads, low salaries, and frequent staff turnover are all challenges. Job satisfaction is associated with workers seeing the success of their clients, having strong supervision, and feeling that agency staff and administrators are concerned for their well-being. Clinical supervision of staff is essential within all human service organizations, but especially within child welfare organizations, where the stakes are so high.

Child welfare organizations must hire staff that hold at least a bachelor's degree, and supervisors should have child welfare experience plus a master's degree to be hired. In addition, child welfare organizations can and should do much more to ensure the well-being of their staff. This includes more staff-training opportunities and more appreciation and attentiveness when caseworkers themselves have problems. Finally, child welfare workers deserve greater recognition for the important work they do.

DISCUSSION QUESTIONS

1. Discuss the challenges associated with being a child welfare worker.

2. What personal and professional characteristics should child welfare workers possess?

3. What can be done to reduce the high caseloads of child welfare workers?

4. Discuss the role of ethics in the provision of child welfare services.

5. Why is quality supervision important in child welfare services?

6. Describe the role of leadership in child welfare organizations.

7. Discuss the importance of the NASW Standards for child welfare practice.

8. What kinds of activities can support self-care for child welfare caseworkers, supervisors, and administrators?

9. What should be done to reduce staff turnover within child welfare organizations?

10. What are you own ideas for improving working conditions for child welfare workers?

REFERENCES

Alperin, D. E. (1998). Factors related to student satisfaction with child welfare field placements. *Journal of Social Work Education, 34*(1), 43–54.

Barth, R. P., Lloyd, E. C., Christ, S. L., Chapman, M. V., & Dickinson, N. S. (2008). Child welfare worker characteristics and job satisfaction: A national study. *Social Work, 53*(3), 199–209.

Brenner, E., Kindler, D., & Freundlich, M. (2010). Dual relationships in child welfare practice: A framework for ethical decision making. *Children and Youth Services Review, 32*, 1437–1445.

Center for Advanced Studies in Child Welfare. (2009, Winter). *Practice Notes. Supervision: The key to strengthening practice in child welfare* (Issues No. 22). Retrieved from http:// cascw.umn.edu/wp-content/uploads/2014/01/Practice-Notes-22.pdf

Child Welfare Information Gateway. (2010). *Caseload and workload management.* Washington, DC: U.S. Department of Health and Human Services, Children's Bureau.

Child Welfare League of America. (2013). *National Blueprint for Excellence in Child Welfare. Executive Summary: Raising the bar for children, families and communities.* Washington, DC: Author. Retrieved from www.cwla.org/wp-content/uploads/2013/12/Blue printExecutiveSummary1.pdf

Child Welfare League of America. (2014, May 22). *Quality improvement report.* Retrieved from www.cwla.org/wp-content/uploads/2014/02/MA-EOHHS-cwla-final -report.pdf

Children's Services Practice Notes. (2008, March). Supervisors and the future of child welfare. *Children's Services Practice Notes, 13*(2). Retrieved from www.practicenotes .org/v13n2.htm

Cohen, B. J. (1992). Quality of working life in a public child welfare agency. *Journal of Health and Human Resources Administration, 15*(2), 129–152.

Crimesider Staff. (2015, August 21). Vermont woman accused of killing social worker, charged in 3 more murders. *Crimesider.* Retrieved from www.cbsnews.com/news/ vermont-woman-accused-of-killing-social-worker-charged-with-3-more-murders

Dane, B. (2000). Child welfare workers: An innovative approach for interacting with secondary trauma. *Journal of Social Work Education, 36*(1), 27–38.

De Varon, R. J., Costello, T., & Edwards, M. T. (2008). The study of workload in child protective services. *Protecting Children, 23*(3), 3–19.

Drake, B., & Yadama, G. N. (1996). A structural equation model of burnout and job exit among child protection services workers. *Social Work Research, 20*(3), 179–187.

Edwards, M. T., & De Varon, R. J. (2008). Work, case, and time: Setting standards for workload management. *Protecting Children, 23*(3), 74–88.

FoxNews.com. (2015, July 2). *Kentucky social worker fears for job after helping child no longer assigned to her*. Retrieved from www.foxnews.com/us/2015/07/02/kentucky-social -worker-fears-for-job-after-helping-child-no-longer-assigned-to.html

Goodman, D., & Hurwitz, H. (2008). The Canadian experience in conceptualizing and evaluating child welfare workload: A moving target. *Protecting Children, 23*(3), 28–42.

Hess, P., Kanak, S., & Atkins, J. (2009). *Building a model and framework for child welfare supervision*. National Resource Center for Family-Centered Practice and Permanency Planning. Retrieved from http://www.hunter.cuny.edu/socwork/nrcfcpp/ downloads/Final%20Building%20a%20Framework%20and%20Model%20for%20 CW%20Supervision%20Report%20042309.pdf

Jayaratne, S., Chess, W. A., & Kunkel, D. A. (1986). Burnout: Its impact on child welfare workers and their spouses. *Social Work, 31*(1), 53–59.

Landsman, M. J., & D'Aunno, L. D. (2012). Developing a framework for child welfare supervision. *Journal of Family Strengths, 12*(1). Retrieved from http://digitalcom mons.library.tmc.edu/jfs/vol12/iss1/10

Ledbetter, S. (2015, August 12). *Hundreds mourn death of Lara Sobel*. WPTZ.com. Retrieved from www.wptz.com/news/hundreds-mourn-death-of-lara-sobel/34660188

Lizano, E. L., & Mor Barak, M. (2015). Job burnout and affective well-being: A longitudinal study of burnout and job satisfaction among public child welfare workers. *Children and Youth Services Review, 55*, 18–28.

Lohrbach, S., Sawyer, R., Saugen, J., Astolfi, C., Schmitt, K., Worden, P., & Xaaji, M. (2005). Ways of working in child welfare: A perspective on practice. *Protecting Children, 20*(2 & 3), 93–99.

Maluccio, A. N., Pine, B. A., & Tracy, E. M. (2002). *Social work practice with families and children*. New York, NY: Columbia University Press.

Meltzer, J., & Paletta, R. (2014, September). *From crisis to opportunity: Child welfare reform in Massachusetts*. Boston, MA: The Center for the Study of Social Policy for the Boston Foundation and Strategic Grant Partners.

Mor Barak, M. E., Levin, A., Nissly, J., & Lane, C. J. (2006). Why do they leave? Modeling child welfare workers' turnover intentions. *Children and Youth Services Review, 28*(5), 548–577.

Mor Barak, M. E., Travis, D. J., Pyun, H., & Xie, B. (2009). The impact of supervision on worker outcomes: A meta-analysis. *Social Service Review, 83*(1), 3–32.

National Association of Social Workers. (2013). *NASW standards for social workers in child welfare practice*. Washington, DC: Author.

National Child Welfare Resource Center for Organizational Improvement. (2007, Fall). Strengthening child welfare supervision. *Child Welfare Matters*. Retrieved from http://muskie.usm.maine.edu/helpkids/rcpdfs/cwmatters6.pdf

National Conference of State Legislators. (2006, September). *Child welfare caseworker visits with children and parents*. Retrieved from www.ncsl.org/print/cyf/caseworkervisits.pdf

Pace, P. R. (2015, April). Workforce plays important role in child welfare, experts say. *NASW News, 60*(4), p. 4.

Perry, R., & Murphy, S. J. (2008). A critical appraisal of what child welfare workers do: Findings from a task analysis study in Florida. *Protecting Children, 23*(3), 44–73.

Rathke, L., & Gram, D. (2015, August 9). Suspect in social worker's death linked to 3 relatives' slayings. *The Boston Globe,* p. B4.

Siegfried, C. B. (2008, March). *Child welfare work and secondary traumatic stress* (Child Welfare Training Toolkit: Secondary Traumatic Stress). Retrieved from http://www .nctsnet.org/nctsn_assets/pdfs/CWT3_SHO_STS.pdf

Smith, B. D., & Donovan, S. E. F. (2003). Child welfare practice in organizational and institutional context. *Social Service Review, 77*(4), 541–563.

Tham, P. (2007). Why are they leaving? Factors affecting intention to leave among social workers in child welfare. *British Journal of Social Work, 37*, 1225–1246.

Thompson, R. C. (2015). *Understanding disproportionality: Exploring cultural competency and racial bias among child welfare workers in San Joaquin County.* Retrieved from https://scholarworks.csustan.edu/bitstream/handle/011235813/912/ThompsonRC .spring2015.pdf?sequence=1

U.S. General Accounting Office. (2003) *Child welfare: HHS could play a greater role in helping child welfare agencies recruit, and retain staff.* Washington, DC: Author.

U.S. News and World Report. (2016). Careers. Retrieved from http://money.usnews.com/ careers/best-jobs/child-and-family-social-worker/salary

Vandervort, F. E., Gonzalez, R. P., & Faller, K. C. (2008). Legal ethics and high child welfare turnover: An unexplored connection. *Children and Youth Services Review, 30*, 546–563.

Vinokur-Kaplan, D. (1987). A national survey of in-service training experiences of child welfare supervisors and workers. *Social Service Review, 61*(2), 291–304.

Wagner, D., Johnson, K., & Healy, T. (2008). Agency workforce estimation: A step toward more effective workload management. *Protecting Children, 23*(3), 6–19.

Wallach, V. A., & Mueller, C. W. (2006). Job characteristics and organizational predictors of psychological empowerment among paraprofessionals within human service organization. *Administration in Social Work, 30*(1), 95–115. doi:10.1300/J147v30n01_06

Weaver, D., Chang, J., Clark, S., & Rhee, S. (2007). Keeping public child welfare workers on the job. *Administration in Social Work, 31*(2), 5–25. doi:10.1300/J147v31n02_02

Whitaker, T., Reich, S., Reid, L. V. B., Williams, M., & Woodside, C. (2004, June). *"If you're right for the job, it's the best job in the world."* Washington, DC: National Association of Social Workers.

Yetter, D. (2015, June 29). Social worker helps girl, faces firing. *USA Today.* Retrieved from www .usatoday.com/story/news/nation/2015/06/29/29social-worker-helps-girl -faces-firing/29488235

INNOVATIONS IN THE CHILD WELFARE SYSTEM

*T*here are many innovative practices and approaches to reduce child maltreatment and much that can be learned from examining them. However, developing and maintaining innovative practices in child welfare "can be a challenging process" (Rauktis, McCarthy, Krackhardt, & Cahalane, 2010, p. 732). Chapter 11 reviews the most recent literature regarding innovative and effective child welfare interventions that promote healthy families and children. The chapter examines new thinking about child welfare interventions including assessing the risk and protective factors in families. If families and communities can learn to build on protective factors, the risk of child abuse and neglect can be reduced. This chapter showcases examples of programs that successfully meet the needs of children and their families.

In recent years, family engagement has garnered much attention in protective service planning for children. The values underlying these innovative approaches are centered on client and family participation in planning that feature cooperation and collaboration within a mutually trusting relationship between the worker and the family. Indeed, family engagement has taken on such importance that it underlies many contemporary child welfare strategies.

Today, most child welfare practices address risk and protective factors within families. The risk factors for child maltreatment have been discussed throughout this book, and refer to challenges such as poverty, intimate partner violence, substance abuse, child behavioral problems, and mental illness (Barth, 2009;

Child Welfare Information Gateway, 2014). In the words of Martin and Citrin (2014), ". . . poverty is still the greatest threat to child well-being and the best predictor of abuse and neglect" (p. 1).

Current approaches in child protection focus on the strengths and protective factors within a family that offset risks and support the healthy development of children. In the past, child welfare prevention and intervention activities focused almost exclusively on reducing and eliminating risk factors (Child Welfare Information Gateway, 2014). The most recent attention to programs that support family engagement de-emphasize the negative and emphasize the things that are going well in the family. Included among protective factors in families are problem-solving skills, involvement in positive activities, supportive school environments, strong social connections, and having economic opportunities (Child Welfare Information Gateway, 2014).

An important effort to review research findings on the effectiveness of child welfare interventions was completed in the United Kingdom (MacMillan et al., 2009). Programs offering nurse–family partnerships were successful and reduced injuries and overall child abuse and neglect as determined by official reports of child maltreatment. It was found that outcomes could be better for children in foster care than for those who remain at home or return home after foster care placement. Also, enhanced services for foster children with mental health disorders can have better outcomes than traditional foster care (MacMillan et al., 2009). Home visitation programs were found to be ineffective in the reduction of abuse and neglect. There was also no evidence that efforts to prevent exposure to violence against mothers in the home were successful in reducing abuse and neglect.

Parent-training programs, known in the United Kingdom as the Positive Parenting Programme, showed effectiveness in cases where there was substantiated child maltreatment (MacMillan et al., 2009). Parent training will be discussed in Chapter 12 as important child maltreatment prevention programs that can assist struggling parents.

FAMILY ENGAGEMENT PROGRAMS

Many innovative programs emphasize a strong working relationship between the family and child welfare professionals, which is a departure from earlier practices where child welfare workers made decisions for children without family input. One model is the Family Group Decision Making Program in child welfare that places the family at the center of decisions. A trained independent professional coordinates a meeting between the family and the child welfare agency to develop a case plan (Kempe Center for the Prevention and

Treatment of Child Abuse and Neglect, 2013). Over time, the child welfare workers come to accept families as partners in making decisions. Family members have the freedom to meet on their own without the presence of child welfare workers. When safety is ensured, preference is given to the family's plan over the child welfare agency's plan. The group process is not limited to devising a case plan, but also includes ongoing resource support and follow-up (Kempe Center, 2013).

The Family Group Decision Making Program in Pennsylvania is an example of a major change in focus in service provision. The approach transformed from child welfare professionals determining the needs of client families to a model where families themselves determine their own needs and then develop and implement solutions. See Box 11.1 for a discussion of the Family Group Decision Making Program in Pennsylvania.

BOX 11.1 Implementation of the Family Group Decision Making Program in Pennsylvania

The Family Group Decision Making Program began in Pennsylvania in 2002 in a system with county provision of child welfare services under the oversight of the state. The University of Pittsburgh monitored the implementation process. The family and agency conferences are based on considerable preparation; a discussion of family strengths, resources, and concerns; and the opportunity for private family consultation. The family-devised plan is then accepted and monitored by the child welfare agency (Pennsylvania Child Welfare Resource Center, n.d.).

In a study of responses from child welfare workers, supervisors, and private providers, there were some negative worker attitudes toward giving the family the power to make decisions as well as concerns about insufficient time, funding, and staff (Rauktis et al., 2010). The program required significant training and support of staff. Strong leadership was needed to overcome initial resistance to change.

Generally, there is a major shift in orientation from the power of the child welfare workers to the increased power of the family. This can be uncomfortable for child welfare workers who maintain responsibility for case outcomes yet have to cede control of the plan.

Sources: Pennsylvania Child Welfare Resource Center (n.d.); Rauktis, McCarthy, Krackhardt, and Cahalane (2010).

The Signs of Safety Program in Minnesota is another innovative illustration of family engagement and the benefits of improved professional collaboration with the family to identify ways to improve the safety of children. The Signs of Safety Program shows evidence of reducing the number of placements outside of the home. It also reduces the number of children who experience family reunification with a successive placement, and results in fewer situations of having to reopen previously closed cases. See Box 11.2 for a description of the Signs of Safety Program.

BOX 11.2 The Signs of Safety Program

The Signs of Safety Program is an example of a strengths-based program focused on child welfare safety issues for working with children and their families. It was developed in Western Australia in the 1990s by Andrew Turnell and Steve Edwards. One major question is addressed: "How can the worker build partnerships with parents and children in situations of suspected or substantiated child abuse and still deal rigorously with the maltreatment issues?" (Signs of Safety, 2015, p. 1). The process begins with a simple assessment and moves on to a deep collaboration among the child welfare professionals, the parents, and the child. The model prioritizes safety of the child and balances safety with family strengths.

The Signs of Safety Program was introduced into several counties in Minnesota. Among the positive changes were the increase in family participation in the child welfare process and a stronger feeling of working with parents and the family rather than working on their behalf. Greater respect for families and greater transparency on the part of the child welfare professionals was noted as well. The process encouraged families to develop their own support network through extended family and friends. Child welfare professionals felt the use of the Signs of Safety Program created the opportunity for greater efficiency and better organization of services with a stronger emphasis on the development of standardized practices. This in turn created better opportunities for evidence-based evaluation practices. Positive outcomes included clearer expectations of family members and realizing that they are better able to take on more responsibility. Child welfare professionals found that family problems were more likely to be resolved quickly, that children were safer as a result of the program, and that fewer children were in need of having to leave their home

(continued)

BOX 11.2 *The Signs of Safety Program (continued)*

for foster care placements. Also, fewer cases were reopened that had been closed for 6 or more months.

Some problems with the Signs of Safety Program were that workers could be too lenient with families. Another concern was that the program might work better in families with young children and less well with teenagers who have behavioral problems. There was also some concern about the possibility of maintaining children in dangerous environments by the overutilization of safety networks. Finally, there was concern for a lack of effectiveness in cases of chronic child neglect.

The program has been used in the United States, Australia, and in European countries with positive outcomes. Rather than a fixed-in-time intervention, an important strength of Signs of Safety is that it will continue to be fine-tuned and evolve over time.

Sources: Rothe, Nelson-Dusek, and Skrypek (2013); Signs of Safety (2015).

THE CHILD AND FAMILY SERVICES IMPROVEMENTS AND INNOVATIONS ACT

The 2011 Child and Family Services Improvements and Innovations Act opened up opportunities to use federal funds (Title IV-E) in new ways, especially by giving attention to the well-being of children in foster care placement (Cabrera, 2014; Stoltzfus, 2011). It worked to increase safety by requiring child welfare workers to visit foster children on a monthly basis, at a minimum. It allowed some states to conduct demonstration projects to determine whether alternative approaches were sufficiently innovative and effective to be expanded. The Act also required states to provide trauma services to children in foster care, and required guidelines and monitoring for the use of psychotropic medications in children (Committee on Ways and Means, 2011). It also provided funding to improve how court systems handle child welfare cases (Stoltzfus, 2011).

Nebraska used these federal funds to develop an "alternative response" program that rates families on a continuum of risk for maltreatment. Nebraska began its "alternative response" program in 2015 as one of 23 states (Stoddard, 2015). Families at low risk can receive intensive services within the home to try to avoid foster home placement. The adversarial, investigative approach to child welfare was replaced by a family engagement approach in which families determine their own needs and child welfare workers provide assistance in connecting families with needed resources. Initially, there was skepticism in Nebraska child welfare circles because a 2009 effort to privatize child welfare services failed when four of the five private contractors chose to end their contracts or had them terminated (Snell, 2013).

To qualify for the "alternative response" approach in Nebraska, families are screened for the risk of abuse and neglect and overall child safety. However, only about 25% of families are eligible to participate in the program, and families could be disqualified because of ongoing family violence, sexual assault, or use of illegal drugs (Stoddard, 2015). The fact that only one quarter of families can qualify for the program can be referred to as "creaming," where only those likely to be very successful are accepted into programs.

THE ROLE OF TECHNOLOGY IN CHILD WELFARE INTERVENTIONS

New technology has been developed to help child welfare organizations pinpoint cases where children are most likely to suffer extreme abuse (Levenson, 2015). These computer models, known as "predictive analytics," have been used in business and sports to forecast likely outcomes, including what kind of pitch a professional pitcher will throw next. The idea is to better determine which children are at highest risk for severe abuse and/or neglect and even death. Risk factors for safety concerns include whether a parent or other adults in the home have a criminal history including incarceration, have been in a rehabilitation program for alcohol and/or drugs, have received mental health treatment, or were themselves clients within a child welfare system when they were young (Levenson, 2015).

One computer program, known as Rapid Safety Feedback, began in January 2013 in Hillsborough County, Florida (Levenson, 2015). Two years before the implementation of the program, nine children were murdered, and this provided a powerful incentive to search for innovative interventions. In Hillsborough County, the computer parameters were determined by a review of 1,500 child abuse cases. It found that deaths were more likely to occur under the following circumstances: when the child was very young, when a mother's boyfriend was in the home, drug use or family violence was present, or there was a parent who had been a foster child. Since the program's inception, no children in the child welfare system have died of abuse, a very strong endorsement of the program (Levenson, 2015).

Computer programs do allow for flexibility to meet the needs of specific child welfare organizations. These programs are now in use in Maine, Connecticut, and Pennsylvania, and in 2015 were being considered by the Massachusetts

Department of Children and Families (Levenson, 2015). In Pennsylvania, the system is designed to give a "risk score" to adults in the home as determined by the aforementioned issues, and to ensure that families with individuals with high-risk scores will definitely be "screened in" to receive services.

These predictive analytic child welfare programs are indeed controversial. Those who favor this computerized approach point to the success that has already been achieved in saving lives, whereas those opposed to it point out that these programs focus on the poor, people of color, and those with criminal backgrounds, a critical concern in systems that already target these groups. Another concern is reducing the professional judgment of child welfare workers. The legal director of the American Civil Liberties Union of Pennsylvania commented: "It scares the beejeesus out of me. That should scare anybody. It's like putting a name into a machine and making a determination about whether that person can have their child or not" (Levenson, 2015, p. A9).

LEADERSHIP INNOVATIONS

As discussed in Chapter 10, leadership in the child welfare system is of critical importance and can be problematic, especially when leaders lack the knowledge, training, and experience in child protection. In 2012, the Child Welfare Management Innovations Institute was established as part of an existing partnership between the Indiana Department of Child Services and the Indiana University School of Social Work. Their leadership development program focuses on providing leadership seminars to child welfare professionals, developing mentorship relationships, increasing knowledge and applying it to child welfare practices, and measuring results (Indiana Child Welfare Education and Training Partnership, 2013).

The Annie E. Casey Foundation (2015) has published an excellent guidebook for improving leadership within child welfare organizations: *10 Practices: A Child Welfare Leader's Desk Guide to Building a High-Performance Agency*. See Box 11.3 for the list of 10 recommended practices to assess the strengths of an agency, create an agenda for positive change, and implement agency and service improvements.

PRIVATIZATION OF CHILD WELFARE SERVICES

In recent years, more states have been privatizing all or some of their child welfare services. Kansas privatized almost all of its child welfare services in 1996, although it is one of only a handful of states to do so (Snell, 2013). The

BOX 11.3 10 Practices: A Child Welfare Leader's Desk Guide to Building a High-Performance Agency

A number of systemic and frontline practices can help agencies become outcomes focused, better manage caseload practices, and better respond to families and staff. These 10 practices are clear and explicit and can help resolve the most challenging of child welfare agency problems.

Practice 1: Focus on Child and Family Outcomes. Examine the quality of services provided, monitor outcomes for children, and promote a culture of ongoing quality improvement.

Practice 2: Emphasize Human Resources, Training, and Supervision. Improve planning by recruiting and retaining highly competent staff, ensure that training and supervision are in alignment with the chosen practice model (Practice 5), work with unions, and support high morale among all staff.

Practice 3: Develop a Broad Service Array. Build effective partnerships with community resources that have their own evidence-informed service practices and that provide prevention services, in-home services, foster care and residential placements, and postpermanency services.

Practice 4: Measure and Address Racial and Other Disparities. Acknowledge that the agency can reduce disparities by using best practices for collecting and analyzing quantitative data and reforming agency practices.

Practice 5: Use a Practice Model. A practice model is based on the philosophy and mission that permeates the agency and incorporates proven and innovative approaches.

Practice 6: Develop Competent Front-End Decision Making. Ensure that quality child and family assessments are provided very early on and utilize the least-restrictive services. Child welfare investigators should have no more than 8 to 10 new cases each month. Workers performing both abuse/neglect investigations and handling ongoing cases should have no more than 10 to 12 cases.

Practice 7: Promote Expert Casework. Limit caseloads to 12 to 15 cases where each family receiving services at home is a case and each child placed with a foster family is a case. Support frequent family visits and available services within the context of a strong family case plan.

Practice 8: Make Family Relationships and Permanence the Focus of Casework. Support parents and caregivers and engage them at every point where decisions need to be made. Use evidence-based practices to recruit foster and adoptive families. Ensure that 75% of children have

(continued)

> **BOX 11.3 10 Practices: A Child Welfare Leader's Desk Guide to Building a High-Performance Agency (continued)**
>
> achieved permanence in 2 years and that children do not remain in child welfare custody beyond 3 years.
>
> *Practice 9: Meet Teens' Needs for Family and Other Supports.* Promote alternatives to placement, and especially emphasize prevention efforts for youth with behavior problems. For adolescents in placement, provide trauma-informed services.
>
> *Practice 10: Build a Health Caregiver Network.* Formal and informal kinship foster placements should have preference over other kinds of foster care. Ensure that caregivers are well trained and supported in their critical roles.
>
> _____
> *Source*: Annie E. Casey Foundation (2015).

impetus for privatization has come from a desire to lower costs, improve quality of services, and have a more efficient use of taxpayer money (Freundlich & McCullough, 2012; Loson, 2009). An increase in the number of lawsuits filed against state child welfare organizations can also provide support for privatization (Loson, 2009).

Those who support privatization point to the ability to save money, the ability to use more flexible and innovative approaches, and faster implementation in less bureaucratic environments (Freundlich & McCullough, 2012). Competition among agencies vying for child welfare contracts can lead to lower costs. Opponents of privatization point to lower-quality services resulting from financial incentives for private agencies and that privatization can create opportunities for conflicts of interest and corruption (Freundlich & McCullough, 2012). Additionally, privatization can reduce the accountability of state government. Other problems include pricing and payment issues, inadequate financial oversight, and lack of outcome measurements to determine the effectiveness of privatization (Loson, 2009).

We need a better understanding of the consequences of privatization of child welfare services, especially in Kansas and Florida, which have used privatized services since 1997 and 1998, respectively (Loson, 2009). Florida has seen a reduction in the number of children in foster care, reduced abuse that occurs in foster homes, and has moved children more quickly into permanent living situations (Snell, 2013). Other states in various stages of privatizing services include Kentucky, Nebraska, Oklahoma, and Pennsylvania (Snell, 2013). Overall, it remains unclear whether outcomes for children and their families are better or worse with privatization (Children's Rights, 2014). For those leaders and agencies considering privatization of some or all child welfare services, Children's Rights offers recommendations for the issues that need careful consideration. See Box 11.4.

BOX 11.4 Children's Rights Lessons Learned and Recommendations Regarding Privatization

1. Determine the goals of privatization, the model to be utilized, the groups to be served, the types of organizations that will be considered as the lead agency, and the financial arrangements.
2. Private agencies should expect that the public system will try to save money. In reality, the public child welfare system should not expect to save money because much financial investment is needed in developing and overseeing services.
3. A more efficient child welfare system will not necessarily be the result of privatization.
4. Start with a few rather than many outcome measures and performance targets.
5. Leadership must be committed to develop and continue relationships between private and public agencies.
6. Determine clear role and responsibility expectations of private and public staff.
7. Ensure strong community support through a shared mission and strong management supports.
8. Support approaches where pilot projects are utilized and services can be phased in over time.
9. Determine the number and location of families in need of services.
10. Ensure that information management systems are up-to-date and can include outcome data.
11. Where services are contracted out, ensure that the guidelines and process are very clear from the initial point of seeking bids through to contract finalization.
12. Contracts must be readily understandable and explicitly state all conditions.
13. The state child welfare agency must provide strict oversight and monitor the performance of the private agency.
14. Adequate funding is a prerequisite, and payment rates and schedules must be fair to all parties.

(continued)

> ## BOX 11.4 Children's Rights Lessons Learned and Recommendations Regarding Privatization (continued)
>
> 15. Be very cautious about the use of "at risk contracting," where private agencies become financially responsible for covering costs when financial ceilings have been exceeded.
> 16. When at "risk contracting" is used, protections must be in place to prevent considerable financial losses to the private agency when circumstances are beyond their control.
> 17. Families receiving services need to be involved at all stages of privatization including program design, implementation, and the measurement of outcomes.
>
> *Source:* Children's Rights (2014).

RECOMMENDATIONS AND PROMISING PRACTICES

It is never easy to implement changes within child welfare organizations and there is no one correct way to do so (American Public Human Services Association, 2012). Often, one change can lead to others, and any child welfare model must stay focused on the safety of children within the family. To be innovative in practice, child welfare agencies and the organizations with which they partner must understand their respective jurisdictional and other requirements. It is important to remember that early interventions are important but that children who have languished for many months in foster care must be a priority as well (American Public Human Services Association, 2012).

The Chadwick Center for Children & Families at the Rady Children's Hospital in San Diego, California, opened in 1976 and has a long history of providing innovations in child welfare practice. It offers child advocacy and trauma-informed services within the context of family-centered care using a multidisciplinary approach (Chadwick Center for Children & Families, 2015). The Medical and Forensic Services Program assists children in providing verbal and other kinds of evidence for abuse they endured or witnessed. The Kids and Teens in Court Program helps children and adolescents prepare to provide court testimony in abuse cases. The Trauma Counseling Program offers individual, group, and family therapy to address the full range of issues in the aftermath of trauma.

The Chadwick Trauma-Informed Systems Dissemination Project began receiving federal funding in 2012 to promote the development of trauma-informed child welfare practices throughout the United States. The child welfare workforce must be educated on how trauma affects an individual at any stage of development. This includes developing a system for screening children for a history of trauma and stress responses to trauma. For those with a positive screen, a trauma mental health specialist provides an assessment to determine the reaction of the child and the parents. This program assists workers in developing a trauma-informed case plan to provide an understanding of behaviors connected to the traumatic experience, and helps to guide treatment (Chadwick Center for Children & Families, 2015).

Innovations in child welfare can also improve the provision of physical and behavioral health services. One example is the effort to improve health outcomes for children by developing partnerships among child welfare agencies, health care providers, and the Medicaid program. The Center for Health Care Strategies, Inc. Quality Improvement Collaborative provides speedier health screenings and assessments, family engagement, coordination of health care, and improved monitoring of psychotropic medications for children (Allen, Pires, & Mahadevan, 2012).

A multiagency collaborative and innovative model in Hampton, Virginia, is enjoying great success in helping children and families (Horne, 2015). The model focuses on having committed agency and judicial leaders, ensuring a wide variety of human services available to children and their families, adequate funding, and a focus on intervention outcomes. A distinguishing characteristic is the "one child at a time" approach that places the child's needs above all else. A Family Assessment and Planning Team develops individualized case plans, and a critical feature is that the team continues to monitor the care provided by all agencies involved. The Hampton, Virginia experience has been very successful in reducing the use of residential programs and foster care for children. In 2002, 281 children were in foster care, and since then the number was reduced by 85% to 40 children in 2014. Children receiving services within their own families increased from 330 to 506 between 2002 and 2014 (Horne, 2015). This is convincing evidence of what can be achieved when agency professionals are committed to working together on behalf of a troubled family.

Through the years, federal funding has been available to cultivate university–child welfare agency partnerships to enhance the knowledge and skills of child welfare workers. In 2014, 13 university–agency partnerships were awarded federal funds to bolster child welfare practices through traineeship programs, and to develop the future workforce through the development and offering of specialized curricula focused on child welfare (National Child Welfare Workforce Institute, n.d.). Included here is the development of social work programs that offer stipends for students interested in child welfare that support field placements and specific courses focused on child welfare. This enhances the workforce by ensuring the appropriate preparation of students before they obtain child welfare positions. Some of the partnerships receiving funds were established between child welfare agencies and the University of New Hampshire, Case Western Reserve, Indiana University, University of Minnesota–Duluth, University of North Dakota, and the University of Alaska–Anchorage (National Child Welfare Workforce Institute, n.d.).

The National Child Welfare Workforce Institute offered a number of recommendations from traineeship programs that took place between 2008 and 2013. From the perspective of the social work programs in colleges and universities, the Institute recommended compensation for faculty who provide support for developing trainee programs, and more in-depth child welfare field placements. A best-practices approach was recommended to review and revise curricula including the infusion of child welfare knowledge throughout existing courses as well as the development of specific courses to address the challenges to the workforce. Support from the leadership of the college or university is also crucial (National Child Welfare Workforce Institute, 2013). From the perspective of the child welfare agency, strong supervisors of students must be recruited and trained to provide an excellent field experience for students. The types of child welfare field placements need to be expanded. Overall, university–agency partnerships should be monitored and strengthened over time. Over the 5 years of partnerships, it was concluded:

> The potential for schools of social work to impact future generations of social workers in child welfare is enormous and traineeship programs which continue to emphasize recruitment of diverse students, preparation for leadership, and trauma-informed practice will be successful in assisting child welfare agencies to meet on-going practice challenges. (National Child Welfare Workforce Institute, 2013, p. 16)

Another approach to cultivate innovations in child welfare practice is to have a formal assessment of existing system-wide policies and practices. The importance of independent child welfare professionals reviewing an existing system to recommend changes should not be underestimated. A recent example is the Division of Children, Youth and Families, the child welfare organization in New Hampshire that will undergo a review after the recent death of a toddler (Associated Press, 2016). This evaluation provided by the Center for the Support of Families in Maryland focuses on case reviews regarding child health and safety as well as risk of harm. Of course, the evaluation itself is just the initial step. Improvement requires a serious commitment on the part of child welfare agencies and the political will to actually implement recommendations.

SUMMARY AND CONCLUSION

Innovations in child welfare systems are essential to keep the field moving forward. Although innovations can be complex, they can also be straightforward by cultivating communication and collaboration among child welfare professionals, parents, children, and community service organizations. Today, family engagement practices by child welfare agencies are helping families become strong participants in case planning, an important step in turning an adversarial relationship into a collaborative one. New models of child welfare interventions share the focus on family participation to determine family needs as well as to determine the services families want to receive. The Family Group Decision Making Program and the Signs of Safety Program are examples of innovative approaches to working with families. The Child and Family Services Improvements and Innovation Act of 2011 created federal funding opportunities for the development of innovations in child welfare.

The role of technology in child welfare interventions will continue to grow and find new applications. At this time, there is no definitive determination regarding the overall usefulness of privatization of child welfare services. Strong leadership, agency collaboration, and the development of university–agency partnerships all contribute to the development of innovations in child welfare practice. Rather than finding a definitive model, all approaches must be continually monitored, improved, and updated.

DISCUSSION QUESTIONS

1. Discuss why innovative programs and practices in child welfare are so important.

2. Describe the importance of family engagement practices in innovative child welfare services.

3. Discuss the Signs of Safety Program as a model for the provision of child welfare services.

4. What did the Child and Family Services Improvements and Innovations Act of 2011 accomplish?

5. Discuss the potential role of computer technology in child welfare interventions.

6. Discuss the leadership practices that ensure the child welfare services are up-to-date and innovative.

7. Discuss the positives and negatives regarding the privatization of child welfare services.

8. In your opinion, is lower cost a good reason to privatize child welfare services?

9. What are some of the roles of university–child welfare partnerships in providing child welfare services?

10. What are your own ideas for introducing innovative practices into child welfare?

REFERENCES

Allen, K. D., Pires, S. A., & Mahadevan, R. (2012, February). *Improving outcomes for children in child welfare: A Medicaid managed care toolkit*. Trenton, NJ: Center for Health Care Strategies.

American Public Human Services Association. (2012, October). *Practice innovations in child welfare*. Washington, DC: Author.

Annie E. Casey Foundation. (2015). *10 Practices: A child welfare leader's desk guide to building a high-performance agency*. Baltimore, MD: Author. Retrieved from www.aecf .org/resources/10-practices-part-one

Associated Press. (2016, March 9). *Review approved of New Hampshire's child protection division*. Retrieved from http://www.washingtontimes.com/news/2016/mar/9/review -approved-of-new-hampshires-child-protection

Barth, R. P. (2009). Preventing child abuse and neglect with parent training: Evidence and opportunities. *The Future of Children, 19*(2), 95–118.

Cabrera, M. (2014, May 30). Government innovation in child welfare. *Stanford Social Innovation Review*. Retrieved from www.ssireview.org/blog/entry/ government_innovation_in_child_welfare

Chadwick Center for Children & Families. (2015). *Chadwick Trauma-Informed Systems Dissemination and Implementation Project* (CTISP-DI). Retrieved from http://www .chadwickcenter.org/CTISP/ctisp.htm

Children's Rights. (2014). *Privatization of child welfare services: Challenges and successes, executive summary*. New York, NY: Author. Retrieved from www.childrensrights.org/ wp-content/uploads/2014/09/privatization_of_child_welfare_services_exec_sum.pdf

Child Welfare Information Gateway. (2014, February). *Protective factors approaches in child welfare*. Washington, DC: U.S. Department of Health and Human Services, Children's Bureau.

Committee on Ways and Means, Democratic Staff. (2011, September 9). *The Child and Family Services Improvement and Innovation Act*. Retrieved from https://www.fos terclub.com/files/House_PSSF_Inno11.pdf

Freundlich, M., & McCullough, C. (2012, October). *Privatization of child welfare services: A guide for state advocates*. Washington, DC: State Policy and Advocacy Reform Center.

Horne, T. (2015, January). *A model for collaboration and results: How cross-agency collaboration helped Hampton, VA., build a broad array of child and family services*. Baltimore, MD: Annie E. Casey Foundation.

Indiana Child Welfare Education and Training Partnership. (2013). *Child Welfare Management Innovations Institute*. Retrieved from http://childwelfare.iu.edu/educ-cwmii.html

Kempe Center for the Prevention and Treatment of Child Abuse and Neglect. (2013, May). *Family Group Decision Making in child welfare: Purpose: Values and processes*. Retrieved from www.ucdenver.edu/academies/colleges/medicalschool/departments/

pediatrics/subs/can?FGDMWebPages/AboutFGDM/FGDMPurposeValuesandprocesses
.pdf

Levenson, M. (2015, October 7). Computers may spot abuse risk. *The Boston Globe*, pp. A1, A9.

Loson, K. (2009). Improving privatization: How federal procurement concepts can solve lingering problems in state contracts for child welfare. *Public Contract Law Journal, 38*(4), 955–974.

MacMillan, H. L., Wathen, C. N., Barlow, J., Fergusson, D. M., Leventhal, J. M., & Taussig, H. N. (2009). Interventions to prevent child maltreatment and associated impairment. *The Lancet, 373*(9659), 17–23. doi:10.1016/S0140-6736(08)61708-0

Martin, M., & Citrin, A. (2014). *Prevent, protect, & provide: How child welfare can better support low-income families*. Washington, DC: Center for the Study of Social Policy.

National Child Welfare Workforce Institute. (n.d.). *Traineeships & university–agency partnerships*. Retrieved from http://ncwwi.org/index.php/teams-services/university-partnerships

National Child Welfare Workforce Institute. (2013, September). *Twelve NCWWI traineeship programs: Comprehensive summary of legacies & lessons learned*. Albany, NY: Author.

Pennsylvania Child Welfare Resource Center. (n.d.). *Family group decision making*. Retrieved from www.pacwrc.pitt.edu/FGDM.htm

Rauktis, M. E., McCarthy, S., Krackhardt, D., & Cahalane, H. (2010). Innovation in child welfare: The adoption and implementation of Family Group Decision Making in Pennsylvania. *Children and Youth Services Review, 32*, 732–739.

Rothe, M. I., Nelson-Dusek, S., & Skrypek, M. (2013, January). *Innovation in child protection services in Minnesota: Research chronicle of Carver and Olmstead counties*. St. Paul, MN: Wilder Research.

Signs of Safety. (2015). *The Signs of Safety approach to child protection casework*. Retrieved from www.signsofsafety.net/signs-of-safety

Snell, L. (2013, April 22). *Child welfare privatization update: Subsection of Annual Privatization Report 2013: State Government Privatization*. Retrieved from http://reason.org/news/show/apr-2013-child-welfare-privatizatio

Stoddard, M. (2015, June 15). Nebraska child welfare workers test gentler approach instead of "us versus you." *Live Well Nebraska*. Retrieved from www.livewellnebraska.com/health/nebraska-child-welfare-workers-test-gentler-approach-instead-of-us/article_f9b13a9b-35ef-5e6c-81a4-d0b330db61ca.html

Stoltzfus, E. (2011, October 5). *Child welfare: The Child and Family Services Improvement and Innovation Act (P.L. 112-34)*. Washington, DC: Congressional Research Service.

PREVENTION AND FUTURE ISSUES IN CHILD WELFARE

*I*t is an overwhelming challenge to prepare for the future of child welfare services. Chapter 12 examines child abuse and neglect prevention and the need to strengthen research and intervention efforts. Prevention of child maltreatment is described from the perspective of primary, secondary, and tertiary prevention, with an example given of a parenting program. The chapter concludes with a discussion of moving beyond clichés about the importance of children toward genuine progress. Child welfare policies reflect American culture and must improve to benefit children, families, and child welfare professionals.

The fact that there are no standard definitions for each kind of child maltreatment makes an understanding of each extremely difficult. Definitions of physical abuse, sexual abuse, emotional abuse, and neglect can be established by agencies, counties, states, and at the federal level. Different definitions used by child welfare organizations and by child welfare researchers make difficult work even harder. Standardization of definitions of the kinds of child maltreatment and the collection of data on children and families can vastly improve the quality of research and allow for comparisons among separate research studies. This includes collecting data on the demographics of children and families as well as the circumstances under which they come to the attention of child protection agencies. Efforts to achieve consensus on definitions of the varieties of child maltreatment can be a significant advance in the field.

There are many advantages to using consistent definitions of the forms of child maltreatment. Chief among them is the ability to quantify the prevalence of each and determine specifically how many children and families are affected. This information could be used to determine the allocation of federal and state funding, based on the most significant needs. Beyond obtaining a more accurate estimate of the extent of child maltreatment, research practices can be advanced, as discussed later. See Box 12.1 for definitions of child abuse and neglect as

BOX 12.1 Definitions of Child Abuse and Neglect

The federal Child Abuse Prevention and Treatment Reauthorization Act (CAPTA) of 2010 defined child abuse and neglect this way:

Any recent act or failure to act on the part of a parent or caretaker, which results in death, serious physical or emotional harm, sexual abuse, or exploitation, or an act or failure to act which presents an imminent risk of serious harm. (p. 1)

Physical abuse: Any nonaccidental physical injury to the child that can include striking, kicking, burning, or biting the child, or any action that results in physical impairment of the child. (p. 2)

Sexual abuse: The employment, use, persuasion, inducement, enticement, or coercion of any child to engage in, or assist any other person to engage in, any sexually explicit conduct or simulation of such conduct for the purpose of producing a visual depiction of such conduct. Also, the rape, and in cases of caretaker or interfamilial relationships, statutory rape, molestation, prostitution, or other form of sexual exploitation of children, or incest with children. (p. 2)

Emotional abuse: Injury to the psychological capacity or emotional stability of the child as evidenced by an observable or substantial change in behavior, emotional response, or cognition. This includes injury as evidenced by anxiety, depression, withdrawal, or aggressive behavior. (p. 3)

Neglect: Failure of a parent or other person with responsibility for the child to provide needed food, clothing, shelter, medical care, or supervision to the degree that the child's health, safety, and well-being are threatened with harm. (p. 2)

Source: Child Welfare Information Gateway (2014).

established by the Child Abuse Prevention and Treatment Reauthorization Act (CAPTA) of 2010 and the Children's Bureau of the U.S. Department of Health and Human Services.

PREVENTION

There is often much talk about the need for child abuse and neglect prevention within child welfare realms, but the goal of preventing child maltreatment has yet to be realized (Martin & Citrin, 2014). Child abuse prevention efforts have expanded considerably since the 1980s with much greater public awareness (Child Welfare Information Gateway, 2011). In the 1980s, new programs were developed including child abuse crisis intervention hotlines as well as parent education and support groups. In addition, efforts were made to reduce child sexual abuse by offering both educational programs to help children avoid sexual victimization, including "good touch versus bad touch," and supports to children to report sexual abuse experiences (Child Welfare Information Gateway, 2011). However, these prevention efforts were limited to those families who had knowledge of their existence, and did not reach others in need. In the 1990s, more prevention supports were offered in the form of home visitation and increasingly addressed the needs of pregnant women. These models of providing in-home services supported bonding between parent and child, bolstered the acquisition of parenting skills, led to increased access to health care, and provided an early opportunity to identify whether children were experiencing developmental delays (Child Welfare Information Gateway, 2011).

Prevention within the realm of public health often focuses on definitions and interventions labeled "primary," "secondary," or "tertiary" prevention. *Primary prevention*, also known as "universal prevention," refers to efforts to reach all with the aim of keeping child maltreatment from developing. This includes public service announcements that promote healthy parenting and can include dissemination of knowledge, especially informational brochures. Another strategy within primary prevention is the parent education program model where parents learn the basics of healthy parenting. In the words of Barth (2009), "Improved parenting is the most important goal of child abuse prevention" (p. 96).

Skills-based curricula are designed to help keep children safe by teaching them ways to protect themselves. The Safe Child Program is one model for teaching children to protect themselves from abuse by recognizing inappropriate or dangerous behavior, how to speak up to a potential abuser, and how to get help (Promising Practices Network, 2010). Evaluations of these programs have found them effective in promoting child safety. For example, in one meta-analysis, a review of 27 sexual abuse studies found that children who participated in sexual abuse prevention programs were better able to protect themselves than children who had not participated (Davis & Gidycz, 2000).

Secondary prevention refers to intervening in families that have risk factors for child maltreatment such as poverty, substance abuse, and mental illness. In this context, prevention is defined as intervening at an early stage to prevent problems from escalating. Secondary prevention efforts include referring clients to family service agencies, home visitation programs, or support groups for parents under stress. Parent-education programs can be considered primary prevention, but can also be secondary prevention when there are risk factors or maltreatment that has already developed. Parent-education programs in the U.K. and the United States have shown effectiveness in working with families that are experiencing problems. For example, the Triple P–Positive Parenting Program is a widely used parenting program designed to address parent responses to a child's health and behavioral problems (Barth, 2009; World Health Organization, 2007). See Box 12.2 for a description of the Triple P–Positive Parenting Program.

Tertiary prevention as applied to child abuse refers to situations where abuse and/or neglect have already occurred. It is designed to reduce the negative consequences of abuse as well as to prevent the situation from worsening by offering professional interventions. This kind of prevention can include providing intensive family preservation services, parent-mentoring services, and mental health services for children and/or adults (Child Welfare Information Gateway, n.d.). Many of the child welfare programs described in this book are examples of tertiary prevention.

Recent prevention efforts are less likely to be placed within one of these three categories and are more likely to be seen along a continuum of prevention (Child Welfare Information Gateway, n.d.). Today, prevention considers not only the family but also the community and system-wide supports for prevention within an integrated service model. As described in Chapter 11, today's prevention efforts are more likely to focus on reducing family risk factors and augmenting protective factors in the family (Child Welfare Information Gateway, 2011). Current prevention strategies focus on greater public awareness activities and campaigns through the media, child sexual abuse prevention classes, parent education and support groups, and home visitation by nurses and social workers.

Ongoing challenges in the prevention field are the search for improved ways to reach at-risk families to determine the right balance between formal support services and informal supports of family, friends, and the community. Prevention efforts must also discover ways to use technology such as videoconferencing to access services. Additional strategies should be developed to enhance

BOX 12.2 Triple P–Positive Parenting Program

Based on social learning theory developed in Australia, the Triple P–Positive Parenting Program was founded on the premise that parents who feel confident in their own skills and actions, such as problem solving and decision making, will have a positive impact on their child's behavior. The basic principles regarding positive parenting focus on providing a comfortable learning environment, cultivating strong discipline, having realistic expectations of children, and parental self-care.

The program relies on five levels of intervention: Level 1, *Universal Triple P*, relies on a media campaign to enlist parents in parenting programs; Level 2, *Selected Triple P*, targets specific parental challenges such as getting a child to sleep or how to toilet train; parents can attend a seminar or have a home visit or phone consultation with a professional; Level 3, *Primary Care Triple P*, addresses physical development of children and managing children's difficult behaviors; this is typically provided in four sessions; Level 4, *Standard Triple P*, is for parents coping with severe behavioral issues such as diagnosed conduct disorder; 12 individual or group sessions are typically offered; and Level 5, *Enhanced Triple P*, is for child behavioral problems within a context of other significant family problems.

According to their website, the Triple P–Positive Parenting Program has shown effectiveness as evidenced by "580 published papers, trials, efficacy and dissemination studies conducted throughout the world." Triple P has been implemented successfully in 25 countries across cultures and socioeconomic groups and due to its numerous positive evaluations, is ranked by the United Nations as the top parenting program in the world.

Sources: Barth (2009); Triple P–Positive Parenting (n.d.).

prevention efforts that are respectful of ethnically and culturally diverse groups (Child Welfare Information Gateway, 2011).

A number of organizations take as their primary goal the prevention of child abuse and neglect. An important nationwide resource is the Childhelp National Child Abuse Hotline (1-800-422-4453). The hotline uses professional counselors, rather than volunteers, who provide information on prevention and crisis intervention, and make referrals to local human service organizations. Prevent

Child Abuse America (2016), a national organization, provides a variety of services including sexual abuse prevention, shaken baby syndrome prevention, and peer abuse prevention. Their Healthy Families America program provides home-based services to over 85,000 families each year. Still another approach to prevention emphasizes developing partnerships among the variety of organizations with which children and families come into contact. See Box 12.3 for a description of prevention partnerships in Fresno County, California.

As we have seen, there are various ways to intervene at various points, all as part of the quest to prevent child maltreatment. Regardless of the methods

BOX 12.3 *Prevention Partnerships in Fresno County, California*

Prevention of child maltreatment must include cultivating partnerships among human service agencies, schools, and other public welfare agencies. Fresno County established a system of advocacy to assist families dealing with the child welfare system to make services more accessible. Over time the "community representatives" who were informing families of community resources and providing support through the child protection process transformed into "cultural brokers," with a more formalized approach to advocacy for children and families. Cultural brokers evolved into a community-based organization known as the Cultural Broker Program, which provides a range of services to families.

The cultural brokers are required to complete a training program that explains the child welfare and court systems and provides information on "best practices" within child protective services. Cultural brokers can work with child welfare professionals in their response to reports of abuse or neglect, and to cultivate family engagement. Cultural brokers maintain a relationship with the public welfare department that includes employment and other services to meet the financial needs of families. Partnerships with schools through the program Project ACCESS work to prevent entrée into the child welfare system, if possible. Cultural brokers are recruited from the same communities of color as their clients to ensure that services are provided in culturally respectful ways.

The Fresno County experience is an excellent illustration of the ongoing communication and collaboration by child welfare agencies with community services.

Source: Martin and Citrin (2014).

used, all child abuse and neglect prevention strategies need to be infused with important and explicit principles. See Box 12.4 for a description of best-practice principles for child maltreatment prevention.

Overall, child maltreatment prevention programs are effective and typically less expensive than treatment programs (Rosenzweig, 2015). One cannot overestimate the importance of prevention services and practices. Strong prevention programs can have lifelong positive effects for both children and their families.

RESEARCH ISSUES

The lack of research on child welfare issues has delayed innovations in child welfare policy and practice (McGhee, Mitchell, Daniel, & Taylor, 2015). We lack

---

BOX 12.4 *Practice Principles for Prevention Services*

Best practices are an important consideration in prevention practice and need to be reviewed and updated. The following principles need to be infused within all child abuse prevention efforts:

1. An underlying framework that identifies specific strategies and curricula to determine the anticipated prevention outcomes.
2. Identification of the target population including eligibility criteria and how to engage the population.
3. A method of determining the intensity of services and over how long a period of time prevention services will be provided to the target population.
4. Strategies to train staff and to deliver prevention content in ways that recognize the challenges and cultural considerations of the target population.
5. Strategies for staff training and providing staff supervision on an ongoing basis.
6. Ensuring that all prevention workers have reasonable and manageable caseloads.
7. Adhering to a method of evaluation that includes characteristics of staff and participants and service outcomes. If a specific prevention model is utilized, ensure that the model is delivered as intended.

Source: Child Welfare Information Gateway (2011).

systematic ways of collecting data on the characteristics of abused and neglected children as well as the characteristics of parents and/or the abusers. The gold standard in research is the randomized controlled trial, yet the complexities of child abuse and neglect cannot be easily measured. As described in this book, the intersection of race, class, and culture all affect child maltreatment and add to its complexity. Child welfare policy must be focused on an in-depth understanding of maltreated children, their abusers, the services they receive, and the short- and long-term outcomes of children and families in the child welfare system (Jonson-Reid & Drake, 2008).

Further, the quality of child welfare research needs to improve. New research methodologies must be developed in order to synthesize administrative data with outcome research and to develop longitudinal studies over extended periods of time (McGhee et al., 2015). Self-reports of victimized children have been shown to be reliable and valid, although it is important to remember that victimization occurs for children who are not old enough to self-report (MacMillan et al., 2009). Research also cannot rely solely on self-reports of caregivers who have a vested interest in portraying themselves in a favorable light to avoid stigma and possible legal sanctions (MacMillan et al., 2009).

Greater research attention needs to be directed to the specific services used, and child and family responses to those services. More work is required to determine the impact of the services, especially defining measurements of "well-being" (McGhee et al., 2015). It is critically important that child welfare professionals and researchers work together to establish the study design, the data to be collected, and the parameters used to determine whether programs and services are successful (McGhee et al., 2015).

The Center for the Study of Social Policy recommends that data collection should include gender, age, race, ethnicity, and the Indian Child Welfare Act (ICWA) eligibility (Martin & Connelly, 2015). The Center recommends longitudinal data collection, that is, data collected over a long period of time and data that focuses on key decision points. These decision points should include information on case referral, assessment, placement in foster care, and termination of parental rights. Child protection data also needs to be made publicly available and accessible within the bounds of confidentiality (Martin & Connelly, 2015). Better management of data by practitioners and researchers can lead to more effective child welfare interventions.

The environment for child welfare research has changed over time, and this can be attributed to several issues. Reductions in available funding for social science research have had a negative impact on child maltreatment research (McGhee et al., 2015). As discussed in Chapter 11, technology, both computer hardware and software, has changed rapidly, making it critical to stay current with technological advancements. In the future, computer technology will play a significant role in assessing families for risk of abuse and neglect and will likely help to identify specific services families will receive. Also, the greater emphasis on evidence-based practices has pushed for both greater efficiency of research and greater effectiveness of child welfare services (McGhee et al., 2015).

LOOKING AHEAD

The Center for the Study of Social Policy recommends a child welfare agenda for the future that focuses on both policy and practice considerations (Martin & Citrin, 2014). Services need to be provided within a context that avoids the stigma of abusive and neglectful parenting. Work requirements to comply with the Temporary Assistance for Needy Families (TANF) program should be suspended, and if that is not possible, participation in a family child welfare case plan should count toward meeting TANF requirements. Resources must be included in early intervention services to prevent deeper and more serious involvement with child welfare systems. Families receiving child welfare services should receive priority for subsidized housing.

As discussed throughout this book, partnerships with other human service organizations should simplify the delivery of services provided to avoid receiving services from numerous agencies, each with its own rules (Martin & Citrin, 2014). Partnerships between medical and legal programs can help ensure that families receive necessary health care and cope with problems associated with child protection issues.

Recent efforts have been made to define the critical elements in the medical evaluation of suspected physical abuse of children (Campbell, Olson, & Keenan, 2015). The development of assessment guidelines and protocols significantly improves the quality of medical evaluations, reduces frustration of medical professionals expected to complete evaluations such as emergency room physicians, and reduces the variability in this type of assessment. Adherence to a specific physical abuse assessment protocol can also improve the quality of research by ensuring standardization of evaluation, and reducing any potential bias on the part of medical professionals (Campbell et al., 2015).

The Center for the Study of Social Policy recommends that priority should be given to young children in high-quality early childhood programs that create strong learning environments (Martin & Citrin, 2014). Multigenerational approaches can improve the economic stability of a family. Significantly greater efforts must be made to reduce societal and systemic racial inequities that impact so many families of color within child welfare. Additional cultural issues such as language barriers and illegal immigration status make things that much more difficult (Martin & Citrin, 2014).

The Center for the Study of Social Policy also recommends mapping areas of high poverty and child welfare involvement to concentrate prevention services in these neighborhoods (Martin & Citrin, 2014). This is a highly controversial recommendation because it chooses an exclusive focus on the poor as the target of services.

As with change in the health care field, change does not come easily in child protective services. A new medical treatment shown to be effective in research demonstrations can typically take 17 years to be adopted by medical professionals and health care organizations (Balas & Boren, 2000; Green, Ottoson, Garcia, & Hiatt, 2009). This time frame is totally unacceptable within child welfare services. We must make changes quickly to protect children. The search is constant for what works and what does not.

Massachusetts has been responsive to making changes under the direction of a new governor. In response to child deaths, new policies have been initiated within the Department of Children and Families. These include ending the system of classifying families as high risk or low risk. The New England Center for Investigative Reporting found that 10 children whose families were categorized as low risk had died between 2009 and 2013 (Scharfenberg & Miller, 2016). Clearly, making a distinction between high- and low-risk families was not an effective way to conceptualize families and their service needs. Assessment protocols have been revised to give greater emphasis to substance abuse and family violence, and to require that assessments be updated every 6 months. New policies will address protocols for maintaining children within their own homes including contacts with each child's schoolteacher. Additionally, new policies will determine when and how child welfare cases should be closed (Scharfenberg & Miller, 2016). Clear and cohesive child welfare policies benefit children, their families, and child welfare workers.

In reality, child welfare policies and practices are a reflection of American culture. We have seen that child welfare cases are correlated with families living in poverty. Poverty in the United States must be reduced if we hope to reduce child maltreatment. We have also seen that child maltreatment is associated with additional significant social problems such as racism, homelessness, substance abuse, and mental illness.

We need to muster the political and social will to make children our priority in American society so that basic needs are met and children are given the opportunity to thrive. See Box 12.5 for quotes from the famous on the importance of children. It is time to move beyond platitudes to genuine interest in the health and safety of children that is reflected in our federal, state, and local child welfare policies and practices.

BOX 12.5 On the Importance of Children

The following is a selection of quotes that emphasize the importance of children to societies and the future of the globe:

There can be no keener revelation of a society's soul than the way in which it treats its children—Nelson Mandela, Former President of South Africa

Children are our greatest natural resource—Herbert Hoover, 31st President of the United States

It is easier to build strong children than to repair broken men—Frederick Douglass, abolitionist and statesman

It's the children the world almost breaks who grow up to save it—Frank Warren, creator of PostSecret

Anyone who does anything to help a child in his life is a hero to me—Fred Rogers (Mr. Rogers) of television fame

Nothing you do for children is ever wasted—Garrison Keillor, author and radio personality

What we instill in our children will be the foundation upon which they build their future—Steve Maraboli, author and inspirational speaker

Children are likely to live up to what you believe of them—Lady Bird Johnson, Former First Lady of the United States

When I approach a child, he inspires in me two sentiments—tenderness for what he is and respect for what he may become—Louis Pasteur, French chemist and microbiologist

Children learn from what they see. We need to set an example of truth and action—Howard Rainer, Taos Pueblo-Creek

If we are to teach real peace in this world . . . we shall have to begin with the children—Mahatma Gandhi

Sources: California Indian Education (2008); Compassion International (2016); Gandhi Worldwide Education Institute (n.d.); Good Reads (2016).

SUMMARY AND CONCLUSION

Standardized definitions of physical, sexual, and emotional abuse, as well as neglect, will be a significant contribution to the field of child welfare. Standardized definitions contribute to higher-quality research that results in more effective prevention and treatment services, and a better determination of how scarce resources can best be utilized.

Primary prevention programs are aimed at preventing any maltreatment from taking place. *Secondary prevention* is aimed at working with children and families that are at risk of child maltreatment. *Tertiary prevention* programs are treatment services that reduce the consequences of maltreatment and keep the maltreatment from getting worse. Prevention programs can target improvements in parenting skills as well as in services offered to families. Parent-training approaches such as the highly regarded Triple P–Positive Parenting Program can provide parents with the tools they need to become stronger and more effective parents.

There are many emerging approaches designed to reduce child maltreatment that will need to be evaluated for their effectiveness. There are no definitive policies or strategies that will work under all conditions. Therefore, we must seek new interventions with our knowledge, skills, commitment, and patience.

DISCUSSION QUESTIONS

1. Compare and contrast primary, secondary, and tertiary prevention of child abuse and neglect.

2. Discuss the importance of parent-training programs in preventing child maltreatment.

3. What are the advantages of using standardized definitions of physical abuse, emotional abuse, sexual abuse, and neglect?

4. Discuss your own recommendations for the prevention of child maltreatment.

5. Discuss the importance of providing education to children about protecting themselves from sexual abuse.

6. Discuss the practice principles for providing high-quality child maltreatment prevention services.

7. In what ways can research on child abuse and neglect be improved?

8. What are the advantages of using a specific protocol for medical professionals to assess physical abuse of children?

9. Why can it be difficult to implement change in child protection organizations?

10. What are your own ideas to create a successful child welfare system of the future?

REFERENCES

Balas, E. A., & Boren, S. A. (2000). Managing clinical knowledge for health care improvement. In J. Bemmel & A. T. McCray (Eds.), *Yearbook of medical information 2000: Patient-centered system* (pp. 65–70). Stuttgart, Germany: Schattauer Verlagsgesellschaft.

Barth, R. P. (2009). Preventing child abuse and neglect with parent training: Evidence and opportunities. *The Future of Children, 19*(2), 95–118.

California Indian Education. (2008). *Inspirational quotes: Traditional knowledge & education.* Retrieved from www.californiaindianeducation.org/inspire/traditional

Campbell, K. A., Olson, L. M., & Keenan, H. T. (2015). Critical elements in the medical evaluation of suspected child physical abuse. *Pediatrics, 136*(1), 35–43. doi:10.1542/peds.2014-4192

Child Welfare Information Gateway. (n.d.). *Framework for prevention of child maltreatment.* Retrieved from https://childwelfare.gov/topics/preventing/overview/framework

Child Welfare Information Gateway. (2011, July). *Child maltreatment prevention: Past, present, and future.* Washington, DC: U.S. Department of Health and Human Services, Children's Bureau.

Child Welfare Information Gateway. (2014, June). *Definitions of child abuse and neglect.* Washington, DC: U.S. Department of Health and Human Services, Children's Bureau.

Compassion International. (2016). *Famous quotes about children.* Retrieved from www.compassion.com/poverty/famous-quotes-about-children.htm

Davis, M. K., & Gidycz, C. A. (2000). Child sexual abuse prevention programs: A meta-analysis. *Journal of Clinical Child Psychology, 29*(2), 257–265. doi:10.12097S15374424jccp2902_11

Gandhi Worldwide Education Institute. (n.d.). *9 wonderful quotes from MK Gandhi.* Retrieved from www.gandhiforchildren.org/wonderful-quotes-gandhi

Good Reads. (2016). *Quotes about children.* Retrieved from www.goodreads.com/quotes/tag/children

Green, L. W., Ottoson, J. M., Garcia, C., & Hiatt, R. A. (2009). Diffusion theory and knowledge dissemination, utilization, and integration in public health. *Annual Review of Public Health, 30*(1), 151–174.

Jonson-Reid, M., & Drake, B. (2008). Multi-sector longitudinal administrative databases: An indispensible tool for evidence based policy for maltreated children and their families. *Child Maltreatment, 13*(4), 392–399. doi:10.1177/1077559508320058

MacMillan, H. L., Wathen, C. N., Barlow, J., Fergusson, D. M., Leventhal, J. M., & Taussig, H. N. (2009). Interventions to prevent child maltreatment and associated impairment. *The Lancet, 373*(9659), 17–23. doi:10.1016/S0140-6736(08)61708-0

Martin, M., & Citrin, A. (2014). *Prevent, protect, & provide: How child welfare can better support low-income families.* Washington, DC: Center for the Study of Social Policy.

Martin, M., & Connelly, D. D. (2015). *Achieving racial equity: Child welfare policy strategies to improve outcomes for children of color.* Retrieved from https://ncwwi.org/files/Cultural_Responsiveness__Disproportionality/Achieving_Racial_Equity.pdf

McGhee, J., Mitchell, F., Daniel, B., & Taylor, J. (2015). Taking a long view in child welfare: How can we evaluate intervention and child wellbeing over time? *Child Abuse Review, 24,* 95–106. doi:10.1002/CAR.2268

Prevent Child Abuse America. (2016). *Learn about Prevent Child Abuse America.* Retrieved from http://preventchildabuse.org/about-us

Promising Practices Network. (2010). *Promising practices for preventing child abuse and neglect* (PPN Issue Briefs). Retrieved from www.promisisngpractices.net/briefs/briefs_childabuse.asp

Rosenzweig, J. F. (2015, March). Understanding child maltreatment 2013 (Executive summary). *Prevent Child Abuse America.* Retrieved from https://www.ounce.org/pdfs/PCA_America_Understanding_Child_Maltreatment_2013.pdf

Scharfenberg, D., & Miller, J. (2016, March 29) Agency gets new rules on family, child monitoring. *The Boston Globe,* pp. A1, A7.

Triple P–Positive Parenting. (n.d.). *Triple P at a glance.* Retrieved from www.triplep.net/glo-en/triple-p-at-a-glance

World Health Organization. (2007). *Preventing child maltreatment in Europe: A public health approach* (Policy briefing). Copenhagen, Denmark: WHO Regional Office for Europe, Violence and Injury Prevention Programme.

INDEX

CPSIA information can be obtained
at www.ICGtesting.com
Printed in the USA
LVHW101941121119
637142LV00006B/173/P